Everyday
Magic

Everyday
Magic

VIVIEN SINGER SCHAPERA

November 2002

To Dear Ruth,
I hope your journey through life
is filled with many magical
blessings and that this book inspires
you to let your light shine
brightly in the universe,
Love,
Vivien

Four Winds Academy Press
Cincinnati, Ohio

First published in the USA in 2002
by FourWinds Academy Press
Cincinnati, Ohio

New Age/Self-Help/Memoir

ISBN

Edited by Kevin Cole
Design and illustrations by Kathleen Noble
Photographs by Dana Kadison

Printed and bound in the United States of America
by Thomson-Shore

DEDICATION

To Lynn Goodwin Borgman mother, wife, quilter and writer of great magic. Thank you for guiding me to Women Writing For (a) Change. And thank you for sitting with me, in spirit, keeping me company, as I wrote.

CONTENTS

AUTHOR'S NOTE

*In the following pages, you will read about the first half of my life,
from the time I was born, until my forties, when I envisioned Four Winds
Academy, a college for training healers.*

*With consent, I have used the real names of my family, friends
and teachers. In a few instances, to respect privacy, I have used pseudo-
nyms. If you should recognize someone, despite this disguise, I request
that you honor my choice, and hold your peace.*

*These events are written from my memory, formed at whatever age
I was then. There is no plot; there are no villains. I describe how I felt and
how I reacted.*

*I intend no criticism and no judgment, because this book is not about
'other people.' It is about me, as author, and you as reader.*

Childhood

I AM

Come with me, I want to tell you my story, all of it, from the beginning — the story of how I discovered everyday magic. Everyday magic is the funny side of sad, the truth in paradox and the reality which hides behind the illusion of everyday life. And me? I'm Vivien. That's where coincidence ends and the magic begins. My name means Life, from the Latin root, lending me the opportunity to penetrate an existential mystery. I am called to inspire you, show you how the pieces of life fit together, in a magical whole. This is a case-study. As you read, don't think about me, think about yourself. I want you to find everyday magic.

I was born in Cape Town, South Africa. My family lived in the protectorate of South West Africa in a small town called Keetmanshoop, but for my birth Mom went home to Cape Town, to be with Becky, her mother. When Mom went into labor, her brother, Uncle Harry, took her to the hospital. Mom says I 'slipped out' in five hours. My brother, Michael, had opened the way — he had struggled forty-eight hours to be born.

Uncle Harry was a professional man with means and foresight. As soon as I was born, he did the same for me, as he had done for Michael — he opened an investment in my name, which would mature when I reached the age of twenty-one.

Dad was still in Keetmanshoop. He wasn't in time for my birth because I had 'slipped out' one month early. When he heard the news that he had a baby daughter he said, "Oh, I wanted another boy."

I was born three days before Michael's third birthday. To ease his pain of no longer being the only child, Mom and Dad represented me as his birthday gift. He was brought to the nursery to see me, expecting a present. "Give it to me, it's mine," he said. No, he could not have his gift. No, he could not hold it. No, he could not take it home with him. He must leave empty-handed.

Mom says she could hear him from her hospital bed. "Give it to me, its mine. Give it to me, its mine," a voice trailing all the way to the parking lot, until the car-door slammed shut.

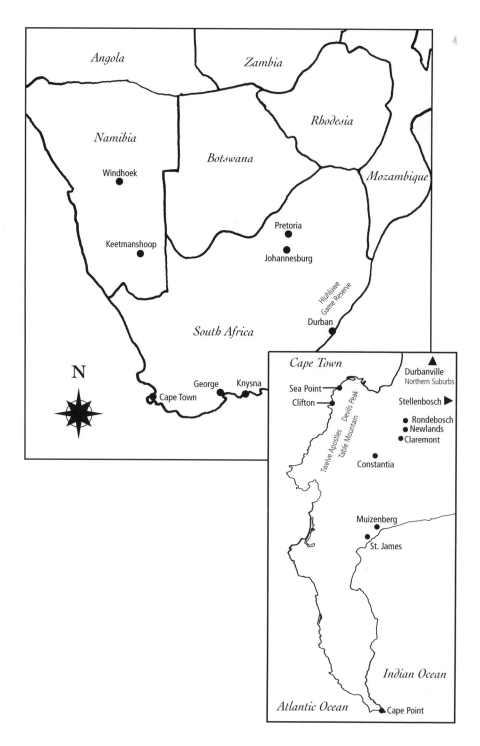

Michael and I were two halves of a whole, a yin and yang circle, one unit — the children. Possessions and talents were shared out between us. Michael was artistic, witty, athletic — so I wasn't. Then again, Michael's traumatic birth left him with attention deficit and a broken nose. He saved me from such a fate, allowing me the option of focus and integrity.

We should have been rivals, but Michael loved me from the heart, the other half of himself. I know, because there is a photograph of him, three years old, sitting knock-kneed on the step. He is smiling with sheepish pleasure at the camera, as he cradles me, his birthday present, in his arms. I was a new-born, too young to remember that day, but I remember the feeling of Michael loving me through childhood, loving me through teenage years, loving me on into adulthood.

After I was born, we moved to Cape Town. At first we lived in the sparsely populated northern suburbs, then we moved to the southern suburbs and lived in a house on Newlands Avenue, in the shade of Table Mountain and Devil's Peak.

We had a cook and house cleaner, Sophie, who had trouble walking. She seemed so old to me, but Michael told me, "No, Sophie is young, she's only fifty. Eighty is old." Sophie would sit outside the back door, in the sunshine, rolling dough, making lokshen, the noodles for Jewish chicken soup.

"Sophie," I asked, "why can't you walk?"

"I don't know," she replied, "one day I had to run for the bus and ever since then I couldn't walk." I wished I could help her walk again, but I couldn't, so I decided that I would never run for the bus, just in case.

My nanny's name was Jacoba. She was slender, timid, only sixteen. She bathed me and dressed me, made our beds and tidied our rooms. She stood by me while I brushed my teeth, called me "Viv" and fed me breakfast and lunch in the kitchen, when Mom and Dad were away at work and Michael was at school.

One night, after dinner, I wanted something sweet and chocolatey. "I want some cocoa," I said. I didn't know there wasn't any cocoa in the house.

"Bring Vivien some cocoa," Mom told Jacoba.

"Yes, Madam," Jacoba said, but then she signaled from the kitchen and Mom got up from the table, to see what she wanted. I could hear Mom and Sophie and Jacoba whispering. I could feel them looking over their shoulders at me. Mom came back to the table with her eyes down, a closed expression on her face. We all waited, while the milk was heating. Eventually Jacoba set a cup in front of me. "What's this?" I wondered. I was expecting a rich chocolate drink. This looked pale and gray. I took a sip and pushed the cup away. "This cocoa tastes like milo," I denounced. The maids burst out laughing. They'd known all along that I wouldn't swallow it. Of course I'd be able to tell the difference between cocoa, an honest chocolate drink, and milo, a fortified, chocolate-flavored malt drink. The sentence became a family joke, a code. Whenever something seemed off, not as it should be, we would look at each other knowingly and say, "This cocoa tastes like milo."

Then the maids cooked up a bad joke. They put the cat in the oven pretending they were going to bake it. When they opened the oven, the cat fled. Michael chased after it and ran through the glass front door, slicing his arm open. The maids walked him to the huge maroon bathroom and helped him hang his arm over the bath. We watched the blood pump from his arm.

"I need stitches," he told them, "you must call the doctor, you must call Uncle Sonny." They were too scared. Their joke had gone wrong.

"Oh, my God, look how he's bleeding," Jacoba said, kneeling next to him, shaking her head, muttering prayers and cuss words, then more prayers, in Afrikaans.

"Call Uncle Sonny," Michael insisted.

"The child is right," Jacoba agreed, "Go call Dr. Katz."

The next day, Mom took us down to the surgery so that Uncle Sonny could take another look at Michael's arm. Aunt Alicia, Uncle Sonny's wife, a full-figured woman with auburn hair, who was also a doctor and Mom's childhood friend, tilted her head, chuckling with praise, "Oh, Renée," she said, "Michael was so grown up. He sat there in the chair and said, 'Just let me pull myself together, then you can do the stitches.'" She chortled, savoring the taste of a child's emerging personality, then repeated the words with an admiring shake of the head, "give me a second, just let me pull myself together."

Aunt Alicia's respect sealed it for me — Michael was a hero, an almost grown-up, an authority — even Aunt Alicia thought so. Besides he had a string of twenty-two stitches running the length of his left arm, terrible scars, a lifelong tribute to his bravery.

I stayed home with Sophie and Jacoba, until I was four. Then I went to nursery school. Every day Dad asked me, "What did you do at school today, Vivien?" and every day I said, "I rode the tricycle."

One day he asked, "Do any other children ride the tricycle?"

"Oh yes," I replied.

"Well then, how come you can go on the tricycle every day? What happens if someone else is on it?"

"Oh," I said, "I just tell them to get off." Dad beamed at me and told the story to everyone who would listen.

Actually, I wasn't brave enough to tell anyone to get off the tricycle. I just waited until they were done. I wasn't brave or physically capable. I watched the other children swinging upside-down on the jungle gym. I wanted to do that too. It looked so free, so exciting to hang upside-down. I didn't want anyone watching me. I didn't want horrible children pointing at me and laughing, so I did something out of character. I broke a rule. I hid behind the tractor tire, when all the other children went back into class.

Alone. I pulled myself up to the first tier, swung my legs over the bar, and let myself swing backwards. Disaster! I crashed to the ground, slammed into the earth, shock. I hadn't bent my knees enough. For a few minutes, I just lay there, waiting for the siren in my ears to stop, waiting for the bad, ugly feeling of failure to go away so that I could stand up. I knew I couldn't lie there for the rest of the day. I forced myself to sneak back into class. The teacher didn't even notice me. I thought I'd got away with it — no repercussions — except . . . I'd just set my destiny in motion. This fall had jarred my spine, causing a disalignment that would undermine my strength and energy; and jarred my mind, undermining my confidence. This fall was going to shape my body and my life, sending me in search of ways to undo the damage it had done. But it would be twenty-three years before I would know its significance.

AWARENESS

Finally that first year at nursery school was over, but I was five, too young, for 'real' school the public elementary school down the road, that Michael went to. Mom rescued me from boredom by arranging for me to go to Anela, a little private school, in a Victorian house, in Kenilworth. My teacher's name was Miss Wilson. An older woman, crisp and knowledgeable, she was a firm apple. Everyone from kindergarten to grade three was in the same classroom. Each morning she gave us our exercise books. Our assignments for the day were laid out inside. We went at our own pace. The seats and desks were solid. I could smell the wood. I could feel the learning. Next to me sat a boy with unruly curls. One day he came to school with a white mouse hidden in his hair. This was paradise.

In the middle of that year, during the winter holidays, Mom took Michael and me to Keetmanshoop for ten days — my first ever vacation. We came home to Dad's proud news. He'd bought a house in the longed for Paradise Estate. When Mom saw the house, I saw her cry with disappointment. The house wasn't good enough.

"What do you want me to do, Renée?" Dad asked helplessly, "It has a prunus tree like you wanted."

"How're we going to fix it Alec, how are we going to fix it? It's in such bad condition."

"What's this?" I wondered, to myself. The house seemed fine to me. "Why is Mom crying, why is Dad helpless? Something must be wrong." The threat of deeper issues infiltrated my childish sensibilities. There must be things I didn't know about, things Mom and Dad weren't telling. There was evidence in the trail of dried up tears on Mom's cheeks, the stoop of Dad's shoulders.

My world was an unsafe place — unsafe and unstable. It was 1961, the year of the Sharpeville massacre — the Black uprising, where police had opened fire, shot people dead. Apartheid, begun in 1948, when the National Party won control of the government, was showing its rotten teeth. Many South Africans, and the rest of the world, predicted that the systematic oppression of the Black and lower classes, would bring doom and destruction on South Africa. Snatches of conversation entered my five-year-old mind and stuck like lint.

Mom took me to say goodbye to our friends, the Bleimans. They were emigrating to England. Packed boxes stood in the middle of each room. Except for dust, and a rocking horse too big to transport, the corners of the house were already empty, deserted. I climbed up on the horse to try it out, but the springs squeaked, a loud, insistent complaint. I climbed down again.

The Bleimans were part of a major wave of emigration from South Africa. I didn't know about Sharpeville, or Apartheid, but I could tell that Mom and Dad didn't have control of the world, after all. There was a bigger power that had control of them — and if it controlled them, it could come and get me. There *was* a hand under the bed. It could reach up and grab me in the night. Anxiety took root in my little body. By the time we left the Bleimans' house, in my silent heart I knew, that one day I would be leaving South Africa, too.

It was because of Sharpeville, the emigration, the drop in the property market, that we could at last afford a home in the dream neighborhood. I loved the house Dad bought, a 'double-storey' with a window in the roof. It was called the 'Gingerbread House.' There were three fig trees, a mulberry tree, a poinsettia, a lime tree, two lemon trees and a grenadilla vine in the back yard; a purple prunus tree, a yellow broom tree and a prolific red rose bush, blue, pink and purple hydrangeas, a red bottle brush, two pink tea trees, white, red and purple fuschias and a bush covered with dainty abelia blossoms in the front yard.

Aunt Alicia and Uncle Sonny lived round the corner on Eden Road. My one best friend, Phillipa, lived across the road from them, also on Eden Road, and my other best friend, Ilana, lived round the corner on Talana Road. I could walk to school in the mornings, I could walk to Hebrew school in the afternoons, and I could walk to my friends' houses in less than five minutes. This wasn't luck, it was by design. Mom and Dad needed us to be independent, because Mom and Dad both worked.

Mom worked full-time. She was a social worker. She came home sad and smoked cigarettes to get the smell and taste of poverty off her tongue, off her clothes, off her mind.

Mom didn't have time to volunteer at school, fetch and carry me in the afternoons, do the things that other mothers did. She worked during the week, and then, on the weekends, she spent all day playing tennis. One Saturday afternoon, she had to drop me off at my second cousin's birthday party. All the other mothers were sitting on the verandah, when we arrived. "Is this Vivien? Look how she's grown!" then they turned to each other, back to their cake and sandwiches, while my mother went off to play a match. I felt like a spare part, a girl on her own, someone to be pitied.

I longed to be like other children, to have a gentle mother who cuddled me and had time to be nice to my friends. Mom's voice was so loud, penetrating the house, interrupting my thoughts. There was no room for nonsense, no pink dresses, no frills. I watched her on the tennis court, pounding her way to club champion, coming off the court, sweating, putting on her heavy black jacket, to keep her muscles warm, everyone shaking her hand, "Congratulations, Renée, well done." Nobody, besides me, cared about the sunglasses tan on her nose.

I felt angry and frustrated. I felt cheated. And I felt sorry for Mom, because I could tell that she felt cheated too. I could tell that she hated her work, that she wanted to be at home. This was the early sixties, when women still stood proud in their role as housewives. Just as much as I wanted Mom to be like other mothers, she wanted to be supported in middle class ways, like other wives. I could tell because it was in her conversation, in the frown on her forehead, the purse of her lips. It was in the words she spoke to me, "Never become a social worker, it's a no-win job. There's nothing you can do. The laws work against you."

Mom was resigned to her fate, but she'd figured out a better way: "Get a job you can do from home. Then you don't have to give up work when you have a family. You can have the best of both worlds." I had no idea what she was talking about, but I understood perfectly — I was living the conflict. Mom's words tunneled into my psyche, writing a script for the future.

Mom didn't seem to have time for me, but as soon as Dad came home from work he'd call me over. "Come Viv," he'd say, and I'd climb into his lap. He'd play games with my fingers and toes, distract me, part his knees so I'd tumble through the gap in his lap, make me laugh louder and louder. It was delicious.

On Sundays he took me down to the beach, and we'd walk along holding hands, stopping to look at shells, play in the waves, breathe the free air. He told me stories, about his horses and dogs — the ones he had before I was born — like Tina, his loyal dog, part pointer, who fell off the back of the pick-up, and had to be traced by an Ovambo tracker.

Dad could explain the puzzles of life. He was clever. He could speak three languages. His eyes twinkled and he made funny jokes. My best feeling in the whole world was to see Dad's face break into a smile, in response to the things I did and said.

After one year at Anela I was old enough to go to 'real' school. On my first day, I woke up before everyone else, put on my stiff, plaid uniform and hard, black shoes and clumped around the house.

"You were up early," remarked Dad, "what time was it?"

"I don't know," I responded tersely. He knew perfectly well I couldn't tell the time yet. "But it was still misty."

Dad laughed, "That wasn't mist, it was four in the morning. It was still dark!"

On arrival at Grove, I found out that my new teacher was away on honeymoon. We would need to double up with the other class, which was taught by the thin-lipped, steely-haired Mrs. Engelbrecht. Oh well, I would still find out what happens in real school. The teacher stood in front and talked and talked. We didn't do anything except sit and listen. No wonder the boys were getting restless and noisy. Where were our exercise books, our math problems, when were we going to get a chance to read?

Mrs. Engelbrecht had seventy-two six- and seven-year-olds. The room was crowded and hot. She'd already told a boy to be quiet three times. In desperation she called him to the front, put blue soap in his mouth and gagged him with a dirty dishcloth. I thought he was going to get sick from all the germs on that gray gag. I faded into the seat. I sat out the week, in silence, and met my own teacher the following Monday.

Mrs. Galombik was younger and less threatening, but real school was so slow! It seemed like the other children weren't listening properly. They didn't know anything, they couldn't remember anything — and there were so many of them. I wanted to go back to Anela. Why didn't anyone warn me about this horrible place? Why did they lead me to think it would be a step forward, when, in truth, it was a thousand steps backwards? I sat in my desk, looking across the classroom, hoping and hoping, to learn something new.

I didn't like it at school, but I didn't like it at home either. There was something extra living in our house, along with the good pieces, getting in the way, causing a divide between mother and father. Rage and resentment lurked on the other side of the front door, squatted in the shadows under the stairs, contaminated the landing leading to the upstairs bedrooms. I didn't know how it got there, who brought it into the house, or why, but I knew that whatever it was, it wasn't friendly. It was too strong and too powerful, and worst of all, it could burst out and engulf us at any moment.

Mom and Dad fought frequently, sometimes every day, always on the weekend. The house turned into a battleground and Michael and I would run for cover, hide under the bed. Michael would say, "Shh, be quiet, don't cry, they'll stop soon, don't worry, they'll stop," comforting me, and himself, as we waited for the storm to pass.

That's how I found out how important teachers are. I needed to find something to like. More than that, I needed to find something to love. There was one other possibility — I could love my teacher and, if I were lucky, my teacher would love me. Third grade worked out fine. Miss Templeton seemed to understand me. Fourth grade was so-so because my teacher went on sabbatical for a quarter, abandoning me to a sharp-nosed Mrs. Rick, then in fifth grade disaster struck. I had a personality clash with Miss de Smidt.

Michael claimed Miss de Smidt was still young, only in her fifties, but her hair was already completely white, her lips were thin, her face was parched and tired. Our favorite entertainment was to actually see the moment when her bony hands wound the crank to start her beige 1950's Austin, to ride home, to take care of her aging mother.

I tried to like her. At least her lessons were interesting, different. She taught us about the Bushmen, including some of the popular myths at the time, like Bushmen can see the details of the stars with the naked eye. She introduced us to the wonders of the dinosaurs — in the 1960's — when nobody else in school had even heard of them.

Miss de Smidt knew how to teach, but she was too hard and cold. I needed my teacher's eyes to soften when she looked at me. I needed her to say my name with a note of warmth in her voice. I couldn't manage without it. I went home from school sobbing.

"What's wrong?" Mom asked, helplessly.

"I hate Miss de Smidt! I hate her, she's mean."

Mom tried, Miss de Smidt tried, but the problem wasn't in the doing. There wasn't something to change, to do differently — something was missing. I was yearning for love from a woman who didn't have enough for herself.

That was 1966, the year all four of us, Mom, Dad, Michael and I, went to Keetmanshoop again. We drove through the desert for hours and hours, eventually arriving at this small town. Michael read the sign. It said, "Population: one thousand." The roads were wide and spacious, the yards around the houses were generous. Here in the desert, there was more land than needed, but that didn't disguise the poverty, the isolation.

The air was too dry, too brown, it stuck in my throat. We went to visit my parents' friends. Inside the screen door, the house was cool, the bathroom had shiny pink tiles and turquoise towels, the kitchen was spacious. I looked up at the strip of sticky fly paper hanging from the ceiling. I felt reassured by the familiar.

Across the road lived our former neighbor and good friend Carl Wurth. His front yard was an oasis. I could see a trimmed green lawn and red hibiscus in full bloom. We went there next. Carl opened the door in welcome, and led us through his house. As we walked from his kitchen to his back yard, I stopped and stared. In front of me a pile of glowing pink rocks rose out of the dust. Succulents grew in the crevices — a rose quartz rock garden.

Carl owned a mine. "Oh," he said, "That. That's in the way, we have to dynamite through that to get to the precious stuff. But it's quite nice, I thought I'd bring some home." In the way? Something more precious? I couldn't imagine. I felt a thirst that went beyond the dryness of the desert, a desire stirring inside me.

Miss de Smidt couldn't give me love, but she had given me another gift. She'd turned me into a budding naturalist. I was primed to notice that South West Africa was rich in minerals. We went to the museum in Windhoek and Mom bought me a small, blue feldspar stone, set in a bubble pack on a printed card. I couldn't reach the stone to touch it, but it was reaching me. This stone, and this place, were telling me about my life. I looked past the desert, over the horizon, into the distance, and said, "Dad, one day I'm going to collect minerals."

"That's an expensive hobby," he said.

Soon after we got back from Keetmanshoop, Becky died. Becky had always been ill, at least as long as I had known her. Mom told me that she had a debilitating disease, her lungs were collapsing, she couldn't breathe. We used to visit every Sunday afternoon, and I knew that Mom went during the week as well, on Thursdays. Becky's room was lined with oxygen tanks. She was confined to bed. She terrified me because every time we visited her, she made Mom cry.

Who could make Mom cry? And why? I could hear Becky summoning the maids and the nurses, on and on, ordering them around, never satisfied. It was tiring just listening to her. I used to hide in the dining-room.

I didn't have a relationship with Becky, because she was always sick, but there was a good part about visiting her — being with her maid, Jacky. Jacky hardly knew me but I could feel that she really loved me.

I hadn't felt safe for a few years, since Jacoba left to marry Freddy, but Jacky could make me feel safe again. When I looked at Jacky — really looked at her — I couldn't see why she had such a calming effect on me. There wasn't a visible reason, but it was tangible. The air around her was warm; the room she was in felt warm, different from the other rooms, where the air felt sharp in comparison. There was a big loving space all around Jacky and I was welcome in it.

"Do you want a glass of milk, Vivien?" Jacky asked.

"Yes, please," I answered, and I drank every drop, even though I hated milk, and wouldn't consider drinking it elsewhere. But I wanted to see Jacky take down a glass, pour the milk and hand it to me. I needed to drink something that Jacky had held.

That same year Dad followed his dream — he became self-employed. Dad was an inventor. In the evenings he'd sit in his chair, eyes half-closed, looking like he was dozing. Then he'd reach for a pencil and a piece of paper and sketch out plans in words or drawings, or both. Once he invented a toilet that could be flushed again and again, without a wait, but someone in France had already invented it, years before. I saw Mom and Dad comparing the drawings. They were exact. This time he'd come up with a formula for a wood finish that could replace varnish. Once applied, the wood wouldn't need to be sanded down again. The oil could be reapplied over the old. Wooden doors and gates and window frames could look like new, year after year, without the effort. Dad went into production.

There was less money and more fighting than ever. The air in the house formed itself into invisible eggs. Mom would greet us at the front door, fingers to her lips, hissing "Shhh, don't disturb Dad." We had to tip-toe around, tread softly, for fear of bumping and breaking the fragile eggs we couldn't see.

For years, I'd had headaches and stomach-aches every day. I'd learned to live like that, but now, with a teacher I didn't like, Becky's death, and Dad's new job, I developed a new symptom. Every night I woke up at midnight, crying, and couldn't go back to sleep.

Mom took me to see Uncle Sonny. He was still our family doctor. He referred me to a specialist, Dr. Mervish. Dr. Mervish was going to hypno-tize me to sleep at night. I heard Mom and Dad talking about the cost. I felt guilty, spending so much money we didn't have. Uncle Sonny and Dr. Mervish said I would need twelve sessions to benefit. It seemed such a lot, but I couldn't help it. There was something the matter with me.

"You're doing what?" Michael jeered, "Being hypnotized to sleep at night!" Michael was thirteen, he could recognize an oddity. "Do you think that will help?" he asked. I didn't know, but I wasn't ready to give up trusting grown ups, yet.

We started in Dr. Mervish's office, at his desk, Mom and I on one side, him on the other, while he explained stuff to Mom. Then he led me to another room, where I had to lie on a bed while he repeatedly told me, "You are feeling sleepy and tired."

Each time I went, he described two or three different scenarios, and said, "You are feeling sleepy and tired." I best remember the one which went like this: "You are all camping on the beach. You look up at the stars and yawn. You want to go to bed. You are feeling sleepy and tired."

After the twentieth or thirtieth version of "You are feeling sleepy and tired," I got bored and let my attention wander. I became preoccupied with wanting Dr. Mervish to think I was a particularly graceful young lady. So I kept pointing my toes hoping he would notice that I was a natu-rally endowed ballet dancer, and would advise my parents accordingly.

Dr. Mervish had to discourage this. "Let your body relax, let your whole body relax. You are feeling sleepy and tired." What a nuisance, he didn't understand.

The hypnosis must have worked, because I began to sleep through the night again, and that was good enough. I already knew how to survive the headaches and stomach-aches.

After Miss de Smidt, I hit the jackpot. I got Mr. Goodacre. Mr. Goodacre had just arrived from England, and he wasn't just a teacher, he was an educator! He had new and improved ideas about teaching and he had a completely different set of beliefs about children — he believed that children had infinite capacities and all they needed was encouragement.

We didn't just do boring old "themes" like in all the other classes. Mr. Goodacre took the time and trouble to sit with each one of us and test our reading age. He gave us a reading list, and demanded that we write regular book reviews. We each wrote a book in serial form. We each published a magazine. We did research and wrote reports. In math we learned the binary system and how to do calculations in different bases.

Mr. Goodacre nurtured my interest in creative writing. I knew exactly which day we wrote in class, when we handed our compositions in and when we got them back, graded and critiqued. I would flip my book open, seeking my grade, anxiously reading Mr. Goodacre's comments, then reading them again to extract the hidden nuances, wanting to know what my teacher thought about my work.

It would have been a perfect year, except for Sheila Kennedy, my "best friend." Mr. Goodacre wasn't the only import from England, Sheila's family had come too. The Kennedys were Jewish.

"Kennedy? That's not a Jewish name," Mom sniffed. I couldn't tell which names were Jewish and which weren't. I didn't know what Mom meant.

One day Sheila told me a secret. "Don't tell anyone," she said, "but Kennedy isn't our real name. We changed our name from Cohen." Mom was right.

"From Cohen to Kennedy?" Michael sneered, "Who do they think they are? The presidential family?" He thought it was hilarious. He was up on history and current affairs. I didn't get the reference, I thought he was being nasty.

Sheila always came first in class, me second. Worse than that, Sheila won the positions of leadership. She was so secure in the advantage of being almost a whole year older than me. She was supposed to be my friend, but she would form 'clubs,' with my other two school-friends, Ilana and Panagoula, and exclude me, leaving me to wander the playground alone at recess.

I had to admit, Sheila was very talented, especially in creative writing. Mr. Goodacre gave me high grades, but Sheila's grades were even higher. One day I opened my essay book, to find I had nineteen out of twenty. Sheila opened her book — nineteen out of twenty. We'd tied. We both glowed with achievement. Mr. Goodacre had given us the highest scores ever. Nobody expected to get more than seventeen, perhaps eighteen out of twenty. We were like siblings, wishing the other away, wanting this moment of glory for ourselves.

Actually, I didn't write to compete with Sheila. I wrote for the love of it. I wrote pages and pages of rough draft in my scribble book, too much to copy into my essay book. I had to shorten my stories. My hand cramped from all the writing.

The next week I wrote a story about an American Indian brave. It was the longest story I'd ever written. I really had to leave a lot out when I copied it into my neat book. Mr. Goodacre handed out our essay books. I opened mine. I had twenty out of twenty! My face went cold. This was impossible.

"Something unusual happened," Mr. Goodacre told the class, "I did something I never expected to do. I gave someone a hundred percent for her composition." He paused, then called me up, "Pass me your book, Vivien, I want to read your essay to the class." He read my story to everyone and explained why he'd given it such a high grade. I didn't look left, I didn't look right. I didn't look at Sheila. This was not about us. This was for me.

I couldn't blame all my misery on Sheila. Three afternoons a week I had to go to Hebrew school, where I was teased by the other children. I was almost two years younger than this group, one grade behind them in school.

It was probably only once in a while, but it felt like every week, the Jewish princesses would circle around me, snickering. One of the girls, the oldest and prettiest, would start by saying, "Look at your shoes, Vivien. My brother has shoes like that. Why do you wear boys' shoes? And those shorts, where did you get those shorts? Aren't those boys' clothes? I'm sure that's what my brother wears. And why do you always wear brown?" There was nothing to say. I didn't know the answers. That's how my mother dressed me.

Their words hurt me. What they were saying was true. I was dressed like a boy, because I was wearing Michael's hand-me-downs and I looked like a boy because my parents thought it suited me to have such short hair. I was always being asked: "Are you a boy or a girl?"

In answer, Dad would grin, and say proudly, "A boy, of course." It was our little joke — people would believe him. That proved to both of us that even if I wasn't a boy, I was as good as a boy. No-one could tell the difference.

Trouble was, I was ten going on eleven. The joke wasn't funny any more. I still wanted to please Dad, but I didn't want to keep up the fiction. Secretly, I cherished a dream of having long flowing hair and long flowing clothes and being the most graceful dancer in the universe.

This was before unisex clothing, before the Twiggy look became fashionable. Mom would take me shopping twice a year to supplement the hand-me-downs. "Here, try this."

"No, I don't like it."

"Why not? It's your color. Go in the changing room and try it on for size." If it was 'my color' how come I hated it?

"I don't want brown," I muttered.

"Just try it on for size. What's wrong with brown anyway?"

"The others will tease me."

"Which others? About what? Brown? What do they know, that's stupid, don't take any notice."

"I don't want a brown dress." I turned my face away, trying not to cry.

"Well then, what about this navy one?"

"I don't like navy either. I like that one," pointing to a floral dress with puff sleeves and lace.

"You can't wear puff sleeves. Your shoulders are too broad. It won't suit you."

"And this one?"

"That's got darts, its for someone who's already got a bosom. It won't fit you, you're too flat." That word! 'Bosom!' It made me squeamish. What a choice, flat-chested or a bosom.

"This one. I like this one."

"That's got a belt, it's for someone with a waist. You haven't got a waist. You're shaped like a boy."

I hated going shopping. I hated my body. And it was worse when I went to the hairdresser. Mom dropped me off. "I want to grow my hair," I said to Auntie Merlin, "can you just trim it?"

"Sure," said Auntie Merlin. She left my hair a little longer. I felt better, even a little excited. I was going to grow my hair. I waited for Mom outside.

"What's this?" Mom scowled, when she came to pick me up, "That's not short enough, I'd have to bring you back next week!" She marched me inside, "Give her a proper haircut." All the hairdressers and apprentices in the salon stared at me as I sat back down in the chair. I really understood Samson, not just the pain and loss, but the shame and humiliation also.

The puzzle was that while I seemed more like a boy, Michael was more like a girl. Michael was very shy. I considered myself a solitary type, I spent hours by myself, nesting in the fig tree, contemplating the world. But I did have some friends. I did go out and play with other children. I felt like an outsider, especially at Hebrew school, because of the way they treated me, but Michael really was an outsider. He didn't even have one school-friend.

Dad told me Michael was always like that. "I used to go down to the school in the middle of the day, and watch," he said, "I'd stand behind the tree, at the fence, so Michael couldn't see me. All the other children would be playing, enjoying themselves and there would be Michael, off to one side, watching the games, not joining in."

I knew that one of the things that made Michael shy, was his appearance. He had a very sensitive face, hurt eyes with long pale eyelashes and a Mick Jagger mouth, dominated by a big nose, which he hated. It was too big, and it was noticeably crooked from being broken at birth.

Michael wasn't shy and reserved at home. He was full of ideas, dominating. He always decided what games we would play. He was really imaginative. While Mom and Dad napped on Sunday afternoons, we played in the back yard, building intricate villages, picking flowers to create exquisite miniature landscapes. "We're going to keep this, aren't we?" I'd ask him. ""Oh yes," he'd assure me, but that wasn't true. He was just stringing me along, already planning the bombs and floods that would destroy our work.

In the winter we'd stay inside, play board games, which mysteriously he always won. We designed houses, compiled quiz games, and made elaborate wardrobes for paper dolls. In the evenings we listened to the radio together.

That was when Mom and Dad were home. When they were out, it was a different story. As soon as the front door closed, Michael dashed for Mom's wardrobe, slipped on a dress and high heels, put a towel on his head to represent long hair, and dragged me through a reenactment of the Russian Revolution. He, of course, was the lost princess, Anastasia. I had no idea what was going on, and I especially didn't know who Anastasia was.

Sometimes I'd get bored with this continual dressing up. "Can't we play something else?" I'd request, and Michael would glare at me like the evil snake that I was. After all, he'd been waiting all day, maybe all week, for this important time.

It was important time, because it was the only time Michael was happy. It was the time when Michael was himself. Michael always looked sad, but I have a photograph of him in my album, when he was nine years old. He's grinning from ear-to-ear, because he has a blanket draped round him, a fez on his head, and he is wearing high heels.

One day my friend, Ilana, told me about a magazine article she'd seen, about men who dressed up as women. "They're called 'transvestites'," she said. The word sounded bad, too bad to remember, or be able to say properly. "It's dangerous," she said. I didn't see how dressing up as a woman could be dangerous. Michael did it all the time and nothing had happened to him, yet.

"No, no, it's dangerous," Ilana warned, "it says so in the article."

"Show me," I challenged. Ilana went over to her closet and pulled out the magazine. I looked at the pictures, and the captions. Ilana was right. It was scary. There was definitely something sleazy and menacing about being a transvestite. I understood that dressing up was Michael's special secret. He didn't have to explain that to me. But I needed to save Michael, I needed to tell Mom. I had to choose my moment.

I heard Mom and Auntie Merlin talking about E.V.. E.V. was someone who came to the salon to have her hair done, except it wasn't clear that E.V. was a her, because Auntie Merlin kept interchanging the 'his' and the 'her' and the 'he' and the 'she.' "You should have seen him on the ship, hanging on the railing, with a low cut sweater, so everyone could look down and see his breasts, I mean her, breasts," Auntie Merlin giggled, "and you know, he wears shorts under his dresses, because he's still a man down there."

This was too good to be true. I was getting an opening. "Who is E.V.?" I asked.

"She's someone who comes to the salon," Mom tried to fob me off.

"What's wrong with her?" I pursued.

"Nothing," Mom said.

"Then what are you talking about and why are you laughing?" I wasn't going to let them off the hook. I was on a mission.

"E.V. used to be married to my physical therapist," Mom said, hoping this would satisfy me. How could it satisfy me? How could E.V. have been married to Mom's physical therapist?

"What do you mean?" I was unrelenting, "How could a woman be married to a woman. Tell me who E.V. is."

"It's very sad," Mom said, "E.V. was married when she was a man, but then her body started to change into a woman's." Mom made it sound like spontaneous combustion.

"All by itself?" It could be something new to worry about, except it didn't have the ring of truth.

"Well," Mom hedged, "a little bit by itself, but then the doctors helped it along."

"If the doctors could help her change into a woman, why didn't they help her change back into a man?"

Mom was stumped. "I think by that time she decided she wanted to be a woman." The perfect lead in, handed to me on a plate.

"That's what's wrong with Michael," I stated, "he's a man who wants to be a woman. He's a transvestite." Auntie Merlin's eyebrows shot up. She dropped the brush she was holding.

Mom didn't miss a beat, "Nonsense," she said, "there's nothing wrong with Michael. You don't know what you're talking about, you're lying." It was a strange feeling, a door slamming in my face. Mom knew I never lied, just as well as she knew Michael was always lying. I felt bad and guilty. I'd failed to save Michael, and I'd let his secret out and I'd embarrassed Mom in front of Auntie Merlin. My perfect timing was a perfect mess.

It's just as well Mom chose not to believe me. It left her free to see her son the way she needed, and it left Michael free to express himself the way he needed. In any case, it was already too late. Michael's tendencies were in motion, gathering karmic momentum.

Michael's behavior was unusual, Mom and Dad fought all the time and I was an eleven-year-old, insomniac with daily headaches and stomach-aches. The pressure was building. We needed a safety valve. Just in time, Jacky came to work for us, which meant she came to live with us, because in South Africa the maids lived-in.

After Becky died, Uncle Harry had stayed in her flat, and Jacky had worked for him. Then, after years and years of being a bachelor, Uncle Harry decided to marry Auntie Myra. Auntie Myra knew finger tricks, spoke nicely to children and read stories out loud. Not only that, she already had three children — Maxine, Karen and David.

For Uncle Harry and Auntie Myra's wedding, I got to wear my first pair of high heels, pink, with black patent leather tips and a strappy back. My hair was still short, but Mom got me a pink feather hat that was soft and feminine, almost as good as long hair. For the first time, I felt like a girl.

It was a quadruple bonus — a new aunt, ready-made cousins, pink clothes and we 'inherited' Jacky, because Aunty Myra already had two maids. Jacky stilled our angry voices, cooled our pain and patched our broken hearts. Where did she find the strength? Where did she find the love? It must have come from her belief in God. Jacky was a Christian and she blessed us with her presence.

I still had one more year of primary school. Lucky again — Miss Gouws, my last teacher in primary school, understood me. One day, for no apparent reason, Miss Gouws said, "Vivien, you should look in that magazine, over there. There's an article on Clinical Psychology."

I looked up at her. Clinical Psychology? I couldn't have said it in words, but I felt like I knew exactly what it was. I could hear a little bell chiming deep inside me, telling me "here's a truth," telling me "take note!" It was the first time I heard the words 'Clinical Psychology' and it was the first time I heard my little bell chime.

"That's what I'm going to be when I grow up," I said, "I'm going to be a clinical psychologist." I made the commitment then and there. It was exciting having a new focus. I'd just realized that I didn't want to be a teacher after all. Miss Gouws had told us a story of how she and Miss Howell had been sitting outside on a bench in the park, and they heard a bell ring. Without even thinking they'd stood up to go back to work and then looked at each other and remembered it was Saturday. It wasn't the school bell signaling the end of break. I'd wanted to teach, for as long as I could remember, but I didn't want to spend the rest of my life governed by a school bell.

I never did read the magazine article. I didn't need to know more yet. I set my sights on university, when I would be able to study Psychology. But first I had to get through high school.

REALITY

I looked forward to high school with the same anticipation as I had looked forward to 'real' school. On the way to school, on the bus, on my first day, Michael warned me, "Stay away from me in the playground. I don't want people to know you're my sister. You look like a barrel on stilts." It was a punch to the solar plexus. The air hissed out of me. What did he mean? I thought he was my best friend. I was used to Michael teasing me, taking advantage of being older than me, but this was down-right cruel.

At home I looked in the mirror. I didn't look so bad. At least my hair was almost shoulder-length now. In those last few months at Grove, Auntie Merlin, had intervened, "Let Vivien grow her hair," she told Mom and Dad.

Despite Michael's evaluation of me, I didn't have any trouble being accepted by my classmates. The girl who sat in front of me, Terri Cohen, took a liking to me. It was natural that Terri and I would become friends. We were in the same class, we had similar interests and we lived in the same neighborhood. Terri's house was right on the border of upper Claremont and Bishopscourt, and while the actual house was not exactly a mansion, the property itself was spectacular.

Terri's father, Dr. Cohen, was a dentist, and his hobby was gardening. The stone patio at the back of their house overlooked a Monet of lawns and flower beds, foreground to an unobstructed, panoramic view of Table Mountain. l marveled at the roses, and marigolds, and orchids and impatience and wondered how Dr. Cohen did it. What was his secret?

One Saturday afternoon, Terri and I went to visit another friend, Lesley, at her house in Plumstead. We went upstairs to Lesley's room. There was a book on her bed. "What's this?" I asked scornfully. "Is it junk?"

"It's not junk. It's a thriller," Lesley said, her face flushing at my snobbery, "it's a Modesty Blaise book."

"Modesty Blaise? Who's that?"

"Like James Bond, only a woman. You should try one."

I turned the book over in my hands. I'd never read a thriller. Mom got me all kinds of novels from the library, from the adult section, because I'd already read all the worthwhile children's books. I was always on the look out for a new book, and even better, a new author, because that opened a treasure trove. "O.K.," I said, "I'll try it."

"Good," Lesley said, "I have the first in the series here on the bookshelf. You may as well read them in order."

As soon as I got home I jumped on my bed and opened the book. Usually it took me a couple of chapters to get really absorbed. I had to get into the story, get introduced to the characters, but in this book the action started on the first page. Maybe a thriller wasn't such a bad thing after all. I was taken with the genre, but I was even more taken with the character. I was falling in love with Modesty Blaise.

Modesty Blaise was a dark and slender woman, with midnight-blue eyes, who knew how to take care of herself. Put her in any situation and she could handle it. She used to be a crook, running a crime organization called The Network, but after she'd made enough money, she bought herself several homes in choice locations and went straight. From time to time she'd get a visit from Sir Gerald Tarrant, the head of British Intelligence, and he would request her assistance in pulling England, sometimes the world, out of a spot of trouble caused by an up and coming megalomaniac. Her right hand man was Willie Garvin, who was a little rough to begin with, but she'd given him back his self-respect and taught him how to harness his remarkable skills, which included pinpoint-accurate knife-throwing. Willie called Modesty "Princess" and everyone knew he would gladly give his life for her.

I was fascinated by Modesty's knowledge of the body and altered states of consciousness — the way she was able to concentrate all her energy into her arm and her hand when she was rigged up holding a grenade, so that if she let her arm drop, even an inch, the grenade would go off and kill her. I was interested in the way extra-sensory perception, intuition and psychic skills were woven into the fabric of the story. But best of all, when Willie wasn't off trotting around the world he and Modesty would get together and work out. They had a specially equipped gym and they always finished with the most important part of their survival training — martial arts!

I wanted to be like Modesty Blaise. No, scratch that. I wanted to be Modesty Blaise. I had found a role-model, a heroine. It was just a pity that I wasn't graceful. I wasn't flexible and limber. Because of my gawky, unyielding body I had no hope of ever being a martial artist. Oh well, Modesty had other qualities I could aspire to . . . and I could fantasize. At least Modesty wasn't a blond.

Terri and Lesley taught me about make-up, which shampoo to use, how to condition my hair and take care of my skin; and Michael took charge of my wardrobe. We went on the train, to the city center, to shop at all the big department stores and the boutiques on Adderley Street. We started at Stuttafords.

I stopped at a rack of sensible dresses. "What are you doing!" Michael moaned, "I can't believe you're even looking at that. That's ugly." He grabbed my arm, "Come over here," he said, dragging me by the elbow to a display of tops and bottoms that were strung by loops because there wasn't enough fabric to hang them properly on the hangers.

"Look, this is perfect," he was holding up a skirt. It wasn't brown. It wasn't navy. It was green leather, and it was short, really short. "Try it on for size," Michael said, his eyes twinkling. I tried it on. It was snug. Oh yes, this green leather mini was exactly my size.

"Now we need to find a top and shoes to match," Michael continued.

"Mommy will have a fit," I said. This was a different kind of shopping experience and I was getting nervous.

"It's got nothing to do with her," Michael said, "you can't dress like that anymore, it's embarrassing." I had to admit I preferred the clothes Michael was choosing for me to the ones Mom chose. I was beginning to have a little hope that, if I was wearing that green skirt, someone might even ask me to dance at the next party.

We took our purchases home and showed Mom. I could tell she didn't know what to say. In her way, she was pleased to see me dressed in the fashion of the day. "Well, all right then, you look very nice, if that's the sort of thing you want to wear," she said.

Sure enough, at the next party, I danced all night. Who would have thought clothes could make such a difference? It was like I had a new personality. Everyone was noticing me, paying me attention, wanting to be my friend. Who would have thought that clothes had magic, a magic that could make me glad to be alive?

Soon after that, I went into a growth spurt. My legs grew long and my hair cascaded down my back. The teasing at Hebrew school stopped. By four to six beautiful inches, my slender body topped that of the Jewish princesses, who had all ceased growing at the age of twelve.

After we'd been at high school a year, David arrived. David was an earnest boy. He wore glasses and he stalked around purposefully, always in a hurry, taking long steps to get there sooner. He had a classical education and it seemed like he knew more Latin than our Latin teacher. He was very concerned about South Africa. He wanted to unravel the class and race issues, and he wanted to make a difference. At first I didn't know what to make of him. He was so intense, unusual. Gradually I understood that underneath his old-man-demeanor was a nice boy.

In English class, we had to present oral communications projects. David and I were in the same group. "Come over to my house," David said, "we can work on it this afternoon." After that, I visited David regularly after school, and over the weekend. We'd do our homework together, work on projects, play the piano and read Hermann Hesse.

I felt rich. I had so many friends. I had love. Dad had begun to prosper. *Six Plus*, the wood oil, was doing reasonably well, and in addition to that, Dad had started a factory, building packaging machinery. He had to travel to America, and to Germany and Italy, to sell machines and buy parts.

Even Michael had made a friend — Ian — an oily-haired boy, who played the piano and the organ with great enthusiasm. With his slick black hair, dark eyebrows, red lips and gray skin he looked like a long-lost member of the Addams family. He was always talking about 'Melissa Grupps' the heroine of a horror movie he had seen, scaring me silly with his eerie voice and eerie tales.

I should have been scared of Ian. In keeping with his looks, he was a medium. We set up a table in Michael's room, wrote the letters of the alphabet on pieces of paper and turned a glass upside down. Ian put a finger on the glass, asked a question and the glass began to move towards a letter, spelling out a message from the spirits.

"Will Michael pass his matric exams?" we asked.

"Y-e-s," spelled the spirits.

"Will Ian get a car when he turns eighteen?" we asked.

"Y-e-s, t-w-o," said the spirits.

"Yippee," said Ian.

"Will Vivien get an A average this term?"

"W-o-r-k, d-o-n-'-t w-o-r-r-y," said the spirits.

These were innocuous questions and comforting answers. I had mixed feelings, I wanted the spirits to be talking to us, and I didn't. I was already so anxious, now I had to fear the unseen, the supernatural as well. Was Ian moving the glass? Maybe, some of the time. But even if he was moving it, I could feel a presence in the room, a change in atmosphere. The air was thicker. We weren't alone.

"Let's ask the spirit his or her name," Ian suggested. The first was called Wanda, and she revealed that she was planning to prepare an acid bath for somebody. I prayed it wasn't me. The second claimed to be Jack-The-Ripper. These spirits were not from a high enough class. Their answers couldn't be trusted; and their information sounded suspiciously like Melissa Grupps stories. "We have to stop," I said, "I think this is dangerous."

"Oh, come on Vivien, don't be a spoilsport." Everybody else was enjoying the 'game.' A game was fun, harmless. This had a sinister note. There was some deception going on, some trickery, and it wasn't all Ian. Ian had started by pulling our legs, but there were elements beyond his intention. I could see it in his face.

The next day a berg wind blew through Cape Town. A hot, dry, electrical wind that put us all on edge, made the leaves crackle, kept us waiting for the weather to break. I paced the house. I couldn't find

Michael. The street was empty of all my friends. "Where's everybody?" I asked Jacky.

"I don't know, " she said, "What you people been up to?"

"Oh, nothing." I didn't want to tell her. She was religious. She wouldn't approve of us contacting spirits. She gave me a sideways look. She knew we were up to no good, but if I wasn't going to tell her, then so be it. I couldn't settle down. I had the same sensation as when the spirits came into the room the night before.

Later in the afternoon Michael and Ian came back. "Where've you been?" I asked.

"At Phillipa."

"Why?" What were Michael and Ian doing at Phillipa's house? She was *my* friend.

"Playing the glass game."

"Why'd you go without me? Why'd you leave me out?" I didn't like being excluded.

"But you got scared. You made us stop. You're taking it too seriously." Of course that was true, but I still didn't want my brother and my friends running round the corner without me.

"Well, I could feel it, even though I wasn't there. I could feel what was going on," I said. Michael gave me the 'you're-a-nutcase' look. That night I examined my bath water carefully, for any signs of acid.

Word got out that Ian was a medium and more and more of our friends wanted to participate. We set the table up in Michael's room again, laid out the letters and proceeded. Everyone asked their questions and got their answers. I was handling it quite well, as long as there was no Jack-The-Ripper and no Wanda of the acid bath.

"I wonder if anyone else in the group is a medium," Michael mused. He had an astute mind and was probably planning a business venture, or at minimum a back-up plan in case Ian suddenly became unavailable.

"Let's ask the glass," Ian said.

Ian's finger was barely touching the glass. It took off, whizzing to the letters, too fast to be under Ian's control. It spelled out, "Yes, Vivien."

"No!" I shouted, "No, I don't want to be a medium." Everyone turned to look at me like I was stupid. Why wouldn't I want to be a medium? At that moment they all wanted this special skill. That's because they couldn't feel what I could feel. That's why they weren't scared and I was. They couldn't feel how it felt to be a medium, and I didn't like the feeling. It was uncomfortable and confusing.

But it wasn't the glass that made me a medium, and it wasn't Ian that made me a medium. I was or I wasn't. And I was one already and I knew it.

"Go on Vivien, give it a try," Michael coaxed, "put your finger on the glass."

"I don't want to," I said.

"Just do it, don't be silly."

Reluctantly I put my finger on the glass. Everyone breathed, in and out, waiting for the glass to move. It didn't. "See I'm not a medium." I was relieved.

"Maybe you are, but you're just not old enough yet," Ian said in an unusually kind voice. Mostly he treated me as Michael's irritating younger sister.

"Yes, that's it, you're just not old enough yet," everyone agreed.

I became scared to go to the bathroom by myself, scared to sleep in my room. My insomnia returned. I lay awake at night, scared of spooks. I pulled the bedspread over my head, so that I couldn't glimpse a ghost.

"It's all nonsense," Mom said, "there's no such thing." I wished she was right, but I knew she was wrong. It was like the difference between cocoa and milo. I could tell. I was ready to believe that Ian had pushed the glass, made up the answers, told us stories, but even if he had, I could remember how the room changed when the spirits came in, the thickening of the air. Ian hadn't made that up, no-one else had even spoken about it, but it was as real to me as my reflection in the mirror. Now that I was sensitive to it, recognized it, we didn't need to be playing the glass game. I could feel it at other times too.

I was scared and I was fascinated. I began to read books about the paranormal, quasi-technical books, like Lyall Watson's *Supernature*, only in daylight. There were a few books in the library. I read them all. One was about a husband and wife team, Olga and Ambrose Worrall, who channeled spirit healing. When Olga was five she saved the life of the woman next-door by raising her legs when she was hemorrhaging. She just knew what to do, the spirits guided her. Now that sounded useful, much better than an acid bath. On consideration, I wanted to be able to do that too.

I bundled my fears into manageable phobias. I could barely phone a friend, certainly not a store, or a place of business, to place an order, make enquiries. I really was afraid of ghosts, but it was magnified, exaggerated because I projected my anxiety, building since I was five, onto these unseen, unheard entities.

My muscles were so tight, so sore, that I couldn't uncurl my body to stand at my full height. I would stand in front of the mirror, pull myself up straight, and then watch as my body curled itself back over again, buckling under some unseen weight.

Michael's back was worse than mine. His shoulders pulled around to the front, his chest was tight and narrowed, he joked, "Look I'm a pirate, I have a sunken chest," but he was very upset about it. He wanted a full, strong chest. He advised me not to wear a t-shirt, because it would cling to my back and show just how round-shouldered I was — a trick he'd discovered for himself. He couldn't tell me how to make my neck look longer. Even with his hunch, his neck was long enough, but mine had disappeared, retracted into a secret hiding place, somewhere between my ears and my shoulders.

The tension was trapped in my body. If someone brushed my shoulder I'd jump from the shock, the pain of being touched. I still had headaches, every day, and stomach aches. I had such bad posture that strangers said, "Stand up straight, Girly. It's not good for you to walk like that," as they passed me in the street. No wonder my brother called me "Magilla Gorilla."

Mom took me to a physical education instructor who gave me exercises. Lack of exercise wasn't the problem. I played tennis and field hockey, went dancing and ice-skating, and did yoga. I should have been strong. Mom complained to the doctors, "Can't you do something about her posture. Look at her back." They shrugged their shoulders, "Tell her to stand up straight," they advised. No-one seemed to know a solution.

At school, I examined my class-mates. We were all slumped in our desks. The twist in my friend's neck, gnawed at my mind — the way the skin and flesh were creasing to accommodate the queer angle of her head, the corkscrew of her legs wrapped around each other for support, the whiteness of her clenched hands. She looked like a tired, old woman, when she was fifteen years old. What was wrong with us?

I thought about it carefully. It was a question of change — if I wanted good posture I would have to change the way I was. I knew I couldn't do it on my own. I'd stood in front of the mirror, many times, and tried, and failed. It wasn't about "head up," "tummy in," "shoulders back." There was a hidden complexity. I could sense it. "There must be something, somewhere in the world that can help me," I thought to myself, "I'm going to find it."

I wasn't the only one mapping my path in life. Michael finished school. He was eighteen, he could get his driver's license and he could get his nose changed, two big steps. It would have been exciting, except that something dreadful loomed on the horizon — military service. All the White boys had to serve their country, help protect Apartheid.

Michael was sent to Pretoria for basic training. I didn't know how I was going to manage without him. He'd always been there, as Iong as I was alive. Michael told me, "When we're old, we'll live together again, after our partners have died."

"Yes," I agreed. We wanted the promise of being together forever. We felt sad. Somehow, we both knew it wasn't true.

Sooner than we expected, Michael was back in Cape Town, stationed near home in a make-shift base, as South Africa prepared for a national celebration. The army was supposed to make a real man of you, squeeze out mommy's milk and put fire in your veins, make you rough and tough. It certainly brought out the real Michael. He was put in a tent with five gay men, and realized it was time to come out of the closet.

Michael and his new friend, André, came home for a visit. "Dah-lee-bish!" Michael said, turning his head coquettishly to his shoulder, flicking his chin up and down, holding his eyes dramatically wide.

"What?" I scrunched up my face. Who *was* this?

"Dah-lee-bish," he repeated. We were standing in the kitchen. He was cooking. "Means 'delicious,'" he explained.

"Oh," I commented.

"Ursula," he said to André, over my head.

"Who?" I asked.

"That's you," he said.

"Me?"

"Yes, 'ursula' means 'understanding,' or 'someone who understands.'"

"Understands what?"

"You'll see," he said. I wasn't feeling understanding, I was feeling irritable, because André had used up my expensive new bottle of *Gentle Care* conditioner which I'd bought out of my own allowance.

"Oh," he'd said, "that wasn't shampoo? I was wondering why I couldn't get it to lather!"

Mom went to the linen closet, looking for bedding for our guest. "What about this one?" she asked, holding up a sugar-pink mohair blanket.

"Oooh pink, my favorite color," André crooned. He made a grab for it.

Mom giggled, enjoying the banter. She was having fun with these army men, her son and his new friend. Couldn't she tell they were pretending to joke, sending themselves up?

After the national celebration Michael was due to go back to the Transvaal. He called me to his room. We sat on his bed. "I don't want you to worry. You're going to hear some things in the next few weeks that might upset you, but I don't want you to worry," he said. "I'm working on a plan to get exempted, and you must just trust me. Don't believe what you hear."

"O.K.," I said, "I hope your plan works out." I felt sad for him. I could tell he was depressed.

Within a couple of weeks an army psychiatrist contacted Mom and Dad. "We need to speak to you about your son. We have to put him in hospital. We're sending him to Wynberg base. He'll be back in Cape Town by the end of the week."

A psychiatrist? Michael? Hospital? He'd gone and told them he was gay, and didn't want to be. He'd asked for treatment. They couldn't leave him in the barracks. Too much temptation. Had to take him out of harm's way, hospitalize him, put him on a behavior modification program. Mom and Dad shriveled overnight. Mom got very thin, and Dad's heart suffered a bad turn.

We went to see Michael in the hospital. Wynberg Base Camp was only a couple of miles from our house. He was almost home. He lay in bed like he was sick. The nurse came and took his temperature. We all sat round him. Dad tried to be upbeat. Mom looked around her, as if to say, "How did we get here, in this awful place?" I tried to connect with Michael, let him know that I was on his side, remembered his words. He wouldn't look at me. His face was closed. He was dealing with the pain of wounding Mom and Dad.

At home, I sifted through my feelings. Michael was trying to protect me, and himself — leave the back-door open. He was using being gay as if it were a lie, to get out of the army. He wanted to keep the question open — was he or wasn't he? It was easy and it was hard. It was easy to tell that he was gay, it was hard to admit it.

"Michael is still Michael," I told myself, "the same person he always was. It's only the information that's new — except it isn't — you've known this all along. You just have to get used to the idea."

Michael was shunted back and forth. The authorities were looking for a place to put him. His plan worked. They put him on the train and he was home in two days. Dad, who'd signed up for the army as soon as he was old enough, did not feel proud of his son.

The next year Michael went to the technical college to study art. He met a whole new group of people, a different crowd, they had parties at each other's houses. With his new nose, Michael had a new personality. He was popular. He invited everyone to our house and they all came. I had two years left at Westerford High. I was jealous. I also wanted to be a college student, painting and drawing my days away, not having to wear a uniform anymore, taping Cat Stevens records, partying non-stop with my friends.

It seemed like I still had a long way to go, then, suddenly, it was over. I was on the other side of my final high school exams.

Mom and Dad bought me a graduation gift, a four-week youth tour of Israel. I was really excited. I'd never traveled to a foreign country, I'd never even been on a plane before.

Mom found out that almost all of the others on the tour were from Johannesburg. There was one other person from Cape Town, a boy from the northern suburbs called Jeffrey Kagan.

On the plane, I said, "This is my first plane trip."

"Me too," said Jeffrey.

We fell into an easy conversation, about our schools. Then Jeffrey changed the subject, "Do you like Leonard Cohen?" he asked.

"Like Leonard Cohen? He saved my life," I answered. Mom had brought me *The Favorite Game* from the library at just the right moment of teenage angst and despair. The book had resonated with my soul, connected me in a time of disconnection.

"Saved your life?" Jeffrey echoed, looking directly into my eyes, nodding his head. This was his test question, his make or break — could this person be his friend? Not if they didn't know Leonard Cohen — and here I was claiming a deep personal bond with his hero, awarding him the highest honor. Clearly we were going to be friends for life.

An organized tour, nothing to do but sit back and relax, be driven from one interesting sight to another, be served breakfast, lunch and dinner, enjoy the entertainment. At first I found things to worry about — what was the time? Where were we supposed to be? Worrying was my habit, I was lost without it. Slowly I realized that I didn't have any control, and didn't need it. I could let go, relax, go with the flow. Travel was exhilarating. I loved hearing a different language, seeing different scenery, tasting different food, shopping in a different culture.

When I got back, Ilana and I went to Sea Point. "I can't believe how much you've changed in four weeks," she said.

"Nor can I," I said. I felt so different, I couldn't explain it. It was like my eyes had changed and I was seeing the world differently.

"I think I'll get some nuts," I said. I really wanted the sunflower seeds for sale in Israel, or falaffel from a street vendor, but I was back in South Africa now. I slipped inside the store and bought a bag of pistachio nuts, came back out munching, spitting out the shells.

"Look at you," Ilana said, "able to go in a store, buy what you want — you've grown up." Ilana knew about my phobias, she knew I was too scared to go into a shop and buy something and that I couldn't use the telephone. She paused a moment, "and you're so much more relaxed, I don't think I've ever seen you like this."

No, she hadn't. I'd had a taste of independence, I'd had a taste of being carefree. I wasn't grown up yet, but I had taken a step forward. I was on the bridge, marking my passage from school to university.

University

GREAT EXPECTATIONS

David was going to America as a Rotary Scholar. Terri was following in her father's footsteps, going to Stellenbosch University to do dentistry. I had not wavered from Psychology since the day Miss Gouws drew my attention to that profession. I was impatient to begin. Jeffrey, Lesley and I were going to UCT, the University of Cape Town.

The University of Cape Town is built on the slopes of the mountain. The original sand-color buildings, with their red roofs and ivy-trimmed walls, stand like an honor guard of grand old soldiers, lining University Avenue. The central column of broad, stone steps, which begins far below at the sports fields, rises progressively to the classical majesty of Jameson Hall. In fine weather hundreds of students congregate there, able to look out over the southern suburbs in the foreground, the Cape flats beyond and all the way to the range of mountains known as the Hottentots Holland.

The first week of the academic year was dedicated to registration and orientation. We swarmed up the steps, and along the avenues, thousands of us, stirring the air with our expectations.

My major, Psychology, was predetermined, but otherwise I could choose. I settled on Social Anthropology, Logic and Metaphysics and French. The only thing I knew about Logic and Metaphysics, was that it was offered by the Philosophy Department. Lesley and I sat near the front. The lecturer, Dr. Keaney, came in, took one look at the assembly and blanched. "My, there's a lot of you," he muttered to himself. He walked up to the podium and launched into a philosophical-sounding mumbo-jumbo. Every ten to fifteen minutes he told a joke, which was lucid, but otherwise he made no sense. At the beginning of the following week the room was virtually empty. "That's better," he smirked, "now we can begin."

Dr. Keaney had demonstrated his methods of reasoning: if they can't understand me, then they will leave. He had successfully avoided grading hundreds of essays and exam papers through the year. His intentional lectures were only a shade clearer than his obscure jumble, but he made up for this by telling us the exam questions in advance.

The Social Anthropology department was tightly run. There was a schedule of essays, weekly small-group tutorials and information-packed lectures. Lesley and I sat in Beattie Hall shaking our right hands from all the writing.

The vocabulary was a minefield. We had to pick our way between 'good' words and 'bad' words. South African society was built on prejudice, defined by race and culture. The University of Cape Town was a liberal institution. We had to be sensitive, wash away the language of our upbringing. We weren't 'Europeans' and 'Bantu' anymore, we were 'Whites' and 'Blacks.' Original inhabitants of an area weren't 'natives,' they were 'indigenous peoples.'

We learned to respect the 'preliterate societies,' admire their values and social structure. Our technology didn't make us better, only our spiritual beliefs. The line was drawn at ancestor worship and witch doctors. Clearly these were methods of social control, with no other validity. "If you didn't like your neighbor, you could go to the witch doctor and ask him to cast a spell," Dr. West explained, "and if your neighbor got sick, even if it was ten years later, the sickness would be attributed to the spell — proof that the witch doctor had done his job." We were allowed to scoff a little here, giggle politely behind our hands at these outlandish beliefs. We were cautioned that our spiritual beliefs were also a means of social control — pie-in-the-sky — but at least we had insight. We didn't believe in spells and magic and spirits.

The Social Anthropology class was big, but less than half the size of the Psychology class. I rounded the corner of the lecture theater and looked up at the rows and rows of students. Four to five hundred bodies were crammed along the benches, elbow-to-elbow, and this was one of two classes at the same level. "Look at the size of this group," I thought to myself. I was seriously intimidated. "What if they all want to become clinical psychologists? I'll never win a place in the clinical program." Of course they all wanted to become psychologists. Maybe not all, but at least half of them. They said so.

The lecturer tackled the problem immediately. "I hope you're not all planning to become psychologists," she said, "it's a long and difficult road. The odds are against you. First you have to do your bachelors degree, then you have to get accepted for the one-year honors degree, and then you have to be selected for the masters program. There is only space for six students each year. And those six won't be drawn from this group. They'll more likely be returning students, from all over the country. Professionals, who have been working already, getting life and field experience."

I looked around the room, surveying the faces, gauging the enemy. They all looked cleverer, more capable than me. Is this what I'd waited for? I chided myself. I couldn't give up now — I hadn't even begun. I had to have faith in myself, in my aptitude. Besides I felt a genuine calling to do this work.

We dived into the nature/nurture debate. What was more important, heredity or environment? We would be writing a test the following week, better follow the argument carefully, stay on top of the material. It was a terrible pressure, my future depended on it. We would be writing a multiple choice test. We would be given the answers. All we had to do was choose the right one, a, b ,c or d. I'd never done multiple choice before. It seemed like an opportunity.

It was much more difficult. I longed for essay questions where I could show my knowledge, my grasp of the subject. The answers were obscured, hidden in nuance, confusing my memory, three of the above, or all of the above? Seventy percent of the class failed. "Not very good," said the lecturer, "only three people got honor scores." She handed back our papers. I was shaking with fear and disappointment. There was no way — or was there? I looked at my grade. I was one of the three! It was a miracle. It was fate. It was luck. Whatever it was, it let me know that against the odds, I could be a top student.

I coasted through my undergraduate years, then applied for the Psychology Honors program, the first bottleneck to becoming a clinical psychologist.

The summer break had just begun, when Jacky called me, "Phone for you, Vivien."

"Who is it?"

"I don't know, it's a man," Jacky said.

"Is that Vivien Singer?" asked a voice I didn't recognize.

"Ye-e-ss," I said tentatively.

"This is Ronnie Dickson, I'm in charge of Clinical Psychology at the Child Guidance Clinic," said the voice.

"Oh," I replied, my pulse warming. Ronnie was a man of charm, who had captured the hearts of the vast majority of the women students. His lanky body lent him an attractively boyish air, made all the more pleasing by fashionably long brown hair, skittering brown eyes and an easy grin.

"I see your name on the list of clinical honors students. I don't know who you are. I'd like to meet you," Ronnie explained.

I hadn't received a letter of acceptance. Ronnie was the bearer of glad tidings. "Well, when shall I come and see you?" I asked, barely able to speak.

"What about now?" he suggested.

I looked at my watch. Six in the evening. I'd just come home from working in the perfume department at Stuttafords. With nothing better to do all day, I'd painted my face with meticulous layers of make-up. I felt ready.

"That sounds fine," I said, "it will take me about twenty minutes to get there."

I took the stairs two-at-a-time, singing to Mom and Jacky, "I got into the honors course, I'm going to meet my lecturer." I was jet-powered.

Ronnie smiled at me invitingly as I entered his office. I felt like a queen. I knew how many of my peers wanted to be in my shoes at that moment. We bantered our way through the 'interview.' I knew it had gone well. Ronnie accompanied me to the stairs, chatting, already old friends, reluctant to part. We said 'goodbye' and then, as I descended, he leaned over the banister and called down the stairwell, "And don't wear make-up to class except when you go to medical school."

The words had the wrong flavor. I was only twenty years old, but I knew it was none of his business. There was no rule "Don't wear make-up" at the University of Cape Town. I didn't know how to think about Ronnie's instruction. I focused on my excitement. I'd made it. I was on my way to becoming a clinical psychologist. I wouldn't allow the feeling of accomplishment to be poached by these strange words.

THE REAL THING

I could hardly wait for the summer break to be over. I wanted to rush on with training in my chosen career, but there were other important connections claiming space in my life. "Come play tennis with us on Sunday mornings," David offered.

"My tennis isn't that great," I responded.

"Nor is ours," he disclaimed, "we just have fun, come and join us." That is how I met Henry.

David had told me about Henry, an older man who understood the class and race issues, had influence on the thinking of the younger students who wanted to tackle the politics of South Africa. I don't know what I expected, but nothing could have prepared me for Henry. He came to tennis wearing two shades of gray — a once-white-t-shirt and once-black-shorts that he had obviously slept in the night before, if not the three weeks before. His eyes were more closed than open, and what I could see through the slits looked red. Henry had especially strong arms and shoulders, a large distinguished head with thick, curly hair and, despite his mastery of the science of 'Unkempt-Appearance,' a commanding presence.

Henry did not look like my kind of guy. We took no notice of each other. We played mediocre tennis and went home again.

A few weeks later David issued another invitation, "Henry's having a party at his flat on Saturday night. I think you should go." We wandered in close to midnight. Henry spied me as we walked into the room. Bold with beer, he beckoned me with an assertive index finger. The glint in his eye left no room for doubt.

Henry invited me to go with him and his four-year old daughter, Alexandra, on a day outing to Churchhaven, a little fishing village situated on a lagoon. The long drive gave us time to talk. He was thirteen-and-a-half years older than me. In his original student days he had been politically active, but just in time, he evaded arrest and detention-without-trial, by leaving South Africa to live in London. He had a British passport.

"Why did you come back to South Africa?" I asked. I couldn't understand why anyone wanted to come back to South Africa. Everyone was trying to get out, and the most desirable possession was a British passport.

"Because of Vanessa," he said. Vanessa was his wife. They had a painful on-off relationship. They were both under a spell, or a curse, and were dragging each other back and forth across the world.

We reached Churchhaven and went down to the beach. I sat quietly, while Henry and Alexandra played in the waves, built sand castles with her bucket and spade. I didn't want to intrude. We all watched the gulls, flying free, and the small birds, scuttling to and fro on the shore. Then we ate our sandwiches and got back in the car for the drive home.

"What are you going to do now?" I asked Henry, " I mean, with your life."

"I'm going to do honors in African Studies." He was still committed to social and political change in South Africa. "And I'll go to *The Pig*," he said, "and listen to the blues." *The Pig* was the local student hang-out, a bar. Henry had made a hobby out of drinking beer.

By the time we got back to Cape Town I was charmed by Henry's nature, seduced by his intellect and disturbed by his drinking.

I told Lesley about Henry. "No," she said, "you can't go out with him."
"Why not?"

"He's Vanessa's husband, and she's my favorite lecturer. She's everyone's favorite." Lesley had idolized Vanessa from her first day at UCT. She didn't like the idea of me, her little school-friend, treading the sacred ground where her goddess had walked.

Soon after we met, Henry went to visit friends and family in London and New York. I had extra time. I began an investigation into the subject of nutrition. The smell of coffee made me nauseous. I complained to Jacky that I wasn't feeling well. She said, "You White people never clean your stomachs. That's what's wrong with you. You need to clean your stomach."

Maybe she was right. There were others who claimed that diet affected well-being. It was worth a try. I went to the library and borrowed all three books they had on the subject of nutrition, and then, wanting to know more, I bought a few. After reading several volumes by Adelle Davis, I crept into the local health food store. I overheard the manager talking to another customer: "This is a liver-cleansing diet, follow it for two weeks and you will be rejuvenated. Your cells will be able to throw off the accumulated toxins and your energy will return."

A liver-cleansing diet. That should do the trick. I hummed and hawed at the till, then forced myself to ask for a copy. "You want the liver-cleansing diet? Of course, here's a copy," the manager said. He was only too pleased to share.

I asked Jacky to help me. She looked at the list of foods. "Very good," she said, "this is easy enough, salads and baked potatoes, whole-wheat bread, steamed vegetables and stewed fruit." We decided I would stick to the recommended program for a week. Within three days I was transformed. I was energetic, I was vibrant. Other people noticed. "Vivien, you look different. Your eyes and skin are glowing. What are you doing?" I was elated. I had found a simple secret to a healthy life — a healthy diet!

"I'm doing a liver-cleansing diet," I said. I wanted to pass on the good news.

"What's that?" they asked.

"Salads and vegetables and one slice of whole-wheat bread with a little grated hard cheese."

"Aren't you hungry?"

"No," I said, "I've never felt better." They looked at me skeptically. Even though they said they wanted the results, I don't think anyone else tried it.

The universe was planning to reveal another health-secret to me. After Henry returned from his trip, his sister, Linda, an actress who lived in London, came to visit. We were sitting at the pool, when she turned to me, and said, "I've just come from a posture lesson."

"What are you talking about?" I asked. My little bell was chiming.

"Its called the Alexander Technique," she answered, "I studied it at The Royal Academy For The Dramatic Arts when I was training to be an actress. It's part of the curriculum. When I knew I was coming to Cape Town I asked for the name of a teacher here. There is only one and she lives in Rondebosch."

"Give me her name. Give me her number. I've been looking for this."

Linda gaped at me. Most people didn't show that much interest in the Alexander Technique, or anything else they were hearing about for the first time. I, on the other hand, was electrified. This must be the "something, somewhere-in-the-world" I'd decided to find when I was fifteen.

"Her name is Miss Roberts and she lives on Rouwkoop Road in Rondebosch," Linda replied. How bizarre! Rouwkoop Road was almost opposite Westerford. I'd cast my net to the world, for something that was quarter of a mile away.

"Give me her number," I repeated.

I didn't tell Mom and Dad about the Alexander Technique, even though they would have been glad, willing to pay. I wanted these lessons and I wanted to pay for myself. I still had my telephone phobia, but I wasn't going to let that stop me. I ignored the drumming of my heart in my ears and forced myself to dial the number. "Hello, Miss Roberts speaking," said a sing-song voice at the other end.

"My name is Vivien, and I want to make an appointment," I said.

"Yes," she said, "what kind of a time would you like?" What kind of a time? What could she mean? In the silence, she could hear my confusion.

"You know, what sort of time — morning or afternoon?" she explained, correctly reading my hesitation. We settled on morning, Saturday morning, only a few days away.

Miss Roberts taught from home. Her apartment was in a gracious building called Kingsbury Court. The grounds were kept in the style of an English country garden. A luxurious display of colorful annuals, blossoming trees and flowering shrubs tumbled over the green lawns.

I rang the bell. In due course, I heard deliberately slow footsteps coming toward me. The door swung open, "Hello?"

"Hello, I'm Vivien. I have an appointment with you at ten," I said.

"Yes ... yes ... I see," Miss Roberts said, looking at me more carefully than anyone ever before, "do come inside, this way please."

Feeling like Alice in Wonderland, I followed my new teacher into the dark passage. She showed me into her living-room, to wait. The flat was on the ground floor, the spacious rooms were tranquilly dark. I could hear the rise and fall of her even, measured voice finishing the lesson in another room.

My turn. The teaching room was generously proportioned, with several mirrors, a barre on one wall, and a large folding table pushed against the opposite side. Miss Roberts put me in front of a chair facing a mirror and put her hands on me. She coaxed my spine to lengthen and my head to balance on the tip of my neck. She checked the way my feet contacted the floor and the alignment of my legs all the way into my back. I could see my shape change as she placed her hands, here and there, asking my muscles to unclench, triggering my rib-cage to expand and breathe. I felt like a crumpled butterfly having my wings gently smoothed by a gossamer hand.

Miss Roberts was well into her seventies, but even with her white hair she looked much younger, perhaps sixty. She had lively blue eyes, a spring in her step and a different way of seeing the world. She walked differently and she talked differently. If Miss Roberts was anything to go by, the Alexander Technique not only profoundly affected one's body, but also one's mind.

I fell in love, with Miss Roberts and her technique. Miss Roberts could drain away the dam of tension stored inside me, she could give me back my body, make me feel at home again. It was such a relief to have the one-on-one guidance, the gradual easing into position, the instant feedback from an attentive teacher, after struggling with the hit-and-miss of imitation, in my other physical training.

I watched in the mirror, as she gently shaped me back into what nature intended. There was a bonus. This wasn't 'a treatment,' effective for a few hours, or a few days, or a few weeks. It was a lesson. I was learning how to do this for myself. Miss Roberts taught me standing and sitting, and walking.

After the standing, sitting and walking, I could lie on the table, and Miss Roberts would hold my arms and legs, so that they seemed to unwind. She'd put her hand under my shoulders until the tight balls of muscle flattened and opened. She'd hold my head, letting my back and neck relax into her hands. It was soothing and integrating. Again and again I marveled, "What did I do with all this tension before I came here?"

I was sure that this would have helped Sophie, all those years ago, when she couldn't walk any more. And I thought about Modesty Blaise, and the way she'd been able to focus her mind to control her body. This really was what I'd been looking for.

"Usually my pupils come once a week," Miss Roberts said. I wanted to come every day. I wanted to feel soft and loose and calm all the time, but my budget didn't include this necessity.

"Yes," I said, "I'd like to come once a week."

Henry teased me about my Alexander lessons, "Did you see Mrs. Alexander today?" He knew he could needle me by calling Miss Roberts by the wrong name. "You shouldn't meddle with your posture," he continued, "it's a kind of dishonesty." Then he had an idea which filled him with mirth. "You know who has the best posture? Walter Matthau. Now that's what I call good posture, full of character. If Mrs. Alexander had her way, we'd all go round looking like robots." Considering that Henry had a painful shoulder, which only felt better while Alexandra or I were pummeling it, his opinion didn't count.

When the academic year began, I discovered that there were only five students in the clinical honors course, and that my step-cousin, Maxine, Aunty Myra's daughter, was enrolled in the counseling course. Since we'd grown up and stopped going to movies and restaurants with Uncle Harry on Saturday nights, I'd hardly seen Maxine. We knew each other well in a different context. Here, at university, we were strangers to each other.

"What are you up to these days, Vivien?" Maxine asked.

"Oh, I've got a new boyfriend, Henry, and I'm having Alexander lessons."

"Alexander lessons," Maxine echoed, "with Miss Roberts?"

"Yes," I said, "How do you know her?"

"My boyfriend's been going to her for years. I've watched his lessons a few times." How come everybody else seemed to know about the Alexander Technique and hadn't told me about it? "I think it's time for me to go to Miss Roberts also," Maxine said thoughtfully, then added "and who's Henry?"

"You probably know him. He's married to Vanessa, you know, the Arts lecturer that everyone raves on and on about."

"Vanessa's husband!" Maxine raised one eyebrow, she could smell a drama.

"Yes, but they're separated."

"Separated?" she gave the word a tinny sound. Maxine knew about divorce. She'd been through it with her parents.

It was a great feeling telling Maxine about Henry. I was surfing the wave of love. I was so wrapped up in my naive, twenty-year-old version of our romance that, I didn't realize that because Vanessa was a public figure, Henry and I automatically belonged to the campus too. The grapevine carried the news to Vanessa's ears. "Do you know your husband's in love, Vanessa, saw him drinking coffee with a young woman, in the Arky Union, couldn't take their eyes off each other, saw them holding hands, did you know?"

Vanessa did know. Alexandra had told her. There weren't any secrets, but it must have hurt.

Henry and I were sitting in his apartment. The doorbell rang. We'd just finished dinner. Henry went to answer it, and I heard the low tones of a cultured woman speaking earnestly. Now and then I recognized the higher notes of Alexandra's voice. I couldn't see them. They were outside the front door. I was in the living room, but the presence of Vanessa and Alexandra was so strong, so palpable, that my mind formed a visual memory.

After fifteen to twenty minutes, Henry came inside. His eyes were black pinpoints in a wax face. He held an envelope, his hand trembled. "She gave me a letter," he said, "she said to read it out loud to you, if you'd be willing to hear." I nodded. He tore the envelope open, unfolded the pages and looked at the first few sentences, beginning to cry. Henry read the words he'd been waiting to hear for ten years. I was full of compassion. I was full of love. I was full of comfort. I was too inexperienced to predict what was going to happen.

In any case, I couldn't linger long enough to contemplate these events. My life was moving along. A series of transformative experiences had been lined up for us clinical students.

Ronnie had arranged for the honors and masters students to spend a week at Integra, a unit in the local mental hospital which offered milieu therapy for 'residents' with intractable personality disorders, or severe histories of drug addiction, alcoholism or abuse issues.

"It's very strict," Ronnie said, "you'll have to behave yourselves, no special privileges. There's a strong hierarchy and you will all have to go by the rules. Remember, they will try to break you. The whole idea is to change behavior. Also, the staff will be reporting to me on how you cope."

I walked in. My fellow students were huddling in the doorway. I saw faces I knew. "Look, there's Max and Rosalyn and Debbie," I thought to myself. They were members of the local Jewish community. "I didn't know they were training as therapists. I wonder if they're doing Social Work?" I knew they weren't doing Psychology, because I was in the Psychology department. Max came forward and welcomed us. Donald, one of the older students, drifted forward, chatting with him, engaging him in a description of the system. Others stepped toward the conversation. I hung on the outskirts, listening, not wanting to do or say anything. Donald asked Max, "How long have you worked here?"

Max looked away, then said, "I don't work here, I'm a resident." We each took a half a step back.

I was having doubts, not about Max, but about Integra. I knew Max, and I knew his sisters. I'd been in his home, a beautiful mansion in the choicest part of Constantia. He was just an upper-middle-class Jewish boy who was having trouble finding himself in the shadow of a rich, successful father. I looked over at Rosalyn and Debbie. Were they residents too? Yes, they were. Same story. It didn't make any sense to me. What were they doing in the company of a teenage mother who'd taken LSD at seven months pregnant to 'bring the baby down,' a young man who'd grown up beaten, abandoned and homeless, and a girl who was trying to give up prostitution? And why were their faces blank? Why did it sound like they were speaking scripted lines? Why were they 'owning' feelings and hugging on cue, like robots?

A simple explanation. Their upper crust therapist was the mastermind behind this unit. They were voluntarily here on his recommendation. They could leave whenever they wanted. But nobody wanted to leave, at least not right that moment. They all thought their therapist was a genius, a father figure who loved them dearly, was going to turn their lives around.

Someone came and called Max. He was wanted in the other room. The residents looked at each other knowingly. "What's going on?" we asked.

"Oh, Max is getting a haircut."

"A haircut?" Perhaps this explained the shaved heads.

"No, no, a haircut is a 'measure.' If you break a rule you get a haircut, someone shouts at you for ten minutes, tells you all your faults. You aren't allowed to look away or answer back and at the end you have to say 'thank you.'"

"Why's Max getting a haircut?"

"Because when you all arrived he pretended he was staff." Phew, If I'd been Max I would have pretended to be staff, too. I was glad I wasn't getting the haircut.

"So when does your head get shaved?"

"That's if you want to come back."

"Come back?"

"Yes, if you run away, and then want to come back you have to give up your hair, as a sign of commitment." Give up your hair? None of us wanted to give up our hair. It was the seventies. Our hair was our most precious possession, the longer the better.

"What if your head's shaved and you run away again?"

"Then you have to give up something else of value. Rosalyn had to give Integra her sewing machine."

"That's not fair."

"Oh yes, it's fair. We've all had to do it."

"All?"

"Oh yes, we've all run away, several times. Someone's away right now, but we're expecting him back by next week. If it didn't hurt so much to get back in, we'd all run away all the time."

I was put to work with Debbie in the back yard. We were supposed to hoe the vegetable patch, except there weren't any vegetables and the ground was too hard. I bounced the hoe against the ground a few times, then pronounced, "This is stupid."

"What's stupid," Debbie asked, scowling at me.

"This," I said, "this isn't real work. We aren't doing anything. We're pretending to do something."

"No," said Debbie "this is real work." I think we were talking about different things. I was talking about gardening in clay, she was talking about milieu therapy in her beloved Integra. I hope that's what the problem was because she reported me for complaining, not doing my work, thinking I knew better, and I got a haircut. The haircut wasn't too bad. Nobody knew anything about me yet, so they couldn't quite fill the ten minute list of faults. Still, for a goody-goody like myself, the fact of getting a haircut was humiliating, until I realized that it was a set-up. There was no way any of us were going to get out of there without one. At least my haircut was over. That was the bright side, but I was annoyed with Debbie. I was just trying to have a conversation with her. Who did she think she was reporting me like that? I felt betrayed.

"I don't like Debbie," I said to Donald.

"Why not?"

"She reported me, and besides she reminds me of my mother."

"Your mother? In what way?"

"I don't know," it was a feeling, not a thought. I had to fish around inside to find a phrase or sentence, get it into words. "Well, it's like she didn't listen properly, then she made up her own version of what I said and what I meant, and nailed me for it."

"Oh," said Donald, which was the right thing to say because I was thinking 'oh' too. Both about my mother and Debbie. From a certain angle — mine — that was what they both did.

We all had to do group therapy together. I'd read about encounter groups when I was doing Counseling Psychology in second and third year. People got honest with each other and said what they really thought.

As soon as we were in group, Kevin, one of my fellow clinical students, confronted me about not being nice to him. I didn't want him to confront me, and I didn't want to be nice to him.

Everyone was supporting him, "Yes, Vivien, why are you down on Kevin? What did he ever do to you?"

I couldn't explain. Kevin gave me a creepy feeling. I couldn't fathom how he'd gotten into the clinical program. He couldn't even write a sentence — he'd leave out the verb. Worst of all, I couldn't understand that nobody else saw the problem. I had to think quickly. It didn't matter how honest and open we were supposed to be in group, if Kevin was stupid, I wasn't going to be the one to say so. I might not like him, but I didn't want to hurt him. Besides, there was something angry about him. Not blatant. He acted friendly, smiled a lot, too much. It was under the surface. I didn't trust him.

I had to admit one thing about this Integra place. Usually I had plenty of words, able to say what I wanted, but I was doing a lot of fishing around inside.

"I'm not down on Kevin," I said, "it just feels like he expects something from me and I don't know what it is. He makes me uncomfortable."

"It's true," said Kevin, "I want Vivien to be nice to me. I want her to hug me."

"Are you willing to hug Kevin?" asked the facilitator. Hug Kevin? Why would I be willing to hug Kevin? More quick thinking. I could hug Kevin and get it over with, or I could be forced to work through my reasons for being unwilling to hug Kevin.

"Yes," I said, "I'm willing to hug Kevin." What they didn't know, and I wasn't going to tell them, was that I didn't like being touched, except by Miss Roberts. That was different, because it didn't hurt when Miss Roberts touched me. With everyone else, the lightest brush against my body, seared my flesh. That's why I didn't want to hug, or be hugged, by anyone, let alone the smarmy Kevin.

"All right, then hug each other," ordered the facilitator.

The group made space for us to get in the middle and hug each other. We were kneeling on the floor, hugging each other. "Look," someone said, "Kevin's not hugging properly, he's got one knee up, between them." I knew why he had his knee up. He didn't really want to hug either. I felt smug, like he'd proved my point. He wasn't who he said he was.

"Put your knee down, Kevin," said the facilitator. Kevin put his knee down, we hugged 'properly,' full body contact, while the whole group beamed their touchy-feely smiles.

Everybody was going to get their turn to be the focus of the group. The pressure was off me. I could sit quietly, thinking my own thoughts while the rest of the group baited somebody else. I felt sulky. I liked Kevin even less now. He'd used the group to manipulate me. "I don't like Kevin," I thought to myself, "he reminds me of my mother."

What was that? Kevin reminds me of Mom? How? First Debbie, now Kevin. This was ridiculous. Every time I didn't like something or someone, it reminded me of Mom. Integra was working. My unconscious was sending bubbles of information up to the surface. I was getting in touch with my anger. I was getting in touch with my feelings about Mom. My feelings were like big red boils on my nose and face. I wanted them to evaporate into thin air, but I had to get the pus out. I had work to do.

"What did you do in the loony bin, today?" Henry asked when I arrived at his flat. I described the measures and the methods. Henry's eyes grew wide. He knew about authoritarian structure. "Don't let them get to you," he said, "don't let them get to you."

"They're not security police," I answered, "they're not interrogating me. They're not after my political secrets. They're psychologists and therapists. They're trying to help me."

Henry shook his head. An authority figure was an authority figure and a secret was a secret. As far as he knew, the police studied Psychology too, were quite good at it. Henry was right, and he was wrong. It was hard to make sense of a place like Integra. It was mixed. There were good things and bad things, and it wasn't clear which was which. As the week progressed, each of us cracked under the pressure. In the art therapy class, one of the students drew a picture that described the week for all of us — an army of giant hands, chasing a bug-size version of herself into the corner of the page, coming to crush her. The tears seeped from the corners of her eyes. She was too tired to cry. All she wanted was peace. She wanted to go home to her husband and children.

Monday morning, we met at the clinic. "How was Integra?" Ronnie asked.

We sat back in our chairs, shrugged casually, "It was O.K., interesting, it's an interesting place."

"I heard you all did well," Ronnie said, looking around the room.

We'd all had the weekend to compose ourselves. It was easy to push a week of our lives to the back of our minds. Even if it was a week that reached in and shook the core. No, we didn't need to talk about it. We were ready to review the cases of the week, ready to take a look at other peoples' problems.

Ronnie was intent on serving us a menu of what we would be dishing out to our clients once we were psychologists. Next was an encounter group with a guest lecturer, Aaron, from Canada, which the clinical and counseling students would do together once a week, for two hours. That meant Maxine would also be in the group.

Aaron introduced himself and gave a little sales pitch about his training and credentials, "Of course everything that happens in these four walls must stay in here. If we're going to take risks, share our innermost feelings and fears, we must feel totally safe with each other. You cannot talk about what happens in group to anyone outside, not anyone, no exceptions. I will not be talking to your lecturers about what you say and do here. It's all between us. This is one hundred percent confidential. Is that absolutely clear?" He glared at us as though we'd already trans-gressed the rule. We all nodded solemnly at him. "O.K., then, we can begin. Let's go round the circle and introduce ourselves."

There were the clinical students, the counseling students, and an extra person, a young man in his twenties — a comforting, huggable, plump man with glasses and a beard, a man whose eyes twinkled and whose voice was soft and gold as malt whisky. "My name is Kenny," he said, "I'm doing a research honors. When I heard about this group I asked if I could be in it. Thank you for including me." Kenny was a good speaker and a good listener, and when it came to groups, he was seasoned and we were green.

From the first session, our group started to take shape. Aaron was the facilitator, Kenny was the leader. By the end of the two hours, I was eager for the week to pass, so we could come back in the room and pick up where we'd left off.

One Saturday night, a few weeks into the course, Henry, his friend and I came back from the movies, after eleven at night. Linda was still in town. As soon as she heard our voices emerging from the elevator, she ran out into the corridor, blocking us from going through the front door. "Ronnie Dickson's here," she whispered, "I had to let him in. He wants to speak to you, Vivien." Henry and Brian looked at me, looked at each other, shrugged and scurried off to the kitchen, abandoning me to Ronnie.

Ronnie here to see me? What did he want? I was shy. I wasn't one of those students who knew how to chat to their professors after a lecture. I kept to myself, did my papers and hoped to get grades on the standard of my work. Besides, it was late. Why was he hanging around in Henry's flat, waiting for me on a Saturday night?

Ronnie took charge, rapping about this and that, then gradually steering the conversation to the honors program. "And what do you think of the others on the course?" he asked, sandwiching the question between offerings of his own.

"I don't know. I like them," I said noncommittally. My stomach was beginning to cramp.

"I'm not sure," he said, "I suppose there's some talent, besides you, but it's hard to know at this stage." He expanded his opinions about each of my fellow students, in turn, looking at me with his brown eyes, checking to see if I was in agreement with him. Every now and then I nodded my head. I didn't want to give him too much encouragement. I couldn't afford to discourage him. What I wanted most was for him to leave.

Two hours passed. It was one thirty in the morning. At last Ronnie was ready to leave. I'd been too embarrassed to tell him that I lived with my parents and should have been home long ago. He stood up and smoothed his rumpled pants. "Now, what have you been studying for the test?" he asked.

"Well, just the stuff you said from the text-book and the lecture notes."

"Be sure you know about taking an interview."

"O.K.," I said. I didn't want his hints. I was weary. I couldn't stop someone else from crossing a boundary, I couldn't stop someone else's mouth. I saw him to the door, said goodbye and went to the kitchen, to seek comfort from Henry and his friend.

They looked at me. In the dim light their skin was gray, their eyes were tired. "What was that about?" I asked.

"We don't know. We were in here. You tell us," Henry said. "He was here a long time."

"I don't know either," I said. "He talked to me about the others in the clinical program and he told me what would be in the test next week."

"Tell absolutely no-one about this visit," Henry said. His friend agreed, "tell absolutely no-one."

How could I keep it to myself? Ronnie's visit was an acid, eroding my insides. I took my secret to the group session. Half way through, it burst out of me, "There's something I need to share," I said.

"What?" everyone was looking at me, waiting for me to speak.

"On Saturday night Ronnie was waiting for me at Henry's flat and he had a long conversation with me about the honors program." Their let's-support-you-in-your-emotions faces changed to that's-an-outrage. What? When? How long? What did he say? They fired questions at me, lawyers at a trial, wanting to get at the truth.

I looked to Aaron for help. He was sitting back, letting the group handle it. There was a lot of discussion, "Was Ronnie's behavior O.K. or not?" We were stuck in the gray area, the blurring of right and wrong, the place where emotion takes over. The men in the clinical program were angry. I was taking advantage of being the only woman on the course to get cozy with Ronnie. They were angry at Ronnie for picking favorites. I was angry at them — didn't they understand how helpless I felt and what a risk I'd just taken?

"I told the group about Ronnie's visit," I said to Henry as soon as I saw him.

"You didn't!" he said.

"I did. I had too. I needed to talk and I couldn't keep the secret."

Henry shook his head at me, "How did it go?"

"Not well, they were more worried about themselves than me."

"What did you expect?"

"I expected psychology, not politics," I said.

"It's all politics," Henry retorted, wondering when I was going to learn.

The next day, leaving a lecture, Donald motioned for me to walk at his side down University Avenue. He looked all around him before he began. "I was in the staff dining room after our group yesterday," he said, "and I saw Aaron and Ronnie sitting together. Aaron was telling Ronnie about our group and what you said."

"Are you sure?" It was the heat of summer, but I wanted to shiver. His words were chilling the air around me.

"Yes, I'm sure," he said. Donald was in his late twenties. He had more life experience than me. He knew what he was saying was significant and I was catching it from him, but I was too naive to see further than my nose. I was shivering because Aaron had made such a big deal about the confidentiality of the group and he'd broken the trust; and I was shivering because Ronnie was going to disapprove of what I'd done. I should have been shivering because I'd just blown my life's dream. Ronnie acted as the filter between the applicants and the selection panel for the masters program. What chance did I have now of ever becoming a clinical psychologist?

Innocence is bliss. As my father's daughter, I wanted to believe that achievements came through an honest combination of ability and hard work. None of my teachers said anything to me, so I thought Ronnie's visit lay in the past. I continued forward. At the clinic, Ronnie said, "We have an unscheduled presentation for you today. Dr. Molloy, one of our associate lecturers has a very interesting case to report. We thought we should take the time to listen to him."

Dr. Molloy was a sandy-haired, tubby man with glasses and a nervous tic or two. He was regarded as *the* child psychologist in the city. Raymond Molloy wasn't only a good psychologist, he was a good showman. The material lent itself to skilled story-telling. He was presenting a case of a teenage boy who'd painted his room black and was refusing to come out for any reason. Raymond was so funny! He played the elements of comedy and tragedy. He took us down — we were sad, empathizing with a troubled child, feeling the pain of confused parents. The next moment he had us falling off our chairs, laughing at the bizarre truth of what it is to be human.

I was following my interest, together with these fine professionals, learning to serve people in need. I didn't realize that there was another case in the room that day, the case developing against Vivien Singer. I was being watched.

Henry told me that I was being watched, but he wasn't referring to my professor. We were on our way to have dinner with a friend. "We'll have to park the car far away," Henry said, "and walk to the house."

"Why?" I asked, we were in my car, a red Fiat.

"Oh, because they know your car, they're watching it."

"*They* know my car? Who's they? And why are they watching my car?"

"The security police," Henry answered, "they'll have you on file by now, because you're with me."

"On file? The security police have a file on me?" This did not feel good. This did not feel warm. I did not want the security police coming to get me at four in the morning, dragging me off to jail, detention-without-trial, interrogation all through the day and night, torture and solitary confinement. Every time we ·went to Henry's friends the conversation turned to who had been arrested, who had been tortured, who had sung like a canary within hours of being picked up. Maybe I didn't want to visit his friend. I didn't want anyone making a mistake, thinking I was political, knew anything about anything. Not me.

Henry's friend had been put under a five-year house arrest a few weeks before. To curtail his political influence, he wasn't allowed to leave his house between the hours of six in the evening and six in the morning, and could not be with more than two other people at a time.

"Don't worry," Henry said, realizing I was having second thoughts about being associated with him and his friends, "if they're watching you and your car, they know perfectly well that you're not involved."

We walked a few blocks to the house. Parking three streets over seemed like a puny camouflage. If the police were watching the house, they were going to see us go in through the front door. "They can't stop us from visiting his wife. She can have as many visitors as she wants. The important thing is that they mustn't be able to see inside the house, get photos of him breaking the conditions of his house arrest, because then they'll put him in jail."

I could feel the eyes on my back, but when I turned to look over my shoulder the street was empty. Empty? I wanted the street to be full, full of witnesses, people of conscience who would step in and intervene. No, I wanted the street to be empty, no-one watching us, no threat. It was impossible to feel safe. The police were against us.

Henry's friend was pleased to see us. He'd been depressed lately. Of course he was depressed. All he was allowed to do was work. He was disconnected from community, interests, ideals. He was denied the pleasures of life — movies, parties, outdoor activities, restaurants, all interrupted for the next five years. The authorities knew how to imprison someone without putting them behind bars.

House arrest was the strongest sentence. A whole group of Henry's friends were 'banned.' Banning was one shade lighter. Under a banning order you couldn't go beyond the magisterial district of your residence, but you could still get out a bit, on your own — no parties or social events, no political meetings, no groups bigger than three. We went to a lot of intense foursomes, sitting around kitchen tables, carrying news and stories, trying to lift the spirits of these exiled souls. Banned and house-arrested people were allowed absolutely no contact with each other.

Henry and his friends were deep in the puzzle of social conflict, me and my friends were deep in the puzzle of personal conflict. I hadn't done anything yet about the boils on my face — my feelings about Mom. They came to a head in group. I was complaining, "Whatever I do or say, I should have done the opposite."

"What do you mean?"

"I can't explain. Whatever I do or say, it isn't right. I should have done something else. I'm always wrong."

"Show us what happens when you speak to your mother," Aaron said. "Do a role-play. Vivien, you be your mother." He looked around the group, "Who wants to be Vivien?" Lisa volunteered.

"Paint the scene," Aaron said. "Arrange the chairs, tell us the set-up."

"O.K.," I said, "it's late at night and I go to her room — my parents have separate bedrooms. Lisa, you come in through the door."

"Where will your mother be?" Aaron asked.

"Sitting on her bed, reading a book."

"So you come in, and then?"

"Yes, I come in, on tip-toe, and she puts her finger to her lips, and says 'shhh!'"

"O.K. let's go from there," Aaron suggested.

I pretended to be sitting in bed reading a book, eating prunes and chocolates, listening to the radio and knitting. Just pretending that I could do all those things at the same time made me feel powerful. Lisa, who was role-playing me, tip-toed into the room, "Shhh!" I hissed at her, "you'll wake Dad."

Lisa jerked back at the ferocity of the hiss, and turned to leave. "Where are you going?" I asked, "I thought you were coming to talk to me."

Lisa turned again, "I was," she said, "but it seemed like you didn't want me to." She sat on a chair, the equivalent of sitting on the couch in Mom's room, watching me sitting on the bed doing four things, all at the same time.

"Nonsense, of course I want you to, it's you who doesn't want to talk to me. You never tell me anything. I don't know what you're doing, where you are, when you'll be home, who you're with."

"You know where I am. I'm with Henry."

"Humph!" I sniffed, using Mom's all-purpose sound, indicating that if that's what you're going to say, she didn't want to hear it, indicating that words were too good to be squandered on this information. Lisa squirmed. Where would she go from here? She needed a hint. Just the way I would have felt — needing a hint on how to have a conversation with my mother.

"Yes, Henry," I said meaningfully, "your father and I were wondering. What's an older man, like him, doing with you?" I got the intonation just right. Even I couldn't tell who was buried under a bigger heap of disapproval, the older man, or me. Lisa shrugged. It was an impossible question. No-one could have answered it.

"Will you be home for dinner on Friday night?" I inquired, continuing to read my book, feigning neutrality.

"I'm not sure," Lisa said.

"We're not running a boarding house, you know. You can't come and go as you please. You have to let us know where we stand."

"O. K., then you can assume I won't be home for dinner. I'm probably going out."

"With Henry?" I peered over my knitting daring Lisa to say it to my face.

"Yes, with Henry."

"Where?"

"I don't know where, we haven't decided yet. I'm not even sure that we are going somewhere. You said I had to let you know if I'll be out, so I'm letting you know."

"Then why can't you come home for dinner? What's wrong with staying home, with us, for one night?"

"It's the weekend. I want to go out with my friends."

"Friends? I thought you said you're going out with Henry. Which friends?"

"I don't know, Henry, friends, Henry and friends, I don't know, we haven't decided yet."

"Why do you have to live in each other's pockets? Your father would really appreciate it if you were home for dinner on a Friday night."

"O.K., I'll stay home for dinner," Lisa said, giving in.

"Oh, now you want to stay home for dinner, as soon as I mention your father," I said.

"All right, then I won't come home for dinner," Lisa said.

"Do as you see fit!" I sneered triumphantly, slamming the ball back into Lisa's court. Lisa was beginning to sag. She'd walked into a trap. She had no idea what to do or say. It was better to remain silent. I was realizing that there wasn't right and wrong. There was control.

I didn't have anything to add, I pulled myself out of the role-play and looked at the group. They were all sitting with their mouths hanging open, staring at me.

"What are you going to do Vivien?" someone asked. Do? What could I do? I wasn't thinking of doing anything. I was stuck. I was caught up in how I felt, a mixture of powerful and guilty. I felt powerful because I could maneuver Lisa. I had a come-back for every line, every situation. I could make her feel good, I could make her feel bad, with a twist of the corner of my mouth. I felt guilty because I knew in my heart that Mom loved me, and wanted the best for me, but I'd just revealed to myself and the group that she had me tightly wrapped in a classic double-bind. We all knew, we'd learned it in class, that the double-bind, the no-matter-what-you-choose-you're-going-to-be wrong, precipitates mental breakdown.

"You have to move out of the house," Kenny and Donald both said. I looked over at Aaron. He nodded his head, agreeing with their opinion.

"We have a room in our flat," my friend, Desmond, said. "you can stay with us."

I looked over at Maxine. She was also nodding her head, "Aunty Renée is very strong," she said. "My mother is married to her brother."

Suddenly I felt very tired. I thought of all the years of fighting. Mom barging into my room pointing her finger in my face, going on and on, coming at me again and again, until one day I grabbed her pointed finger, and then her head and banged her against the cupboard doors, so that Jacky had to pull me off her. "What's wrong with you Vivien, have you gone mad? Look outside, all the neighbors are in the street, wondering what the shouting is about." Maybe I wasn't crazy. Maybe I wasn't a bad daughter. Maybe I was just fighting for the right to be me.

It was time to end the session. Aaron pulled us together. We were subdued, all thinking about our mothers. I went home with Desmond, to check out the flat and meet his room-mate, Albie. They lived on the Main Road in Rondebosch, in a spacious but grimy apartment, above La Perla restaurant. I didn't mind the musty green carpet, the yellowing paint, the sink full of dishes and the toothpaste crust on the basin in the bathroom. I didn't mind the extractor fan humming noisily, blowing the odors of the restaurant kitchen past the window of the room that would be mine.

Here was the paradox. I was not one to sit on an insight, ponder my options. I was strong and decisive, able to move forward. I'd been trained by a worthy teacher. I'd been trained by Mom. By the end of the week, I'd left home.

A month after I moved in, Albie said, "You know, we have space for one more person. Let's advertise, and we'll invite anyone who's interested to come for dinner. That way we can really get to know them, see if they'll fit in with us."

We went through a few prospective room-mates, then Tanya came. Straight away we could tell that Tanya had the right feel. She was a social work student. She was still an undergraduate, but she had a maturity. She spoke strong sentences and made insightful comments. Tanya's father had grown up in a concentration camp. She told us a little about the phantom of the holocaust, but she didn't refer to her other scars.

After she left, I asked Albie, "Did you see? Was her face scarred or wasn't it?"

"I don't know," Albie said.

"I didn't notice anything," Desmond said.

"I was trying to see all evening, but I couldn't make up my mind. It looked like her face was scarred, and her eye also, but I couldn't tell. She didn't let on." There were no gestures to acknowledge disfigurement, no hands to the face, no tilt of the head, no hiding or avoiding. It left me wondering. I thought I'd seen something, but I wasn't sure.

Tanya and I became fascinated with each other. She liked the idea of me, "I'm going on a job interview," she said, "can I borrow your dress."

"Sure," I said.

"And can I borrow your jacket?"

"Yes," I said. The jacket went well with the dress.

Tanya looked down at the ground, "Do you mind if I borrow your boots as well? I think I'd like to go to the interview as you." I must have had something that she wanted. I had no idea what it could be, but I understood about dressing up and being someone else. I was used to Michael.

Besides, I knew what Tanya had that I wanted. She had a whole bevy of girlfriends. A stream of beautiful young women, blond hair, brown hair, fresh skins, bright eyes and lithe, dancing bodies came in and out of the flat to be with Tanya. I was full of awe and admiration. I could easily make friends with boys. Tanya could make friends with girls.

I asked Tanya about the scars. I hadn't imagined them. "Yes," she said, "they're from when I was five. There was a horse and cart in the road, the sun was shining in my mother's eyes and she couldn't see. She braked suddenly. I flew through the windshield."

"It sounds bad," I said.

"It was bad. My mother thought I was dead. I just lay in the road, with blood on my face. Then the ambulance came and took me to hospital."

Tanya wanted to be like me and I wanted to be like Tanya. I wanted to be able to heal the wounds of life. Integrate the scars into a wholeness, so that no-one, not even I, could tell, if they were real or imagined.

We were all serious about our studies. It was convenient having Desmond on hand. He was the top student, academically speaking. We could sit and talk about our essays and projects, at breakfast, lunch and dinner. We were supposed to do experimental research and write a journal article according to the guidelines of the American Psychological Association. I felt a pressure to get started. I vented to Miss Roberts, "I have to do a thesis," I said, "it's such a lot of work."

Miss Roberts paused next to the table, weighed her words, and said, "You know, when Nikolaas Tinbergen, the ethologist, received his Nobel Prize he talked about two things in his acceptance speech — the

Alexander Technique and autism. I wonder whether you should put the two together and see whether the Alexander Technique has an effect on autistic children?" Maxine worked at the autistic school, so it was worth looking into.

"I think that's a wonderful idea," Maxine said. "I'm going to speak to the principal. She's very open — she does yoga. I'm sure she'll be interested." Maxine arranged a meeting. The principal showed me around the school, talked to me about the Technique and wanted to know when we could begin.

Everyone was being so helpful. Everyone that is, except for the psychology department. I hadn't even discussed my proposed topic with my professors. I was reluctant to approach anyone, because I knew they'd look down their scientific noses, scoff at the Alexander Technique, and tell me to do something else. I was caught between pleasing Miss Roberts and pleasing the psychology department. I chose Miss Roberts. I decided to go ahead with the project without the support of an advisor.

The principal helped us select five children for the study, and Miss Roberts and I went down to the school three afternoons a week. I sat in the corner of the room, observing, while Miss Roberts gave each child twenty-minute lessons.

She'd put her hands on them. They'd look confused. Then their bodies began to ease up and open. "That's right," Miss Roberts said, "getting taller, getting taller . . . and you can walk," and she'd steer them around the room. As soon as they were on the table they started to talk to her, explain what they'd done the day before, tell her what they'd eaten, who they'd visited. These were autistic children, reticent in communication, limited verbal skills, poor social skills, but they couldn't wait to spill the beans to Miss Roberts. "That's right," she said, holding their heads while they were lying down, "getting longer, getting longer, beau-ti-ful!" all the while letting them prattle on to her in their stilted little voices and strange vocabulary, as though everything that was happening in the room was perfectly ordinary.

Miss Roberts had more than fifty years of teaching children, ranging from severely disabled to extraordinarily gifted. Those five little autistic children knew they could trust her hands and her voice. They lapped up every minute, and so did I.

It was nearly June, nearly time for the winter vacation. Henry wanted to go to Grahamstown to do research at Rhodes University. I assumed we'd go together. "I'm not sure," Henry said, "I don't think you should come."

"Why not?" I felt hurt. Why was Henry ambivalent about me going with him?

Henry couldn't explain himself, "I'm worried you'll be bored," he said.

"Why would I be bored? I've also got work to do."

I consulted Maxine. "It doesn't matter if you do or don't go," Maxine told me. We were standing outside the periodicals library, high up in the library edifice, overlooking the long view of Cape Town.

I frowned at her. What did she mean? "It doesn't matter what you do," Maxine tried again, "going to Grahamstown isn't the real issue. There's something else going on."

She was right. Absolutely right. Her rightness dazzled me. I closed my eyes. I was unwilling to absorb that I couldn't make a difference. I wanted to think that Henry and I had found true love. Henry was drinking less and less. He was much healthier, less depressed. Delicate shoots of self-esteem were beginning to break through the dry ground. We had a deep and comfortable rapport.

I refused to listen to Maxine, or Henry. I insisted on going to Grahamstown. We went in my Fiat. The air was cold and dry, the sky a distant blue. We stayed in an old historic house with a bathtub too big to fill, drafty windows and thirsty wooden floors. The town was desolate. All the students had gone home for the winter break.

On the way home my car started to hum and beat. The engine seals had worn out. Dad paid hundreds to have the car repaired. If I'd understood about metaphors, I would have seen the sign.

BETRAYAL

I was glad to get back from vacation, not only because the vacation was no fun, but because it was my birthday. I was turning twenty-one. Every year I'd asked Mom, "Can I have a party?" and every year Mom said, "Not this year, I'll give you a party when you turn twenty-one."

"Huh," Mom said, " a party? You've got another think coming!" That was mean. I'd waited my whole childhood for this one party.

Michael stepped into the breach. "You can have your party at my house," he said, "I'll give you your twenty-first birthday." Michael had his own house in Harfield Village. We could do whatever we wanted. We invited everybody.

The people poured in. Every room in the house was full. Uncle Harry arrived on the doorstep, smiling and waving an envelope. "Here you are my darling," he said, "see what's in there!" The investment he'd made when I was born, had matured. It was a check for a thousand rand — a lot of money, doorway to the world.

Officially I was an adult now, but I was caught in the gap between being a beginner-adult and an experienced-adult. Every year Ronnie presented an adult education course at the university — a course on parenting skills, using applied behaviorism. After Ronnie's general presentation the participants broke up into small groups, led by the honors and masters students. I knew nothing about children, except that I'd been one myself. Yet I had to get up the nerve to lead a group of parents through child management techniques.

I planned the evening step-by-step. My first strategy was to memorize everyone's names. Usually, names tended to go in one ear and out the other.

We all sat in a circle. Everyone was waiting for me to tell them how to begin. "Let's go round and each say our names," I suggested. I kept pinching myself — listen, listen, listen, remember, remember, remember. Each parent said their name and why they were at the class. There were twelve in the group. I led a discussion, making sure I used each person's name multiple times.

By the end of the evening I had rings of sweat under my arm. The parents were smiling, standing up, stretching, "How did you remember all our names?" they cheered me, "that was quite a feat." I'd done it! I'd won their trust and admiration.

My second strategy was to scour everyone's assignments for topics that held personal meaning. "Anyone have problems with getting their child to do homework?" I asked, looking around the group, knowing there was a single mother who was tortured by her child's homework issues.

"I do," she said. "I'm having a terrible time. I don't know what to do." The group dived into the subject, batting information to and fro, sharing troubles and solutions. Our sessions were so positive that we reached a critical point. The number of parents in my group was expanding, while other groups were shrinking.

"What are you doing, Vivien?" Ronnie asked me, "your group is doing so well. I think I'll have to sit in and see what's happening. I like to know what formula makes for success."

Ronnie came into the room last. We'd all been sitting, open and relaxed, as usual, until Ronnie walked in to join us. Then everyone stiffened, recrossed their legs. I began with my prepared introduction, "I thought we'd explore stealing, and other cries for help, tonight," I said. A woman had written a note to me. Her son was taking money from her purse. I wanted to give her a chance to talk about it in the group. "And . . ."

"We should look in terms of the reinforcement model," Ronnie said, finishing my sentence. He couldn't resist the temptation. He made it his group for the evening. As they were leaving, I could see, by the looks on their faces, that the parents were trying to communicate with me. I couldn't quite get it. Was it sympathy for me, or disappointment and frustration for themselves?

"Oh well, there's always next week," I tried to comfort myself, but there were only two more sessions. It wasn't quite the same. Sightseers from other groups disrupted the rapport we had built over the twelve weeks. The energy had already unwound.

The year was dwindling. I needed to complete my thesis; and to do that, I needed to get an advisor. I ran through all my options and decided on John. He was the least intimidating.

John listened to me describe my project, then said, "Well I suppose it's O.K. I mean it sounds like this Alexander thing affects behavior, so I guess then it would fall into the subject of Psychology." We talked through the different steps and details of my thesis, "It's too late now. You've done so much already. It will just have to do." He shrugged his shoulders in dismissal.

I could tell I wasn't going to get a good grade, never mind that I'd actually planned and executed a real piece of research. Real research just doesn't look good on paper. It's messy. I knew that some of my classmates were fabricating their results, to serve their theories, and worse — fabricating their entire thesis, tailoring it to all the specifications.

Why did I choose Miss Roberts and The Alexander Technique instead of the Psychology Department, when I was desperate for good grades? I thought carefully about what I'd observed, and what I'd learned. I'd witnessed the art and generosity of a master teacher taking the time and trouble to coax open the minds and bodies of trapped little children. Perhaps I'd made the best choice, after all.

I had one more unfulfilled requirement. I went to Ronnie. "I still don't have a patient for my case-study. Please select someone. It's already so late in the year."

Ronnie looked at the waiting-list, perplexed. "Here's one," he said, "although it looks complex. This child is suffering from disturbance in every possible area." He read the list: "Eating, sleeping, school-work, homework, interaction with friends and at home."

"I only have four weeks to go," I pointed out. "There's no way I can see that through. I'll need a regular staff member as a co-therapist, who'll take over the case."

"Yes," said Ronnie, "I'll think of someone." Ronnie decided on Raymond Molloy.

Raymond was supposed to be assisting me and showing me the way. We agreed to meet at the clinic fifteen minutes early to go over the case before the first session. I stood in the waiting room, all dressed up as a professional, looking at the Kliban cartoon of people who don't brush their teeth, waiting for Raymond. The family arrived, all five of them, hoping for help.

"Hi, I'm Vivien Singer," I said, "we're just waiting for Dr. Molloy. He's the therapist. He should be here soon." Mrs. Weinberg wanted to chat to me, get oriented, but I didn't want to do or say anything yet. We sat in silence, watching the door. Where was Raymond?

He arrived ten minutes late, "What's this about?" he mumbled to me from the side of his mouth as we walked to the therapy room, the family trailing behind us.

"Disturbance in all areas," I said, "eating, sleeping, behavioral and social."

"Oh," he said.

We all sat down and Raymond looked over at me, signaling me to begin. I wanted to shout "No, this is my first case, don't do this to me," but I couldn't. They were all staring at me. I was thrust from nothing to primary therapist in one move.

We were in the play therapy room, surrounded by toys. The youngest child in the family was five, she wanted to play with a puzzle, "Can I do this, Mommy?" she asked.

"I don't know," she said, "ask Vivien."

She looked over at me, "No, don't do the puzzle now," I said, "I think we should all try to listen to each other. In fact, let's begin by each person saying what they think and everyone else listening." Mercifully, they were all willing to talk and Raymond picked up on the gist. Somehow we limped through that session. As soon as it was over, I rushed home and collapsed on my bed.

It wasn't only my first therapy session that sent me to bed. I had other worries. Henry and I were at the end of our relationship. Henry had had a good year. He'd become the best student in the history of the department. He was down to a lone beer at the end of the day. Henry felt restored and he wanted to get on with the rest of his life.

"I've got something to tell you," he announced. He looked scared of me. "I want to go back to Vanessa," he said, forcing himself to speak the words.

I remembered Vanessa and Alexandra at the front door, all those months ago, in February. Everyone loved Vanessa. Of course Henry wanted to go back to her. "We're going to wait until Christmas and then get back together again. You and I can still see each other until then," Henry suggested.

That seemed like a strange arrangement to me. "If we're going to break up, we need to do it now," I said, keeping my voice kind, not wanting to chase Henry away with the shrieks of pain pushing against the wall of my stomach.

"You're not angry?" Henry asked.

"No, I'm not angry," I said, "I should have known this would happen. I hope it works out for the two of you."

This was bad. And the timing was bad too. I was about to write exams that would determine the rest of my life and I couldn't move my body or focus my mind.

Tanya helped me. We went for a walk along Sea Point promenade, "I hate him," she said.

"You hate him? Why?"

"I heard him make you cry. I hate him," she was saying what I couldn't say. She was saying it for me, expressing my indignation, validating me.

We watched the waves and listened to the wailing of the gulls. Tanya stood next to me, letting me feel my anguish, not trying to make it go away, not wishing I'd hurry up and get back to being my usual self. The waves were swelling up and down, pushing in and out, swelling up and down, pushing in and out. I could feel infinity and I could feel Tanya's love. I knew it was going to be all right. Life goes on.

Within a few weeks of starting with the Weinbergs, the term was over. I handed the case over to Raymond. "It's all yours," I said, "my course is finished and the Weinbergs are expecting to continue with you."

"O.K.," Raymond said. I thought I was done.

More than a months later, the secretary of the clinic called me. "Vivien, the Weinberg family contacted us in distress. They've heard nothing from you since their last session."

"No!" I said, "Raymond Molloy took over the case. Didn't he continue?"

"No," the secretary said, "they've heard nothing."

"You'll have to speak to Ronnie," I said, "I can't work at the clinic any more because my course is finished. I'm hoping to get in for the masters program, but right now I can't do anything."

My heart was tying itself into a cold knot. I was upset that the Weinbergs had been abandoned, upset that I'd been abandoned. I was supposed to have a supervisor to guide me from initial interview to termination, but I didn't. Without a supervisor, it was my word against Raymond's, and Raymond Molloy was Cape Town's Mr. Child Psychology, while I was nobody. Or worse — the fall guy.

Everything looked bleak, then lo and behold — my grades were good enough to apply for the masters program. The finishing post was in sight. The day had come to apply for the Clinical Psychology training. I filled in the forms and went through the initial interviews. There were six places and six of us made it to the final selection.

We waited in the staff-room, the same room where I'd met with the parents after Ronnie's education courses. Each of us was being individually interviewed by a panel of eight, at the big boardroom table in the meeting room. Every now and then we'd say something polite to each other, but no-one was in the mood for chit-chat. We shifted in our chairs, avoided eye-contact and intermittently allowed ourselves to breathe loudly.

We waited through each person's interview, and then we waited, while the panel deliberated. Ronnie came out with a grave face and said, "I'll speak to you one at a time, in my office."

David's mother was one of the applicants. "Last year they came out and announced that everyone had been accepted," she said. Two little lines appeared above her nose.

"It means one of us didn't get in," Donald interpreted.

My internal bell started to chime. I knew what was about to happen. This time, it wasn't good news. "Don't worry," I said, "it's me who didn't get in. They're going to say that I'm too young."

David's mother was quick off the mark. "Well, if it is," she said, "and that is the reason, there's nothing you could have done about it." I think she had an internal bell too, because she also recognized the truth. She didn't waste time on false comfort, but she did her best to support me.

I replayed my interview in the light that someone had failed, and realized it had not gone well. The head of the department had looked down at a sheet in front of him, cleared his throat, leaned on the table, and challenged me. "It has been said that you are tactless at times. What do you have to say about that?"

The department head was looking at the paper in front of him, referring to something specific. But what was it? No-one at the clinic had ever said anything to me. The label confused me. I was the youngest in the family, I was an honest child, I'd often blurted things out. Mom had said numerous times, "Oh Vivien, shush, you're so tactless." I couldn't tell the difference between my family label and what was going on in the interview. This was the one word that could instantly shame me, make me blush, lose my tongue.

When I walked through the door of Ronnie's office, he looked down at his desk and groaned, "Oh, Vivien." He tried to soften his face sympathetically. "The panel believes you are too young for the course. They recommend that you go out and get some life experience and then reapply."

They were right. I was too young and I knew it, but I also knew the panel didn't base their decision on insight. They based it on false information. I was cheated. My results and achievements proved that I was a more solid candidate than some of the other students they were accepting. Worst of all, only five places were filled. My space, which I'd worked so hard to earn, was left empty.

I went back into the waiting room. "It was me," I said, "I didn't get in. You can all relax now."

"Are you O.K.?" Donald asked.

"Yes," I said. I turned to walk out the door, then turned back and waved, "Well, good luck, see you around."

I ran to my car, and drove down the hill, back to our flat. My place in the program was empty, and I was empty. In just a few weeks, my boyfriend and my professors, custodians of my dreams, shattered my hopes. I should have felt bad, yet I didn't. Another sensation was taking shape inside me, strengthening me.

I walked in through the door. Tanya, Albie and Desmond were sitting at the table, faces turning towards me, waiting to hear. "So what happened?" they asked, expecting a celebration.

"I didn't get in," I said, holding onto my tears, not wanting to part with another piece of myself. "They said I was too young."

Their smiles froze, mid-expression. They knew I'd achieved the academic requirements. They knew I had the interest and aptitude — they knew me. What had gone wrong? They bubbled with indignation. I had to reassure them. "I'm O.K.," I said, "really, I'm fine, don't worry."

"What are you going to do?" they asked.

"I'm going overseas," I said, "I'm going to Europe. I'm going to kibbutz. I'm going to travel for a year."

For ten years I'd had my sights set on a narrow goal. But I couldn't become a clinical psychologist. I had to choose something else — I was free. No boyfriend, no course, no commitments — I was free. I was remembering Uncle Harry's present, doorway to the world — I was free.

Journey

WINGS

I got the idea from Jeffrey. He'd quit law school and gone to kibbutz, the communal farm unique to Israel. In the summer months, especially, during the extended school vacations, youth from all over the world pour into Israel. The youth of South Africa were no exception, and because of the distance, and the air-fare, they combined the kibbutz experience with extended travel in Europe.

Jeffrey had followed the formula. He'd attended kibbutz *ulpan*, a five month program for working half the day, and learning Hebrew, the other half. There he'd met a young American, and the two of them went on to explore Europe together. Not getting into the masters program gave me the opportunity to admit to myself that that was what I really wanted to do.

I went to see Mom and Dad. "I didn't get in for the course," I said, "I'm too young. I need to get life experience and then reapply."

"Oh," they said, "we thought that might happen."

"But I know what I want to do instead."

"What?"

"I want to go to kibbutz *ulpan* and then Europe."

"You? On your own?" They knew I was barely capable of buying something in a store by myself, and incapacitated by the phone.

"Yes," I said, "on my own. I expect I'll meet someone on kibbutz and we'll travel Europe together, like Jeffrey did."

Over the next few days I acquired a one-year, Cape Town/Tel Aviv return air ticket, a passport, an international driver's license, a YMCA card for staying in youth hostels, a student ID card and a wad of travelers checks. I also acquired a gray suitcase and a red backpack.

I went to the Israeli consulate to apply for kibbutz *ulpan*. The consul enjoyed this part of his job. He smiled at me warmly. "I'm going to send you to a very large kibbutz called Magan Michael," he said. We'd visited Magan Michael on my first trip to Israel, a show-case kibbutz, boasting a dining-room overlooking the Mediterranean Sea. We could see the waves hitting the rocks, the spray fanning across the picture windows.

A few goodbyes and I'd be on my way. Top of my list was Kenny. He'd just got married to Barbara, his long-time girlfriend. They were also leaving, emigrating to England. "So, what are your plans?" they asked.

"I'm going to Magan Michael," I said.

"I don't believe it!" Barbara responded, "That's where my sister, Hilda, is going, and Kenny's father will be on the same flight to Tel Aviv. You'll be able to go with them to Kenny's sister, Rochelle, In Jerusalem."

We were all on the same flight. We spent a couple of days in Jerusalem, with Rochelle, then it was my turn to take the role of guardian, escort Hilda on the two-hour bus ride to Magan Michael. Rochelle dropped us off at the bus station. Albie had warned me, "Israelis don't respect queues. Don't expect things to be like here."

"What's Albie talking about?" I thought to myself. All was calm and normal. A motley assembly stood in a loose line, smoking, chatting and eating garinim — unshelled sunflower or pumpkin seeds. Then the bus arrived. Suddenly there was a frenzy of shoving and shouting as the passengers fought their way aboard. It was a Picasso-like blur of black mustaches, black beard stubble and black hairy armpits. We were in the Middle East now.

"Which way to Magan Michael?" we asked, getting off the bus.

"That way," pointed the driver. We looked up the road, saw other young people rounding the bend. We joined the stream. The coordinator of the *ulpan* program greeted us in groups and directed us on how to get our room keys and our work clothes. To me he said, "You shouldn't have been sent to this *ulpan*, we don't have the facilities for you. You already know too much Hebrew and we only have a beginner's class. I've arranged for you to go to Mayan Tzvi. Their classes have already begun, but I am sure that you will be better off there. I have called them and they're expecting you."

Mayan Tzvi was the kibbutz that Jeffrey had gone to! Jeffrey had told me about his Hebrew teacher, Walter. "Brilliant," he'd said, "a brilliant teacher." I was in luck.

I went to find Hilda, tell her the news. We wished each other "goodbye," and I shouldered the gray suitcase and the red backpack and left for Mayan Tzvi.

BLANK SLATE

Mayan Tzvi was a reasonably short distance up the road. Only problem was, it wasn't on the ocean side, where the land was flat. It was on the other side. "How are you going to get up the hill?" the bus driver asked, as he dropped me off.

"What hill?"

"That hill," he said, indicating a steep incline.

"I guess I'll have to walk," I said.

"You must hitch a ride," he indicated, by gesturing with his thumb.

Not me, no hitching. I shook my head. He shrugged his shoulders. He'd let me find out about the hill on my own. A quarter mile up the road, when my arm felt like it was going to break off from carrying my suitcase, a pick-up truck with a crew in the back, pulled up next to me. "Mayan Tzvi?" asked the driver. I was done with shaking my head. I nodded vigorously. He told me to climb in and dropped me off at the entrance gates.

The guard at the entrance called Benno, the *ulpan* director, on a walkie talkie, then sent me down the path, to the dining-room, where Benno would meet me. Benno led me past the kibbutz buildings, surrounded by attractive little gardens and mature trees, the defunct storage tower, the donkey-shed and the lens factory, up to the *ulpan* buildings, where he introduced me to the *ulpan* house-mothers, who handed me shorts and shirts and showed me to my room. "You'll be sharing with Rose, who is from Oklahoma and Ursula, who is from Sweden. They're both very nice girls. Everyone's at work or in class now, so you'll just have to hang around until supper-time. Go to the dining-room anytime from six onwards."

Ursula came back to the room first. "Hullo, who are you?" she asked.

"I'm Vivien, I just arrived."

"Can you speak Hebrew?"

"A little. I'm rusty, haven't had any practice in a while."

"I'm just learning. I really want to be able to speak Hebrew." She took her books from her bag and looked at them.

Then Rose opened the door. "Hello?" she said, eying me.

"This is Vivien," Ursula said, "she can speak Hebrew."

Ursula and Rose were excited to have another person in their room. "Where are you from?" they asked.

"South Africa," I replied.

"Another one!" they exclaimed, "There are more than twenty South Africans on this *ulpan*. With you here, there are more South Africans than Americans."

Ursula, Rose and Rose's boyfriend invited me to walk down to dinner with them. Kibbutz dining-rooms are communal eating halls, catering to the entire kibbutz population. Mayan Tzvi had over seven hundred inhabitants. Albie had said, "When you walk into the dining room, everyone will look at you. They won't even pretend they're not looking." It would have been easier if I'd arrived with the influx, been one of fifty new faces. On the other hand, nobody here knew me. I was a blank slate. There was no image to preserve, no course to qualify for and no professors to impress. There were no judging parents, no sneering brother, and no responsibilities. I had plans to discover a different version of myself.

The big dilemma was selecting the right Hebrew class. "How is your Hebrew?" Benno asked me, "Are you intermediate or advanced?"

"Hmm, I've done Hebrew for years," I said, "but I'm rusty, I'm not sure about the pace and syllabus."

"Let's go talk to the teachers," Benno suggested.

"Sit in on each class and then choose," said the intermediate teacher. She was kind.

I sat one morning in each class. I wasn't sure I could manage the advanced class. I'd missed the beginning. But I wanted Walter. Jeffrey had spoken so highly of him, and even in one morning I could tell he was as brilliant as Jeffrey said. I followed my rule. I chose the best teacher.

The week after I arrived there was a *gius* — a work party — in the banana plantation. That meant that everyone who could be spared was detailed to work in the fields.

Uri, the head of the agricultural division, the same man who'd rescued me from the hill trudge, took us down to the banana groves. The men were going to do the heavy work, replant the banana trees. The women were going to slice dried leaves off the trunks. Uri gave us each a knife, and showed us how to trim away the dead material.

It was spring. The atmosphere among the trees was jungle-like, tropical. I hadn't done any exercise in weeks. The combination of elements fired my blood. I found myself hacking and trimming at a ferocious rate. Uri noticed my speed and energy. After the *gius* was over, he told Raffi, "I want Vivien. She must stay in my team."

"Do you mind?" asked Raffi.

"Mind? No, I'd love to. That's why I came to kibbutz — to work outside."

At the end of my third week on kibbutz it was *Purim*, a festival celebrated with a fancy-dress party. I wasn't very creative and I hadn't brought any dresses that lent themselves to exciting transformation. I went as a boy — a *Hasidic* boy. I was comfortable in jeans, jacket, my long hair tucked up into a borrowed cap, with two ringlets on either side of my head, as sideburns. So much for the blank slate.

The dining-room was full of people who couldn't recognize each other. Even the dining-room had been transformed from a cafeteria into a dance hall. A young man sidled up to me. "And who are you?" he asked, pretending that he hadn't noticed me before.

"I'm Vivien," I said. I knew who he was. He was Amir, one of the eligible young men on the kibbutz. He worked in the fish ponds.

"*Veevyun?*" he repeated in his Israeli accent. "That's a beautiful name." He said it thoughtfully, as though he knew a Vivien already, knew what the name meant. He nodded his head. "My brother had a girlfriend Vivien."

I forced myself to be casual, to dance with him lightheartedly, to continue to look around the room, as though in search of other attractive young men. I already knew I wanted Amir. He was tall and bearded. His strong, muscular body was light and whip-like. His heavy, sensual eyes instantly telegraphed his passion in life — the pursuit of young women.

I knew enough about his type to realize that the excitement lay in the chase, and I could see I wasn't the only object of his interest. There was another young lady whom he wanted and who wanted him. We danced all night, then I stepped aside. "Go with Glenda," I said, "maybe you like her more. I don't mind."

He stared at me. This hadn't happened before. There were more available women than men. If you caught a man you had to hold tight. "Are you serious?"

"Of course," I said, "look — she likes you — try your luck."

He was puzzled, but he couldn't resist. "All right, then next week I'll try you," he concluded, staking a claim. He couldn't wait a week. Within two days he'd ditched Glenda and settled on me.

My life on kibbutz had a rhythm. One week I would go to work in the fields in the morning and study Hebrew in the afternoons. The second week I would go to work very early, three in the morning, to spray the fields before the wind came up. After breakfast at seven, I would go to Hebrew class until noon.

The only problem was that Amir was bored with kibbutz life. He craved something more. "I don't want my life to be just eating, sleeping and working. I want to do other things and you must do them with me," he commanded, adding, "I am the man and you are the woman, I will say when it is bed-time.

He only had to get up at six. It was O.K. for him to stay up until after midnight socializing, watching TV, visiting friends in nearby settlements. I had to get up at three.

He thought I was listening to him and that was fine. Amir always spoke English to me. He had no idea I could speak Hebrew, no idea that I could understand what he and his male friends were saying. He didn't bother to ask, so I didn't tell him. I'd always wanted to be a fly on the wall. I wasn't bored. I was hearing all kinds of interesting information. I truly was listening to him.

Interesting or not, it was hard for me to stay awake in the mornings, and it was especially difficult when I was sitting on the tractor. I struggled against the vibration of the vehicle, the involuntary lowering of my lids, an unending cycle of head falling forward, head jerking back, foot on gas pedal, inch forward, wait to spray the crops, head falling forward again. I thought about people who work night shift. I adjusted by sleeping four to five hours in the afternoons. Even with those extended afternoon naps, I was amazed how much can be accomplished in a day.

After we planted the mature banana trees, we sprayed the crops, then we developed new fields with baby trees. We laid irrigation pipes, picked fruit, painted the cuts where trees had been pruned. Every day I reminded myself to pause, look up at the blueness of the sky, listen to the swish-swish of the Mediterranean Sea and the humming of the bees. I inhaled the sweet and citrus fragrance of the seaside orchards in the early morning and plucked the biggest, juiciest grapefruits from the trees. When we came across ripe bananas, tree-fresh and wet with dew, we ate them. They would have spoiled by the time they got to market. My pockets filled with pecan nuts and I carried home the oversized rich, buttery avocado pears, one in each hand.

I overheard Uri and Chayim, the team leaders, the men responsible for the agricultural success of the kibbutz, arguing loudly with Raffi, almost coming to blows. "Vivien is worth four or five of the others. She works hard. She can do it on her own quicker than a group. She has good ideas. She understands what needs to be done. She's . . . she's better than a boy!" Chayim shouted.

"Exactly," agreed Uri, "that's why I need her! I planned my whole morning expecting to have her help."

Raffi looked from one to the other in surprise. "There's only one Vivien," he said, "you'll have to take turns."

After being rejected in my chosen career, I needed to hear that. Few women got the chance to work outside permanently. Ironically, the innovative model of kibbutz life had sunk into the traditional division of labor along gender lines. The women worked in the kitchen, the laundry, the dining room and the other service sectors, while the men worked in the fields and the fish ponds.

As much as I loved being on the kibbutz, I also loved going to the cities on the weekend. The weekend was short, only Friday afternoon and Saturday, but Israel is a small country. Sometimes I'd visit Mom's cousins, Auntie Nettie and Auntie Chaia in Tel Aviv, sometimes I went to visit Rochelle in Jerusalem.

Auntie Chaia was already well into her eighties, she was small, she looked frail, but she wasn't. She was strong and wiry. As soon as I arrived, she'd sit me down at the kitchen table and serve me fresh cheesecake, watch me eat. We didn't have much to say to each other, we were from different worlds, different generations, but I was family, Renée's daughter. There was so much love, it was like being with Jacky.

When I went to Jerusalem, Rochelle and I would shop for food and vegetables, hurry back to her apartment, chop and cut, cook and eat. I enjoyed the camaraderie. I looked forward to my special treat, a walk through the old city, a favorite place on earth. I could hardly wait to get out and feel the tingle of the air, the glow of the Jerusalem stone, the prickle and push of the people. I loved to wander the cobbled streets, shop the Arab market, surrounded by the religions of the world. Travel enchanted me. Diversity enchanted me. Other ways enchanted me.

It was all about accepting differences, adapting, learning to get on in the world by breaking open my thinking. I couldn't run to Mom, or Michael, or anyone else for help. I had to do it myself. I'd bought myself a pair of leather sandals in Haifa. With each step I took, they clicked loudly. The sound was irritating enough, but I was concerned that the click was caused by a fault in the sandal. I went back to the store.

"I need to exchange these sandals," I said, "they're making a clicking noise."

"What!" the shop owner said, taken aback that I had the nerve to try and return this perfectly excellent footwear. "There's nothing wrong. These are good sandals."

I shook my head at him. "Something is broken."

"Where?" he argued, "I see nothing broken, show me where it is broken."

I put the sandals on and marched up and down the store. "Do you hear that? Listen to that sound, something is broken." The click was undeniable.

"No," he said, "there is nothing wrong. They all do that." He folded a sandal between his hands, to prove how well made they were.

"Then I don't want them. I don't like the sound. Something is broken," I repeated. I did not want to walk across Europe in chirping sandals. The shopkeeper was angry with me. He stabbed the air with his finger, thinking he could intimidate me. He didn't know about Mom's finger. I could stand up to him, and more, I could give it back. It was a gesticulation contest. I was just getting into my stride, discovering a new talent, when he surrendered. He forlornly handed over a brand new pair.

I had become a young adult who, pitted against a male, in a chauvinistic culture, and a foreign language, could exchange a used pair of sandals.

My victory was soon challenged. There was only another six weeks of *ulpan*. It was time to go to Tel Aviv to arrange my journey through Europe. I hadn't met anyone to travel with me. I was going to have to go on my own.

"You're going to Tel Aviv to get a visa for Italy?" someone asked.

"Yes," I said.

"Do you know you have to stand in line at the consulate? They only give a certain number of visas in a day. You have to get there very early."

I got there as early as I could, but it wasn't early enough. The quota for the day was ushered inside the consulate. The rest of us were told to come back another day. That wouldn't be possible. There had to be another solution.

I walked up and down the wide, Tel Aviv sidewalks eying the travel agencies, too intimidated to go inside. They looked so official, so business-like. My phobias returned. It was good the sandal-man from Haifa couldn't see me like this. I'd walked past half a dozen agencies. I was pathetic. "What do you think they do for a living?" I asked myself. "Just go inside, tell them what you want. That's their job. Stop wasting time and get on with it."

I continued to walk up the street, the can/can't battle raging inside me. I reached a pitch of frustration, "Next agency, no matter how it looks, you're going inside." I hated myself. I was pitiful. There it was, another travel agency. I forced myself to open the door, go inside. A young man said, "Can I help you?"

"Yes," I said, "I want to buy an air-ticket to Athens and a Eurail pass, and I need a visa for Italy."

"Of course," he said, "I will need your passport."

"You can do it for me? You can get the visa?"

He gave me a strange look. "Yes, we can do it for you. We're a travel agency. That is our job. It will take a couple of days."

"Are you sure? I was at the consulate this morning. They were so busy. They said we must come very early in the morning."

"You tried to do it yourself? No, no, we'll do it. They make it difficult, because they only want to deal with the agents. We can do it, no problem. Just fill in these forms."

Within fifteen minutes it was all wrapped up. No more worries, except one — here I was, paralyzed at the thought of walking into a travel agency, and I was now committed to traveling through Europe on my own. I could feel the fear hovering on the other side of a thin wall. I pushed it back. Others had done it, so could I.

Only one day in the city and I was relieved to get back to the safety of the kibbutz — until I went to look where I'd be working the next day. I discovered I'd been put in the kitchen. "The kitchen? What's going on?" I asked Raffi.

"Don't ask me," Raffi said, "I can't tell you anything, but there've been complaints that you always get to work outside. You have to work in the kitchen this week."

"That's not fair," I said, "my friends are in the fields. I don't have friends in the kitchen." Raffi couldn't look me in the eye. I'd been off the kibbutz one day and I'd been ousted from my place.

The kitchen staff complained to Raffi that I was surly and they didn't want me. "What about the children's house," Raffi suggested, "will you work with the children?"

"I suppose so," I said. Kibbutz children had a reputation for being hard for outsiders to handle. They were brought up in a pack. They weren't sweet little angels. I made one mistake of trying to befriend the children and they turned into a baying mob, so I kept my distance. Working in the children's house meant making beds, washing windows and polishing children's shoes. As long as I didn't have to deal directly with them I was probably going to survive.

I managed to keep my mouth shut until I came up the stairs of the unit, to find the children tormenting a little girl because her skin was slightly darker than theirs. They were pointing at her, chanting in unison,

"*Shochit, shochit*," meaning "Black girl, Black girl," and she was looking down at herself, trying to hide from her own eyes. "Shut up," I shouted at them, "shut up. Never say that again."

The plight of the little Yemeni girl, with her dark skin, was cause for reflection. It was all about insiders and outsiders. I had been so busy becoming an 'insider' to kibbutz life, that I had only made two friends on the *ulpan* — John, from South Africa and Julia, from England. My insider status in one domain, gave me outsider status in another. I had alienated myself, just like I'd alienated myself in the Psychology Department.

For a couple of weeks I worked in the turkey shed, clipping beaks off turkey chicks. I felt exactly like those poor chicks. There they were, caught in a cage, with nothing to do but peck at their food. Suddenly a big hand grabs them, squeezes them tight and clips off their beak, so they can't peck each other. Droplets of blood fell on my shoes, where they left an indelible stain.

There were only so many beaks to clip. "What am I going to do with you, Vivien?" Raffi asked, shaking his head in despair. "You can work anywhere you want, just not in the fields." He looked as sad as I felt. It was disturbing to feel that my peers resented me, wanted to push me out of my place, take it for themselves.

I turned my attention to my Hebrew studies. Thanks to Walter, I was almost fluent. My first week in the class, when I got the meaning of the word he was explaining, the English translation slipped out of my mouth. He stopped, turned his mouth down theatrically, to let me know that wasn't how we learned language in here. He was recreating the way children learn their mother tongue. He demonstrated the word in different ways — mime, charade, sentences, similes, a rich use of language. We simultaneously learned vocabulary, syntax, grammar and idiom. Walter put patience, energy and love in one end, and a class of students who could speak Hebrew came out the other end.

Now that we were all comfortable speaking Hebrew, I wasn't limited to the South Africans and Americans for friendship. I had a common language with the Spanish and French students. Leaving the dining-room one evening, I fell into conversation with Pnina, who was from France.

Absorbed in conversation, we wandered up the path together, to the *ulpan* and volunteer buildings, and stopped outside the door to the room I shared with Amir.

Amir overheard us. When I came inside, he said: "That was you talking outside wasn't it?"

"Yes," I replied.

"You didn't tell me you can speak Hebrew."

"You never asked," I retorted, "you always wanted to practice your English."

"Wait a sec, does this mean you have understood everything I've been saying with my friends?"

"Yes, of course!" I smirked.

He was looking at me, trying to make up his mind which way to go. "Why didn't you tell me?"

"I never hid it from you. You could have worked it out," I said. "You know I'm in *ulpan*. You know I'm in Walter's class. You know I'm learning Hebrew. What do you think I'm doing every day? Wasting my time?"

"But nobody on *ulpan* learns anything," Amir said.

"That's not true. We can all speak Hebrew. We can all read the newspaper. We can all understand the news on the radio and TV."

"How?" he questioned.

I looked at him in disbelief. Walter lived next door to Amir's parents. "Don't you know what a brilliant teacher Walter is?" I asked.

"Walter?"

"Yes, Walter," I said, "your parents' neighbor. He's one of the best teachers I've ever had." I described Walter and his teaching skills. "Walter doesn't only teach me Hebrew, *he's teaching me how to teach.*"

Amir stroked his beard, "I didn't know that. Imagine . . . Walter . . . such a good teacher." Then he remembered that he was feeling tricked, supposed to be angry with me, "I'm going to speak to him about you!"

Amir was thoughtful and I was thoughtful, too. I was shocked that members of the kibbutz were not aware of the master teacher in their midst. It was a shame. And I was disappointed with an implication of my conversation with Amir — he hadn't noticed that I could 'tell the difference between cocoa and milo.'

Our *ulpan* was over. Uri wanted to hold a farewell celebration for the team who'd replanted the banana fields. He asked Raffi for special permission to schedule me to work outside. One last time I went down to the fields. Uri made a speech. "Volunteer labor is very important to the kibbutz," he said, "and this has been the best group we've ever had." I could smell the earth. It put a sweet taste in my mouth. Until then, I'd carried my sense of self in my academic abilities. Now I had another dimension. I was a hard worker.

It was the middle of June. I mailed my suitcase to Julia's home in the north of England, planning to visit her after my travels through

Europe. I packed my red backpack, said goodbye to Amir, walked to the entrance gates and hitched a ride down the hill, to the bus stop, to catch the bus to Tel Aviv.

VISION QUEST

From Tel Aviv I flew to Athens. I didn't know where I was going to stay that night, or any other night. As a young woman alone, brought up in violent South Africa, safety was my first concern.

On the plane, I devised two rules and a plan.

Rule 1: Reach your destination before nightfall.

Rule 2: Do not indulge in sexual liaisons.

The Plan

Go to foreign exchange at the airport, get Greek currency, then go to the information booth at the airport and find out how to get into town. Find a place to stay, using the guide, Europe on $10.00 a Day.

My plan was comforting, but I didn't need to follow it. Prominent signs directed tourists to the bus into town and a large group of travelers and backpackers were gathering at the bus stop. As soon as I walked up, a tall young man spoke to me. "Is this your first time in Athens?"

"Yes," I answered," and it's my first time in Europe."

"I've been here before," he said. "If you need somewhere to stay, you can come with me. I know a cheap place." I drew closer to him. I wasn't on my own anymore. I was one of a pair.

The cheap place must have been too cheap, it no longer existed. We plodded up and down the hills of Athens, looking for an alternative. My backpack pulled on my shoulders and neck, making my muscles burn. The hip belt was poorly designed, a previously unnoticed flaw. I was beginning to wonder if I wouldn't have been better off with my original plan, when my companion stopped some other young tourists and asked them if they knew a place to stay.

"Oh yes," they said, "go up the hill and turn left, you can't miss it."

They were right, we couldn't miss it. The place was squirming with youth, from all over the world. Naked light bulbs hung from the ceilings, the paint was peeling, the basins were stained and the toilet was a hole in the concrete. It didn't matter, the walls resounded with the cheerful sounds of young people on summer vacation.

Journey To Europe

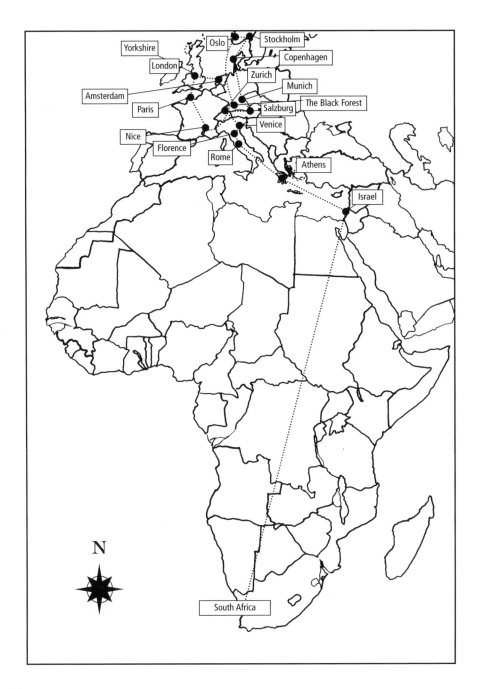

I went into the girls' dorm. "Come up on the roof, look at the view," someone said. I followed the crowd. My airport friend had also made his way up there. We looked at the view of Athens. "This is great," I said.

"Should we go get something to eat?" he asked.

"Sure," I said. I felt so light without my backpack. I felt so light knowing I had a place to stay that night.

The next morning I thought, "I'm traveling alone, so alone I must be." I knew exactly what I wanted to see. Mom and Dad had shown us slides of their trip to Greece. I was going to use my guide book and the public transport, and go and see the archaeological wonders for myself.

I did a day trip, looking at pillars and columns and broken steps. I was safe and bored. I was glad there were lots of people around when I got back to the hostel. We ambled down the hill, in a big group, exchanging stories, looking for a restaurant.

"I want to visit the Oracle of Delphi tomorrow," I announced.

A freckle-faced girl from England heard me. "Can I come with you?" she asked.

"Sure," I said, "we'll have to leave early in the morning. It's a long way."

"No problem," she said, "I'll be up." Her name was Liz. She once had a Greek boyfriend. She spoke a few words of Greek.

The bus-ride seemed endless. "We'll have to be careful," I said to Liz, "the last bus back to Athens leaves at four thirty. We mustn't miss it."

"How do you know all this?" Liz asked.

"I looked in the book and I got pamphlets from Tourist Information."

"Oh," she said.

"Why, how do you do it?"

"I just ask people, see what happens." Obviously Liz didn't have the same travel rules as I did.

We spent the day exploring the ancient buildings, absorbing the imposing atmosphere. The trip made us hungry. "Let's get something to eat," Liz said.

"I don't think we've got time. The restaurant looks crowded."

"We'll be fine," Liz said, "you need to relax. Everything will be O.K."

"All right," I said, "let's go eat." The restaurant was too busy and the service was too slow. "Come, we must run for the bus," I urged Liz. She huffed and puffed behind me, stopping to catch her breath. We got in sight of the stop just in time to see the bus pulling away. "Now what?" I asked.

"We'll have to hitch," Liz said. She seemed so much more cheery now, in charge, in control, doing things her way. I didn't want to hitch, but she had me. It was the only way we could get back to Athens.

Within minutes two fellows in a truck stopped for us. "We just need a ride to Athens," Liz said, "don't be expecting anything from us. We're stuck because we missed the last bus. All we want is a ride." They dipped their heads cordially. They knew the last bus had left. All they wanted was to help us. Back in Athens, Liz recognized a street corner, "There," she said, "we'll get off there." As she took hold of the door-handle, the driver asked, "Come for dinner?" and his friend said, "Drinks?"

Liz shot a glance at me. I was already too far beyond my boundaries. I had 'no' written all over my face. "No," she said, "we just wanted a ride, but thank you, thank you for your help." I felt guilty looking at their three wilted faces.

"It just shows its worth putting effort into the day," Liz said, as we walked up the street, "otherwise you land up just sitting around, like I did yesterday."

I thought about what Liz said. Why would someone travel to a foreign country then just sit around? Didn't they want to see the sights? I realized I was not like the European tourists, casually boarding trains to neighboring countries with sandier beaches and different cuisine, for a two week summer vacation. I was on a quest.

Still, even with a quest, I didn't need to be so scholarly, studying the history and archaeology of the mainland. The conversations in the hostel revealed the fun way to enjoy Greece — to catch the ferries and go island hopping.

I chose Santorini. As the ferry pulled into the dock, a hum started on board. The hum grew louder, turning into a buzz. We all looked up in dismay. The harbor was at the foot of a high, steep cliff and we could see little figures walking up and down a twisting flight of thousands of steps. There was good news and bad news. "You don't have to go up by foot," the person next to me said, "you go up on the back of a mule." On the back of a mule? That was almost as bad as hitching a ride. Half way up the cliff I began to giggle. "Here I am, on the back of a mule, being led up a cliff," I thought. "I may as well unclench my hands — I'm not the one holding the reins!"

Massaged loose by the mule ride, I noticed that wherever I went, an army of colorful backpacks bobbed up and down the road ahead of me. Everyone had tidbits they were eager to trade, everyone was hoping to meet someone, go on a jaunt, share a meal, compare adventures, interact. Mostly people were traveling in two's and three's, but there were also lone travelers like me. It was understood that no-one wanted to keep to themselves. We were a community of transients. It was easy to strike up a conversation, make new friends.

On the ferry I'd met a young Frenchman. We made our way to the beach, unrolled our sleeping bags and slept under the stars. We ate in the small taverns, walked the village and the island, visited the volcanic beach with black sand. Our last night, we slept at the harbor, so that we could embark our ferries early the next morning. Our journeys had overlapped for three days. Now we were going in different directions.

I took the ferry to Italy, landing in the south, at the port of Brindisi. It was a new country, a new language and a new currency. I hobbled across the square, disoriented, looking for lira and directions to Rome. There was no-one in front of me. I looked back, to see what had happened to all the other passengers. They were making a rush on the ice cream vendor. What was the matter with them? It was only nine in the morning. "Onward," I thought to myself, "no accounting for strange tastes, I have to get my *Eurail* pass endorsed, catch a train."

Rome was too big, the roads too wide, the traffic too fast. I hurried on to Florence. The ambience, the markets, the mist on the river teasing the red roofs, enchanted me. I met a young American, Anthony, in the youth hostel. "Come with me on a day outing to Pisa," he said. We went to Pisa, and looked at the leaning tower. It leaned. We walked around it, viewing it from different angles. The angle didn't matter. From every point of view, it leaned.

"How long 'til it falls down?" I asked.

"Don't know," Anthony said, "you can look it up in the book. Let's go have ice cream."

"Ice cream?"

"Yes, ice cream," he said. He gave me a funny look. "You haven't had the ice-cream yet?"

"No," I said, "I can get ice cream at home. I'm counting my pennies, I don't want to spend my money on ice cream."

"You can get Italian ice cream at home?"

"Of course," I said, we have Italian restaurants, and they make Italian ice cream."

Anthony didn't believe me. He shook his head. Then he had one more try, "Oh, come on!" he said, pointing at a plaque on the wall, "look, this place won an award for their Zabaglione flavor. That's what I'm going to have."

I was scared that if I had one, I wouldn't be able to stop. "All right then, I'll try one," I said. The first taste took me by surprise. Suddenly I understood the strange behavior of my fellow ferry passengers at Brindisi. They knew something I didn't know — they knew how ice cream in Italy tastes. Light, fruity flavors blended smoothly with rich chocolate and fragrant vanilla. Why did I ignore the signs? How many precious days of eating ice cream had I missed? And what else had I been missing?

Anthony watched my face change. "Actually," he said, "the most famous ice cream shop is in Florence. I'll take you there tomorrow." That's all I needed — a famous ice cream shop. In the end I had to ration myself to three ice-creams a day.

"Let's go to Venice," Anthony said, "I especially like Venice."

I had new respect for Anthony's suggestions. "O.K.," I said. I wanted to see the canals, the gondolas, the Venetian architecture, subject of so many pictures I'd looked at, when I was a child. Michael and I had dreamed of Venice. We'd wished that Cape Town would be flooded. We wanted to ride a boat to school.

"Let's go to this poster exhibition," Anthony said.

"I can't stand the thought of another exhibition," I said.

"Why? What are you talking about?" Anthony asked.

"I dragged myself to the art museums in Rome and Florence, and I didn't see a single painting I liked," I whined.

"Were you selective?" Anthony asked.

Selective? How was I supposed to be selective? "No," I said, "I just went to the famous museums and looked at the paintings."

Anthony laughed at me. "Well no wonder. That is boring. Don't worry, this will be different."

It was an exhibition of the artists original creations, beginning with posters from the 1800's, progressing through posters of the different war eras and on into the technology and style of the pop generation. I saw the originals of Michael's Toulouse-Lautrec poster collection, as well as other famous posters that had become part of our culture, the recent history of mankind. I was a child of the twentieth century. I knew what posters were for, how they were supposed to affect me. I could tell if they were pleasing, informative, successful. I could relate!

Anthony was younger than me, but he'd been full of good ideas. I was sorry to say goodbye. He was continuing to Chamonix, in France. I was going to Zurich, then on to the Swiss Alps, to Grindelwald, via Interlaken.

From Interlaken I caught a cog train, designed to climb the steep slope to Grindelwald. After all the big cities, I couldn't get enough of looking out the window — the mountain air, the green slopes mottled with yellow flowers, blue skies with wispy clouds, great mountains with white peaks. The radiant sunlight gently bathed the scenery, and my spirit.

There were sightseers, but if they wanted to see anything, they had to be willing to hike the alpine trails. This wasn't about going to restaurants, drinking coffee in the cafes. This was about a robust interaction with nature. The hostel provided cooking facilities. For the first time in seven months I had the choice to cook for myself. I'd been eating bread and fries and ice cream. I decided to follow the liver-cleansing diet. I ate simple, clean food and went hiking daily. By the third day my jeans eased. I felt light. The path through the woods invited me to run and jump and sing. The gradient was a mere nothing.

Rejuvenated, I continued my travels. By the time I got to Denmark, I finally admitted I was under-dressed. It was the coldest summer in Europe in a number of years. In Greece and Italy my ten dollars a day had gone far, but as I traveled north, ten dollars bought less and less. From the backpackers point of view, Denmark was expensive. I looked with jealous eyes at the mountains of fudge and taffy in the candy store. I wanted some. I took a photograph of the store window instead. I could hardly afford a new jacket. My guide-book had anticipated this. It listed a secondhand clothing store. There was one jacket that fitted me. It was good to feel warm again!

All of us backpackers were in the same boat, scratching to get by on our budgets. We found something to take the place of money — camaraderie. We were beginning to recognize each other, "Didn't I see you on the ferry?" and "Weren't you in the youth hostel in Zurich?" At Copenhagen station we bumped into Anna, a train companion from a few weeks before. "I'm just passing through," she said.

"You're not going to see Copenhagen?"

"It's too expensive, isn't it?"

"Yes, but we've found a cheap place to stay, and some reasonable places to eat. We're having fun. Come on, join us," I urged.

"Really?" she inquired, "Should I?"

I told here the name of our hostel. I watched her look up the number in the telephone directory. I wished I could be so confident, so competent, able to make phone calls from public phones in foreign places. Then she surprised me. "You phone?" she requested, holding out her coin to me.

I jumped back, as though she offered a scorpion. The very idea! I could travel across Europe on my own, but phoning — that was going too far.

"No, no, you phone," I said soothingly, disguising my dread as support. "They're very friendly there. It will be O.K."

She dialed the number, conversed and put down the receiver with a smile. "Yes, they have space for me." I was in awe. She must have had her own fears of phoning, or she wouldn't have asked me — and then she did it. I resolved that I would be able to manage that feat, one day.

That evening, in the dorm, getting ready to go out for dinner, the other young women gathered round me. "Where are you from?" someone asked.

"Yes, I also want to know," chimed another. A group gathered round me. The last time I had been surrounded was at Hebrew School. Then the intention was to mock and torment me. I started to writhe with embarrassment.

"Me too, I don't recognize your accent," someone else added, "you sound German, or something." I didn't want to admit I was from South Africa. The shame of being a White South African was worse than the shame of being dressed like a boy.

"I know . . . you're from Greece," tried one.

"No, I think Spain," guessed another.

"Russia!" asserted another triumphantly.

"Close," I said, "all four of my grandparents are from Lithuania. But I'm from South Africa," I confessed, looking from face to face, expecting rejection, wondering what they would say.

They all started to chatter, asking me questions, "I would love to go to Africa," one of them said admiringly, "what's it like?"

"Yes, what's it like? Are there jungles? Are there wild animals? You're so far from home! How do you manage?" It was hard to believe. They thought I was foreign and exotic. They thought I was a lone adventuress from Africa.

From Denmark, I took the ferry to Sweden, first to Stockholm and then to the northernmost tip. For hours and hours the scene from the train window repeated itself — dense conifer woods, punctuated occasionally by blue lakes. There were no signs of life. They may as well have stuck a poster on the window and simulated the motion of the train.

Fortunately, it was the custom to exchange books on the trains, and I'd been handed *Journey to Ixtlan* by Carlos Castenada. I was enjoying the book. It seemed appropriate to be reading about a journey, while I was on a journey. I came to the last chapter. Carlos' teacher warns him that if he fulfills the rituals to initiate him to the next level of his training, he will be alienated from his current world. Carlos decides that he is not ready to take this step. He chooses to drive away from his teacher, go back to his home. I put the book face down on my lap, breathed in and out. It felt like Castenada had written this book just for me, to let me know I wasn't alone. It was obvious to me why he made that choice, then, and equally obvious that he would later make a different choice. These pages spoke to my soul, gave me the courage to face my own path.

After a period of inward reverie, I shifted my attention to my fellow passengers. Across the aisle, a middle-aged American couple were traveling with a gigantic bag of Milky Way candies, popping them into their mouths with comforting regularity. Every now and then, presumably urged by guilt, they offered the bag around, but no-one accepted. We could tell by the way they held the bag inside their body zone, that they didn't want us to take their candy.

Opposite them sat two young ladies who specialized in all the 'don'ts' of train travel. They had started with the heinous act of boarding the wrong train and progressed through the unheeded warning of boarding the correct train, but seating themselves in the carriage which later separates and goes to a different destination. They had story after story of scrapes they had got themselves into and how they'd been rescued, always by at least one man, sometimes a group.

Directly opposite me sat a young American lass whose name was Nancy. Nancy? No-one in South Africa was called Nancy. It was a fictional name. When I was ten, I'd had a paper doll called Nancy and I'd read several books with characters of that name, but I'd never expected a live one, and here she was, proving herself too good to be true. Nancy was a fount of philosophies that she had learned at her mother's knee. Especially after my recent experiences, I thought my upbringing was sheltered, but listening to Nancy, I realized I was a woman of the world.

"My mother told me," she announced to the whole train, "that I should always wear make-up. And if it should happen that the doorbell rings and you open the door, and a man is standing there, and you're not wearing make-up, then you should just continue as though you are wearing make-up." She breathed deeply, pausing, "Don't show him that you're aware that you're not wearing your make-up." She wanted to be sure that we'd understood the point.

We all nodded solemnly, not needing to discuss such profound wisdom. After that my need for scenery was reduced. I silently amused myself constructing a picture of Nancy's world. I imagined the kitchen, including the curtains on the windows, a gingham print, red and blue and white. I wanted to scoff, but I couldn't. I was touched by the way she spoke about her mother, her innocent gratitude for feminine guidance.

From Sweden I went to Norway. The inspiring sculptures of the Vigeland park beckoned me, Edvard Munch's painting, *The Scream*, changed my pulse, the Kon Tiki expedition fired my respect for human accomplishment, the natural wonder of the fjords claimed my breath. In downtown Oslo, I looked through the window of an apothecary and saw a proud father holding up his baby for all the women pharmacists to admire. Changes in sex-roles had not yet reached South Africa. The women stood around in their white coats, smiling, reaching their hands out to the baby, and the man, in jeans and t-shirt, grinned from ear-to-ear, leaning on the stroller. Look at that! I couldn't imagine the end of Apartheid, and less could I imagine fathers taking time off work to take care of babies. This was a different world, and I liked it. What I didn't know, was that this chance tableau, was showing me my future.

I tore myself away from Norway to travel south again, through Germany to another attractive university town, in the region of the Black Forest. I'd been on the road ten weeks, my bubble and fizz had gone. I didn't feel like meeting more strangers, doing the work of making friends. I went on to the south of France. I walked, alone, along the promenades, looking down on the topless sun-worshippers. I took the train from Nice and went to Monte Carlo for the day, where my step-cousins Maxine, Karen and David, spent their summers on their father's yacht. I wanted to be with them — the comfortable, the familiar. I wasn't in the mood to speak French, or be followed by a German tourist hoping for holiday romance. I wasn't even in the mood to eat French pastries. I wanted South African whole-wheat bread with marmalade.

I caught the train to Aix-en-Provence. The train's final destination was Paris. I was feeling tired. Why get off the train? Why try to find my way around another strange city? Why not stay on the train the whole day, go to Paris? Because it's Sunday. It's against the rule. The train arrives in Paris at dusk, the information booths will be closed. So what? I can use my guide book, and the map at the station. I've always been all right, why not today?

The map of the Mètro had been defaced. There was a huge tear across it. I stared at the blank space helplessly, looked round at the scurrying people, heads down, hurrying to get home. No-one to ask, no clues.

I stood around for about fifteen minutes, then decided things could only get worse, not better. It would soon be dark. I slung my pack on my back and started walking down the road in the hopes that a street sign or approachable person would point me to a Mètro station. Within minutes a small French car drew up alongside me. The driver was too big for his car. He'd folded himself into the front seat behind the steering wheel.

"Where are you going? Can I give you a ride?" he asked. I could barely understand his Parisian accent. He was definitely going to struggle to make sense of my South African French. I hesitated. I wasn't sure I wanted to deal with him. "What are you doing walking down the street alone, at this time of the day, dressed like that — *demi nue.*" He outlined the neckline of my sundress, which I'd bought in the Arab market in Jerusalem — suitable attire for the south of France, not so suitable in the unknown suburbs of Paris at twilight. "You're not safe. Get in the car. Where do you want to go?"

"The Mètro," I said.

"Sure, I'll take you to the Mètro. Get in the car." I was doubtful, but I had to trust somebody. I got in the car.

As soon as I was in the car he said, "I can take you to the Mètro, but why don't you rather come to my apartment. We can go out together for dinner this evening." Then he added, in English, "no strings attached."

I rubbed the back of my neck. The hairs were beginning to prickle. Now that he actually had me in his car, he was reluctant to release me. I was running out of time to find a room for the night and I suspected that around every corner lurked another predatory male.

I glanced over at him. He wore glasses. His short hair was dark with grease, his skin looked pale and unhealthy. He had long, skinny arms and legs. He was just a lonely guy looking for a girl. It was impossible to tell from looks, but it felt like my will was stronger than his. I was in need of help, he was in need of company, what the hell. "O.K.," I said, "I'll come with you, but no strings attached."

"No strings attached," he agreed and threw the car into gear and drove us to his apartment. "What's your name?" he asked.

"Vivien."

"Viviàne? That's a French name." He seemed pleased.

"And yours?"

"Philippe."

"What do you do?"

"I'm a medical student," he said, "don't expect anything fancy. I'm very poor." That was the truth. The apartment was green and brown and dark, confined living quarters, heavy with the smell of stale air. He had so little furniture that he didn't even have a bed, just a big old couch.

"Come," he said, "let's go out, see some night life."

Neither of us could afford the shows, or the restaurants. We walked the streets, observing the people, buying food from the street vendors. Slowly his hand moused its way into mine. I pulled my hand away, "No strings attached," I reminded him. A few minutes later his hand crept back into mine. It didn't matter what I said, he was going to try anyway.

Back at his apartment I went into the bathroom to brush my teeth. When I came out a giant bed had sprung out of the couch in the living room — my first view of a sofa bed. With exaggerated movements, I unfolded my sleeping bag and laid out a place, on the floor.

"*Non, non!*" Philippe protested. He would sleep on the floor and I could sleep in the bed. But I'd reached the limit. No matter what promises he made, I knew better than to sleep in his bed. I lay down on the floor, turned on my side and went to sleep. During the night I woke up to find Philippe lying on the floor, pressed up against my body. "*Je t'aime,*" he whispered in my ear.

I wracked my brain for the French. Bed is masculine, use the imperative, "Go back to bed," I said firmly, and he did.

In the morning it was clear that Philippe had had a sleepless night. He was tired and angry, but he dropped me off at a Mètro stop, as promised, and I found my way to the main railway station.

I didn't want to be on guard any more. I wanted to have friendly conversations about common experience and common interests, stay in a home not a hostel. I decided to go to England. I tried to call Julia, my kibbutz friend, keeper of my suitcase, but the number wouldn't connect, so I sent a telegram, "Arriving three p.m. train tomorrow."

Julia was waiting for me at the station, "Let's go for tea," she said. Tea? Civilization at last. I fell upon the scones like a starving person. It was my first visit to England, but the culture, subject of my childhood books and magazines, was familiar enough to feel like home. It was great to recognize a face, stay in a house with a yard, and see my suitcase, filled with my personal belongings.

The next morning Julia took me aside. "I'm leaving for Wales next week, to begin college, and my parents want me to focus on that."

I didn't want to hear these words. I wanted to take a break from the constant traveling, I wanted to stay with Julia and her parents for weeks and weeks. Too bad, my timing was off, I couldn't expect to arrive out of the blue and move into someone else's home.

My timing wasn't just off, it was disastrous. I phoned Kenny and Barbara in London. "Oh," said Barbara, "Kenny's parents are here at the moment and we just don't have room." She paused, trying to think of a plan, not coming up with anything, already over-committed, "But what are you going to do, Vivien?"

I forced lightness into my voice, "I still plan to go to Paris and Amsterdam, so if I can't find somewhere to stay in London, I'll go there for two weeks and then come back."

"Good," she said, relieved, "because then we'll have space for you."

One more try. I called the Bleimans, our friends who'd left South Africa when I was five. "Well, Vivien," Rita said, a sigh in her voice, "I've had some bad experiences and I have a 'no visitors' policy now."

"I understand," I said sadly. I knew what she meant. We South Africans were always taking advantage of our friends in the big cities overseas, descending on their homes in London and New York, staying for free, acting like they owed us something because they'd escaped South Africa and we hadn't.

What was I going to do? I had nowhere to stay. Nobody wanted me. Wait a minute, that's nonsense. I had just spent ten weeks taking care of myself in Europe — I could do the same in England. It would be even easier, everything was in English. I was capable. I was self-sufficient. There was a big difference between *wanting* help and *needing* help.

As soon as I found my inner strength, Rita called me back. "Vivien, I've changed my mind. I thought about it some more and Jack agrees. You can come and stay for a night or two. After all, you're Renée's daughter, I shouldn't put you in the same category as the other visitors we've had."

"Thank you," I said, "I'll stop in on my way to Paris."

Jack was sitting in his favorite chair, in the lounge, reading by the light of a lamp, when I arrived. He nodded kindly in greeting and returned to his book. Rita showed me to the guest room, "Do you have everything you need? Can you think of anything else? Enough towels? Just tell me."

The next morning I rose early, intending to see the sights. Rita was in the kitchen, "What would you like for breakfast?" she asked. She wanted to take care of me, make up for her initial 'no.'

"Oh, some tea and toast, will be nice," I said, also affected by the 'no,' not wanting to be a nuisance.

We sat at the table, "Where have you been?" Rita asked, trying to be interested. Her eyebrows went up in response to my list, "That's a lot of traveling! We've just been to South Africa to visit everyone."

"How was it?"

"It was hard."

"I can imagine," I said, "no-one understands."

That comment hit the nail on the head. "You're right," Rita said, her voice changing from polite to real, "no-one understands. They're so caught in their own little world. I feel like I have nothing to say to them, and I've had such a difficult year."

"A difficult year?"

"Yes," she said, wiping a tear that escaped down her cheek, "and I can't tell anyone about it. It's a secret."

"A secret?"

"Yes, and its not mine, it's somebody else's secret."

"Oh," I said, "that's the worst kind." We drank tea and talked about the burden of other peoples' secrets. Rita worked as a counselor — we had common experience, we had common interests. I was having an intimate conversation with someone who knew me, with the least expected candidate, my mother's friend. When we looked at the clock, it was past two in the afternoon.

My reason for coming to England was fulfilled. Anchored again, I was ready to resume my travels, journey back across the channel, to Paris and Holland.

By now I knew the formula. I stayed one night in the youth hostel, found friends and the next day, four of us moved to a room in a cheap and convenient hotel. We went to see the Mona Lisa, the Palace of Versailles, the Left Bank, Rodin's house, the Eiffel Tower, the Champs Elysées, Notre Dame and Sacre Coeur. We drank *café au lait* at the French coffee houses and ate mounds of *pommes frites*. To splash out we went to a Moroccan restaurant, to eat cous-cous, succulent vegetables, tender meat and spicy sauce.

A pretty American called Mary-Beth asked me, "Are you going to Holland?"

"Yes," I said.

"Can I come with you?" Here were the words I'd expected to hear in Israel. Here was my travel companion, in time for my last port of call.

"Yes," I said.

"Let's take the *Magic Bus*," she said.

"What's that?"

"It's the cheapest way to go. You drive overnight, through Belgium. I know where to get the tickets." This was nice, having a travel companion who knew what to do, where to go. I liked it.

That was the end of Mary-Beth's knowledge. After that she relied on me. I wished she'd speak up, say what she wanted. She had a mind of her own and a will, and it was strong. I knew because she told me her story. "I like skiing," she said.

"I've never skied. I've never been in snow."

"I like skiing because it's the one sport I can still do."

"What do you mean?"

"My knees. I can't run anymore, my knees are damaged."

"Why? What happened?"

"We were on our way to a track meet. We were late. The cab-driver arrived drunk. We got in the cab anyway, because we didn't want to miss the meet, and we crashed. They took the cartilage out of both my knees. That was the end of my athletic career."

"Were you good?"

"Yes," she said, "I was going to the Olympics." Her sweet face, gold hair and soft skin looked too fresh to have swallowed such bitterness. I wanted her to use her strength to make our time more interesting, but she didn't.

The summer was ending, the number of backpackers had noticeably dwindled, the September leaves were beginning to curl with hints of yellow and red. I wanted to go back to London. It was our last night. "Let's not take the tram," Mary-Beth said, "let's walk."

"Good idea," I agreed, "it's not that far." Somewhere we took a wrong turn. Instead of streetlights, neon signs and busy sidewalks, the roads were dark and empty.

"What are we going to do?" Mary-Beth whispered.

"We must retrace our steps," I answered smoothly.

"But I don't know where we are, I don't know which way we came," she was almost crying.

"No, don't worry," I said, "I know where we are, I know which way we came, I've been keeping track." I let myself go very still, listening to something I'd never heard before — a calm voice inside me, a voice that knew what to do. "This way," I said. We turned around, walked three blocks and were back in the familiar downtown shopping area. It was the end of my solo quest.

The words 'retrace our steps' echoed in my head. For me, that meant, back to England, back to Israel and then back home, to South Africa. This time, Kenny and Barbara gave me the guest bedroom at the end of the hall in their home in Golders Green. The house was a pleasant ten minute stroll from the tube station. While they went to work, I went sight-seeing. At night we sat in the living room. "Listen to this one," Barbara said, reading out a job ad from the smalls, "what do you think?" She was looking for a new job.

"Sounds good. Give them a call."

"I don't think the salary is high enough."

"How high does it have to be?"

"I'm not sure, but high enough to get the mortgage we need."

We laid out the property section of the newspaper and looked at the houses, calculating the mortgage costs. Not just a new job, a new house as well.

"Let's go out to eat," Kenny said, "or should I make one of my famous omelettes."

"I feel like Chinese," Barbara said.

"Me too," I said.

"O.K., I know where to go. We can have omelettes tomorrow night," Kenny said. We all jumped in the car and drove around London. The meal was nice, but it wasn't enough.

"I'm still hungry," I said, "I could eat more."

"Me too," Kenny said.

"Me too," Barbara said.

"What about Mexican?"

"Yes, Mexican!" we all shouted in unison. We were a happy family.

"I have to go to Oxford to visit David," I told Barbara.

"David who?" she asked.

"David Stern, my friend from school."

"I don't want you to go," she said, "what will we do without you?"

"I'll only be gone a few days. I'll be back."

I caught the bus. I stood up in anticipation of my stop, and saw a young man, in overalls, with long hair and a beard. "Who's that?" I wondered. He stepped forward to greet me. I recognized his voice. It was David. "Look at you," I said, "you look so different!" Where was the awkward boy? Who was this Oxford student?

"You came on a good day," David said, "we're having a party at our house tonight. But I have to warn you, I have six roommates, all men."

"Can I stay there?"

"Yes, but you'll be the only woman in the house." It sounded ominous, Snow White and the seven dwarfs.

As soon as I walked through the door, David's meaning became clear. "A woman!" said one of the roommates, "can you fix this?" He was holding a baking dish. He looked perplexed.

"What is it?" I asked.

"I'm trying to make apple pie." I thought a moment. Baking wasn't one of my hobbies, but Mom had a great apple pie recipe. Pity I didn't have a copy. "Yes you have." My inner voice was interrupting my thoughts. "I can remember the recipe, trust me."

"We'll have to begin again," I said out loud, "do you have more ingredients?"

"What will you need?" he asked, his face opening with relief.

We made a list and he jumped on his bicycle and raced to the store. I watched myself whip up a giant apple pie. I wasn't so helpless after all. Not only could I travel alone, I could make apple pie without a recipe!

"Come," David said, "let's do the Magdalen college walk, then you can see autumn colors." We wound our way through the glowing trees, across the green lawns mottled with fallen leaves, alongside the tinkling stream, past the old mill and the venerable stone buildings. It was pure poetry. The air was sharp and my heart was warm with friendship.

"I want to do this every day," I said.

"Of course," David agreed, "and tomorrow I'll bring my camera." He took a spool of photos. When I saw them, I gasped. I'm wearing a rust colored shirt and blue jeans. My long, dark hair dances with red lights, my face is open and relaxed, my eyes are smiling. Even I could see that these weren't pictures of a frightened girl. These were the luminous tones of a free and powerful spirit.

Back at Kenny and Barbara's we turned the calendar to November. "I have to buy a ticket back to Israel," I said, "my ticket to Cape Town expires in December."

"So soon?" Barbara asked.

"Yes, so soon. I want to spend a little more time on the kibbutz before I go back to South Africa."

I didn't expect such a big welcome on the kibbutz. "Where have you been? You were away so long!" everyone exclaimed.

"I was in Europe," I said. "I was traveling."

"Well it's good that you're back. Your boyfriend missed you."

"My boyfriend?"

"Yes, Amir. We thought of getting together and buying you a ticket. He was such a misery. We thought you'd gone back to South Africa."

"I thought he'd get another girlfriend," I said, "I'm on my way back to South Africa now."

"You're not back for good?"

"No, this is the end of my trip."

"But you have a home here, a job, we need you to work in the children's house. You have a boyfriend, a life, what more do you want?"

I examined the routines of the other South Africans who now lived on the kibbutz. I would become restless. I would want to study more. I thought of Carlos Castenada. This was not my life's path. I'd survived my time alone in the wilderness and I'd found my inner voice. The final act of my quest was recognizing that it was over. It was time to go home.

Choices

BACK TO THE FUTURE

The plane ride from Tel Aviv to Cape Town was tedious. I was impatient to get home and exercise my new self, explore the territory of my life. I tumbled out of the plane, heavy with anticipation, tears of excitement in my eyes.

Mom and Dad, Tanya and Albie were waiting for me, big smiles on their faces. Hugs all round . . . and then . . . nothing. Nothing to say. Mom broke the silence, "Why are you crying?" she asked, in a puzzled voice. She didn't understand. And I didn't know how to explain — a delicate crack in the new me, a hairline fissure, hopefully just a pencil mark which could be wiped clean.

I couldn't explain myself to my mother or anyone else who thought they knew me. My old life was waiting for me, smothering me in its embrace. It was the no-one-understands conversation I'd had with Rita, only it was different now that it was happening to me.

Tanya, Albie and I were planning to reconstruct the household we enjoyed before I left. "We've found a place," Tanya said. I didn't like the house, or the neighborhood. I wasn't ready to choose. I wasn't really back yet. I didn't want to stay with Mom and Dad. That would make me feel like a child. I moved in with Ilana, temporarily. After a few weeks there I didn't want to move again. "Can I stay?" I asked Ilana.

"Yes," she said, "It seems to be working." Tanya and Albie were angry. Because of me they'd lost the house they wanted, and now I wasn't sticking to my end of the agreement, I'd chosen Ilana over them. The hairline fissure widened to a rift between me and my friends.

While I was away, Mom and Dad helped Michael buy a picture framing business. He spent his days counseling customers — how to enhance their artwork, how to highlight the finer details, how to enliven the meaningful symbols of their lives. He ran up and down the stairs managing his staff. I sat listlessly at his desk, paging through the classifieds. There weren't any jobs for psychology honors graduates. I needed experience in

the field, but I didn't know how to get it. If only I *had* done social work!
I could have got a job, and the experience, and *then* I could have gone on
to apply for the clinical psychology program. Social work was different
now, not like when Mom did it.

At last, an ad with possibility. A family needed someone to take care
of their children in the afternoons. I called the number, heard the familiar
Jewish inflection in the mother's voice, and my bell chimed. I knew I'd
get the job — and I did.

I resumed my weekly Alexander lessons as soon as possible. In April,
Miss Roberts called me. "There's a group of people who want to train as
Alexander teachers," she said. "We are going to have a meeting. I thought
that seeing as you're in Psychology, you might be a good candidate.
Would you like to join us?" Me? An Alexander teacher? Not with my
posture. But the training — that was interesting. That would be the best
way to help myself, really learn the Alexander Technique.

"Yes," I said, "I want to come to the meeting."

"Saturday morning," Miss Roberts said, "ten o' clock. See you then."

There were two other prospects — Yvonne Becker, a school
librarian, and Joan Brokensha, a speech and drama teacher. Miss Roberts
was already well into her seventies, Yvonne and Joan were in their late
forties, whereas I was all of twenty-two years old. We sat in Miss Robert's
living room, stiff and polite. I looked carefully at Yvonne and Joan.
Yvonne had a wide face with strong blue eyes and a purposeful line to her
nose and jaw. Joan was taller, with dark, shoulder-length hair, gentle
brown eyes and pink lipstick. We were self-conscious, aware that in our
little way we were trying to make history, in the Alexander Technique,
and in South Africa. We committed to training on Saturday mornings,
beginning the following week. Miss Roberts would write to the Society of
Teachers of the Alexander Technique (STAT), based in London, and ask
for curriculum guidelines.

STAT wrote back. We sat in Miss Robert's living room, again,
reviewing the letter. "Well, here it is," Miss Roberts said, "there are two
basic requirements, sixteen hundred hours of training, under two qualified
directors."

"Sixteen hundred hours — that will take us nine years!"

"Two teachers? There is only one."

"It's impossible. We won't be able to do it."

Miss Roberts fussed with her china tea, clinking the spoon against
the saucer. I heard myself say, "You know, we shouldn't give up. If we

want to train, we should just begin and in time things will develop." I shocked myself. *Who was I to speak these words? I was just someone who wanted to learn from Miss Roberts.* I didn't care whether STAT said my training was right or wrong.

Everyone's heads perked up. Our backs lengthened. "Yes, of course that's what we must do. We must begin and see what happens." We were unanimous.

"I'll write to London," Miss Roberts said, "explain why we can't comply with the regulations. See what they say."

"Perhaps we can train here, and finish our training in London."

"Yes, that way we aren't training in isolation, and they can check our standard."

"I'll suggest that," Miss Roberts said.

"Let's carry on from where we left off last week." We marched ourselves into the teaching room, and continued our training.

A few weeks later we got a reply. "It seems like a member of the council took up our cause," Miss Roberts began. "She spoke in our favor, persuaded them to let us go ahead. In the interests of the Alexander Technique in South Africa, and the Alexander community in general, they've agreed that a special plan should be made. We can go ahead. I can train you in Cape Town, and then you can finish at a course in London."

"That's good news," Yvonne said with a smile.

"Very good news," Joan and I nodded.

"I think we should celebrate," Miss Roberts said, "black tea or china tea?"

"China tea," we all agreed. Yvonne was already making plans to go to London.

CRISIS AND CALAMITY

Despite my job and my Alexander training, the difference between how I felt during my year away and how I felt back in South Africa was too big. I was falling into the crack between the new me and the old me. I could feel myself lurching but I couldn't stop it. All I could do was watch. I must have known unconsciously that it wasn't enough for my energy to fall, it would have to happen physically, because I predicted it.

Jeffrey came with me to watch my horse-riding lesson. I was getting out of the car, and I turned back and said, "Watch me fall off and break my arm." He raised an eyebrow. I walked away, laughing at my joke.

My regular teacher was away. I had a substitute. "O.K.," she said, "let's warm up with a sitting trot, without stirrups."

"The whole paddock?"

"Yes, the whole paddock." I usually did a small circle, about a third of the paddock. We did one round, then two. Then Noli, Dad's Arab horse, felt the wind and took control, faster and faster, until he was galloping. My legs dangled, helpless. I could feel myself sliding on the saddle, I could see the soft sand of the paddock. I let go the reins, allowed myself to topple to the ground, chopping my wrist on a log of wood, breaking my arm. I looked up at Jeffrey. I could see that he hadn't breathed in the last minute. "What did I say!" I muttered.

Jeffrey drove me home. I walked into the house carrying my arm, holding it at the elbow. "I think I broke my arm," I told Jacky.

"You people, why do you have to go riding? What do you expect?" she grumbled. Dad had also broken his arm falling off his horse.

"You and your father," Mom commented. "Jeffrey can take you to the hospital." We spent the rest of the day in waiting rooms, X-rays, doctors, getting my arm put in a cast. Luckily, it was my left arm. That night Ilana came into my room, "I need to talk to you," she said, she wasn't looking at me, she was looking at the floor. "I want you to move out, this isn't working." I couldn't believe my ears. She didn't say anything else. It was no use arguing, there was nothing to argue with.

I called Michael. "Ilana asked me to move out," I said.

"I'm coming to get you. I'll be there in twenty minutes."

I called Jeffrey. "Ilana asked me to move out," I said, "I'm moving in with Michael."

"Wha-a-a-t! I'll be there in twenty minutes, I'll help you move." I was out of there in less than an hour. Ilana hid in her room until we were gone.

Michael had a two bed-room, Georgian style cottage in Harfield Village, the up and coming trendy neighborhood. He furnished his home with elegant antiques, Persian rugs and inviting easy chairs. The walls were painted every two months in the colors of the moment — dark taupe in the living room, burnt orange in the dining room, blending with the red tones of the floor tiles. Ming vases and intricate pottery on occasional tables complemented the standing sculptures and bold canvasses in opulent frames, hanging on the walls. We put my pine bed and painted desk in the second bedroom, currently painted mint green. I felt like what I was — a poor relative.

Rich, poor — that wasn't the only difference. Michael had a completely different lifestyle. He drew his friends from two communities, the white yuppie gay boys in their unbuttoned, softly draped shirts, pleated pants and smooth, blow-dried hair; and the colored drag queens in their off-the-shoulder sequined dresses, high-heeled shoes, and glittering faces.

Michael went to the clubs almost nightly. "You can come," he said, "because you are 'ursula', but we'll have to get you some clothes, do a make-over."

"What's 'ursula?'" I asked. I remembered the word from when André came to visit, but not what it meant.

"Understanding" Michael answered.

"And 'beatrice?'" I'd heard him say beatrice a number of times, in his shop.

"Means someone's listening in on the conversation, can't speak freely." A whole new world, a whole new language. I wasn't exactly sure that that was where I wanted to be, but beggars can't be choosers. We spent all of Saturday afternoon getting dressed up, doing our faces and our hair, and then going dancing until the wee hours of the morning. I'd certainly never done this with any of my girlfriends. It took my brother and his friends to show me how to dress up like a woman and have fun.

My arm was still in the cast, when I went home for Friday night dinner with Mom — Dad was away on a business trip. We were both miserable, disgruntled with our lives. We perched at the dining room table. "Everything's going wrong," I said.

"Now you know how I feel," Mom retorted.

"Why does it always have to be about you? If you know how it feels, why can't you say something understanding?"

"I was just saying I know how it feels. I've felt this way for years. Now at last you can see what it's like. Maybe you can say something understanding."

"What's the matter with you," I yelled, "I'm the one with a broken arm." I waved my arm in the air.

"I've got a bad neck," Mom yelled back, "I can't see straight when I wake up in the morning . . ."

That old story again! The anger, the frustration, the disappointment of the past few months was boiling inside me, making my face hot, forcing me to jump out of my chair. Mom took one look at me and bolted into the lounge, locking the door. I hovered menacingly on the wrong side, my heavy, useless arm pulling relentlessly on my neck. I could see Mom through the glass, putting on a record to drown out my voice. I balanced on my slippery shoes, and methodically kicked out a pane of the living room door. "Don't lock me out," I screamed, "don't lock me out. I just want someone to listen to me."

"What's going on here now?" Jacky said, coming from the kitchen, "can't you two behave yourselves?"

"She won't listen to me," I grumbled, "she wouldn't open the door."

"But who's going to clean up the glass?" Jacky asked, knowing perfectly well that she always had to clean up our mess.

"Not me," I said, "serves her right."

As soon as the cast came off my arm, I caught a bad dose of flu. I would have to delay the surgery to have my wisdom teeth extracted under general anesthetic. I needed to go see Aunt Alicia.

"O.K.," said Aunt Alicia, "I'll call the surgeon, see when it can be rescheduled." She looked down at the floor next to her desk, tilted her head and said, "I heard about your visit home the other night," looked directly at me, and added "you mustn't behave like that, you're losing points."

Points? Who cared about points? I hunched down in my chair and glared at her. "It's no use believing everything Mom says," I replied, "everyone in my family is crazy. I can't stand it anymore. We need therapy."

"Well, I've thought for a long time that you all could benefit from some help in that department," Aunt Alicia admitted. "Maybe if you go, they'll come too."

"O.K.," I said, "I guess it's time."

"Who do you want to go to?"

"I don't know. That's the problem — we're not an easy bunch."

"No," Aunt Alicia agreed, "not an easy bunch."

"I'll think about it," I said, "ask around and see who I can come up with."

"Good," Aunt Alicia said, "and let me know."

I went home to recuperate from the flu, and while I was lying in bed, thinking nothing more could happen, the doorbell rang. I heard Michael talking, then he came to my room, "There's a man at the door. He just smashed your car."

"No," I said, "you're joking."

I'm not." Michael was mad at me. "*I told you* not to park your car there. *I told you* to park it in the side street. *I told you* they drive down the avenue too fast. Now come to the door and get the insurance information."

I got out of bed, and went to the door. The man's hands were trembling, the bridge of his nose was cut and bruised, my car was unrecognizable. "I'm sorry," he said, "I'm really sorry." He was in pain. For a brief moment I cared about him, then I couldn't hold on anymore, the world went foggy, far away. I ran back to my room, pounded the bed and screamed, again and again. My life was out of control, undriveable, twisted and broken, like my car.

Michael came to stop me, "I'll call the insurance," he said, "I'll organize the quotes, but shut up. Just shut up now." At least my car could go to the body shop. What was it going to take to repair me? I looked at the upcoming months — I still needed surgery.

After the wisdom tooth extraction, I was put in the children's ward to come round from the anesthetic. Groggy and helpless, I was awakened by the cries of a baby in excruciating pain. Before I could call for help, the anesthetic dragged me under into sleep, to be wakened, within a few seconds, by the cries. Finally I managed to keep myself awake long enough to call the nurse. "Can't you do anything for that baby? I can't stand the crying."

"No," she said sadly, "we can't find what's wrong."

"Will it stop?"

"No," the nurse said, "that baby cries all day long."

"Get me out of here," I said, "I have to get out of here."

Mom took me home to her house. My face was unrecognizably swollen. My mouth looked like a post box. I needed to hide. Jacky brought me scrambled eggs on a tray and Mom didn't say anything about her neck. Missy, my chinchilla cat, lay on the bed, keeping me company, glad I was home again. But a couple of days in my parents' house was enough. I got restless and fled to Michael's.

Back in the green room, convalescing for the third time in six months, it occurred to me that I'd last seen Jeffrey six weeks earlier, when he'd helped me move, and since then I hadn't received one single 'phone call. No-one wanted to be with me. I wasn't the same as before — I was depressed and I was sick. To my relief, Tanya came to visit. Not a proper visit, a brief Saturday afternoon courtesy. She brought her new best friend and roommate, Rose-Anne, unrivaled princess of Cape Town, defining member of the in-set. Rose-Anne took one look at me, pointed her finger at my distorted face, and doubled up laughing. My face was the funniest thing she'd seen in years. She was right, I did look funny, but strangely, I wasn't in the mood to laugh.

I'd hoped Tanya and I would pick up our friendship, but it didn't look like that was going to happen. Rose-Anne had taken my place. Terri stepped into the breach, came back into my life. She liked Michael's camp lifestyle. She went for a make-up lesson and discovered all kinds of enter-taining techniques for painting faces. Some evenings we spent hours applying layers of under-base, base, highlight, blusher and powder, and then we hopped from restaurant to restaurant where her musician friends had gigs. Some nights we did the make-up thing, cooked oatmeal porridge, pigged out and went to bed.

In the middle of winter, Tanya did invite me to the big party at her house. The social work students were talking about one of their lecturers, "He's so great," she said, "I wish I could go to him for therapy."

"Yes," said another, "me too. But we can't because we're his students." The atmosphere was thick with agreement.

"Who are you talking about?" I asked.

"Gordon Isaacs. He's so great."

"You can't go to him?"

"No. He won't give therapy to his students."

"But *I* can go to him!" I looked at Tanya.

"Yes," she said, "that *is* who you should go to."

"Yes," Aunt Alicia said, when I reported to her. "I've heard of him, very good. He has a way of putting his finger on the sore spot. I'll write the referral."

Gordon's office was in the social work department, in a white and smoky-glass building on University Avenue. I parked my car, a lump growing in my throat, pressing on my chest. The irony wasn't lost on me. Here I was, going to a social worker, for psychotherapy.

I found the door. What to do? I patted the door. Too light, no response. Knock and go in? I wanted to do this right. I looked at my watch, it was time for my session. I had no idea what lay behind the door. Was it a suite? Was there a secretary and a waiting room? Did I need to go in and let them know I'd arrived? I knocked, more decisively, and opened the door four inches — two surprised faces, a pale youth and a dark man. I had burst in on someone's therapy session — a terrible crime.

"Just wait outside, I'll be with you shortly," said the dark man. I backed out shamefully.

I watched the pale youth leave, then Gordon called me in. I'd been on the giving end of therapy, but I had no idea what it would be like on the receiving end. It was obvious that sooner or later I would have to experience psychotherapy. I knew I had a sea of issues storming in my unconscious. Sometimes I could feel the waves crashing against dangerous rocks, I could see the spray flying upwards, I could feel the churning and foaming — a backwash of emotion claiming me, trying to pull me under. Most of my friends were in therapy, but they had reasons.

They were stuck — they couldn't complete their papers, they quit their courses rather than write exams, they had an alcoholic parent, a manic-depressive parent, a weight problem, a relationship problem, their parents were divorced . . . I didn't have problems, I just felt bad. I didn't deserve therapy. I was just a whiner. I wanted to seem reasonable, intelligent, perceptive and insightful — not needy, like those other clients.

"What can I do for you?" Gordon asked. That's all? No gentle introduction to ease me into the process? Only this uncompromising question? He didn't seem very nice. I tried to force more air into my chest. "My doctor referred me. She wants my whole family to come, but we thought we should start with me," I explained. Then I went on to describe the situation for about twenty minutes.

Gordon sat still, staring at me, showing no active signs of interest. At the end of my monologue, I shot a glance at him, "I don't know if this counts, but I just feel cross all the time." He nodded, his first gesture of engagement. It most certainly did count, probably more than anything else I'd said.

Gordon took a deep breath, "Well, I can't do anything about the other people you've been telling me about, but I can help you." In other words, *if things were to change for me, I would need to focus on taking responsibility for myself, rather than launching into stories of my difficult circumstances.* The pressure on my chest lightened, a great weight was lifting off me. I stopped talking about my family. They weren't in the room anyway. I talked from my heart. The session ended so differently from how it began. With very few words, by some ethereal magic, Gordon had created the right space.

One Saturday in August, at the time I started therapy, Terri said, "Let's stop at *Pilgrim's Book Store* on the way to the restaurant and say 'Hi' to my friend Neil."

"Neil who?"

"Neil Schapera."

"Oh, I know the Schaperas," I said, "they used to live behind us." The Schaperas lived in Doris Road, behind Philippa. I knew his parents and his sister Janis, but not Neil himself. He was older than me. Michael knew him by sight, but I wouldn't have recognized him — or so I thought.

We walked into the bookstore. "Here, this is Neil," Terri said, "Neil, this is my friend, Vivien." I nodded "Hi" but I didn't say anything, and I didn't say anything, because I couldn't. I did recognize Neil, but not in the ordinary way. For as long as I could remember, I had held a picture in my head of my future husband. I'd been so aware of this image that at school, in a history slide-show I'd blurted out, "The man I marry will look like that." I'd thought I was talking nonsense. But now here we were in a bookstore, and Terri was introducing me to "the face" — the high cheek-bones, sculptured nose, brown-black sensitive eyes, the refined mouth and soft, shoulder-length hair. And 'the face' was smiling at me, saying "Hello." I was mesmerized. And not only by the face, but by the faded green t-shirt, and the masculine chest hairs curling over the stretched collar, and the tan arms, strong and muscled. Here was the most beautiful man I'd ever seen. If only I were a heroine in a novel, then I could faint.

No fainting for me — had to make conversation. "Where are the books on the Alexander Technique," I asked. 'The face' got an impish grin.

"The occult section is over there."

"What do you mean **occult**? Alexander Technique isn't occult."

"Just teasing, wanted to see how you would react."

"Well, *do you even know* what the Alexander Technique is?"

"I've got a vague idea," Neil said, "come, you'll find those books under 'health.'"

Forty-five minutes passed in a flash. Terri came over. "It's time to go," she said.

I floated out of the store. My bell was chiming out of control. "Mmm," I said to Terri, as we glided up the escalator, "I like him."

"He has a girlfriend," she said, "don't get your hopes up." No, I was sure. I could feel the chemistry.

Stupid bell, it was wrong and Terri was right. Neil didn't call. Ever since I was depressed I couldn't tell what was going on. I was more dysfunctional than I realized, even my bell wasn't working.

But romance would have interrupted important business — my process of integration. Instead, I took up two consequential hobbies. The first was running. There was a reason I'd parked my car in the wrong spot and it had got smashed. I'd become too reluctant to bend down and open the gate to the off street parking behind Michael's house. It was time to get fit again, buy a pair of Nikes, put on old shorts and a t-shirt, and run up and down the long avenues. Tanya introduced me to Shirley, a social work student, who also lived in Harfield village. Sometimes I ran to Shirley's house and drank tea with her.

"I also want to get fit," Shirley said, "but I don't want to run. I want to play a game, or something."

"Can you play squash?" I asked.

"Yes," Shirley said, "I can play squash, but I can't keep score. I've got a score-keeping disorder."

"That's O.K., I can keep score, as long as you can play squash." I ran on my own three times a week and Shirley and I played squash twice a week. I didn't mind bending down to open the gate anymore.

The other hobby was indoor gardening. Influenced by Michael's sensitivity to decor, I bought a schefflera and a fern for my room, as well as several smaller plants. My room didn't get much light, so one Saturday I set the plants out on the patio to sunbathe. That evening when I went to get them, I found the leaves scorched black, damaged forever.

This was the result of ignorance. Mom and Dad often got plants as gifts. They'd look lush for a while, then they'd get thinner and thinner, until one day, all that was left was dry sticks and Jacky would throw the pot out. Potted plants had a short life span, except for Dr. Cohen's collection. His went on from year to year, getting bigger and bigger, becoming huge strong specimens, with character. I would go to the library, get a book.

There were several references. One stood out — *Making Things Grow* by Thalasso Caruso. It was simple. Growth is inherent to the organism. To make things grow, all you need to do is create the right conditions. The more optimal the environment, the more vigorous the growth. Principles that could be applied to healing. At least that's what I'd noticed, working with Gordon.

"What's this book?" Terri asked.

"I want to learn about plants," I said, "and I want to grow them from seed. It's the least expensive way to get a big collection."

"You should ask my Dad," Terri said. "He grows all his own plants from seed."

Next time I was at her house, I did ask her dad. "Sure," Dr. Cohen said, "go to *Henshilwood's* gardening department, choose what you want, bring it up to the house and we'll see what we can do."

I went to *Henshilwoods*, selected coleus and marigold seeds and went back up to the Cohen's the following Saturday. Dr. Cohen led me over the lawns, through the rose beds, impatience, fuschias and marigolds to the shed screened by the banana tree, to the left of the pool. The shed was Dr. Cohen's other surgery. He reached for a seed tray, layered it with various colored soils, sprinkled the seeds and sifted compost on top, as artful as cooking a soufflé. He then guided me through sowing the second tray and coached me in gently wetting the soil enough, without displacing the seeds. I returned to Michael's house with my two precious incubators.

Michael had been carpet shopping. He was layering Persian and Chinese rugs over the wall-to-wall carpeting in the living room, pulling them this way and that, hemming and hawing, trying to decide which he preferred. I watched from the doorway. He consulted each of his friends in turn, not listening to a word they said, listing his own pros and cons. I was scraping together money to pay him rent and he was layering carpets on carpets.

I took my complaints to therapy. "When I was little, I wore Michael's old clothes and played tennis with Michael's old racquet," I whined. "It's always Michael, Michael, Michael. He always gets everything. Michael has good taste, Michael has a sense of humor, Michael is a gourmet cook, Michael knows how to entertain, Michael has style. He's only twenty-five, and he has his own home and his own business, and I'm living in a room in his house and paying him rent, watching him choose expensive carpets. Michael always gets everything."

I could see by the way Gordon was gnawing his finger, that he knew where I was going with this. He just had to wait for me to find out. I unraveled the yarn and discovered that what I wanted was my own home. Mom and Dad had funded a house and a business for Michael, where was mine? "Oh yes," I reasoned, "I had a university education, but a fat lot of good that was doing me!" Clearly the scales were unbalanced.

I couldn't wait to rush up to the house and confront Mom and Dad. "Now don't tell me about Michael," I said, "This is about me. I need my own place." Mom and Dad listened. I laid out my plan.

"But we're going to need thousands of rands in September to pay Michael's taxes," Mom protested. Her words proved my point. Everything *was* Michael, Michael, Michael. One day I would see that my view was one version of an incomplete story. Mom and Dad's hearts already knew more about Michael and me, than they could ever put into word or deed.

"Renée, didn't you hear a word she said," Dad intervened, before I could start yelling. Then he looked at me and said, "Well, Viv, we've always thought of you as someone who can land on her own two feet and we've always worried about Michael. We didn't know you felt this way. Of course we'll see how we can help you."

Once Dad had spoken, Mom sprang into action and took me flat-hunting. She scoured the newspaper, followed up all the possibilities, helped me find a flat in a small block in Claremont, near the gardens. Shirley helped me move. After nearly two years on the road, I had a home again.

A few months after starting with Gordon my understanding of therapy changed. I realized that I couldn't 'go back' to how I used to be in my 'more functional' days. Therapy wasn't about putting things back in place. It was a journey, like the year before. Except this was an inner journey of self-discovery, an opportunity to finish the exploration, match the inner with the outer. I had changed my way of responding to new experiences, but I hadn't yet changed my reactions to the old. Everything out there would always be the same — I was the one who needed to change. I was so grateful to Gordon. Grateful? I loved Gordon. It was classic transference, but so what, I loved him. He'd given me back my life.

GROWTH

The seeds had turned into a forest of little green shoots. There were hundreds. I bought the smallest size pots available and transplanted the seedlings one at a time, each into its own container. There was no way I could keep them all. As soon as they had three or four strong leaves, I distributed them to anyone who would have them. The marigolds flowered profusely and even began to seed themselves. The coleus developed a spectrum of bright variegations, firm leaves on full green stems.

I gave Shirley four of the best specimens. She put the plants on the window sill of her room. They grew at twice the speed of anyone else's. The shades of the leaves were deeper and brighter. Her plants were wild and free, sturdy as Jack's beanstalk. I shook my head in disbelief when I saw them. Shirley had magic. I wanted to have magic, too.

Shirley and I continued to play squash together. We were becoming lean and fit, our reflexes were improving. Shirley was strong, green-eyed and blond, like a lion. She had a roar for a laugh. She was committed to community work. Shirley's dedication scratched at me, reminded me that I wanted to become a clinical psychologist. After a hard game, fresh from the showers, I said, "You know what? I've just decided I should reapply for the clinical psychology program."

"Haaa!" she bellowed in encouragement, flinging her head back and raising clenched fists. "Go for it!"

"And If I don't get in, I'll do an academic masters," I continued.

I spoke to Gordon. "I'm thinking of applying for the clinical masters again."

"You have to find out why you didn't get in last time," he said. I stared at him, hoping he'd change his mind. What if they said something horrible? Gordon style, he just stared back at me, until I said, "O.K., I'll go speak to Ronnie."

Ronnie's charm was still intact. He leaned back in his executive chair, putting his hands behind his head and flashing his teeth at me. "And to what do I owe the pleasure of seeing you today?" he asked.

"I want to apply for the clinical masters again and *my therapist* told me to find out why I didn't get in two years ago," I said.

"Aaah!" he intoned. He knew the answer right off the bat. "There were two major incidents. The first was when Dr. Molloy, the visiting lecturer, told us the case study of the teenage boy. You laughed *at* him, not *with* him. You laughed a lot more loudly than everyone else. He noticed and he complained to us afterwards at the staff meeting. You hurt his feelings." Why didn't anyone talk to me about it at the time? And what was he so touchy about? Everyone was laughing — what made him think I was laughing at him? And why, if he'd complained about me, did I land up with him as a co-therapist, without any supervision or guidance? I let Ronnie go on. "The second was that you didn't properly complete your clinical case. You simply 'dropped' it at the end of the year." I held Ronnie's gaze intently. How come such a busy man could remember all these details so easily? How come he didn't have to look in a file, cast his mind back, reflect a moment? At a moment's notice, he could cough up well known 'facts' about me that had never been used to train me.

I was the smallest chicken in the pecking order. A whole institution was standing in judgment of me. I would have to swallow it and move forward, hoping that a good attitude in the present would make up for indiscretions in the past. Did I have a chance? I would have to wait and see.

I filled in the application and waited to be called for the interviews. The weeks went by. I heard nothing. The day before the final panel selection I had my usual weekly appointment with Gordon. "What's happened?" he asked.

"Nothing," I said, "I haven't been called for any interviews."

"Why not?" I shrugged my shoulders. I didn't want to talk about it. Obviously I wasn't worth interviewing, obviously they didn't want me.

"That isn't right," Gordon said, "you must go down to the clinic and find out why you haven't been interviewed."

"O.K.," I said, "I guess I have to."

"Let me know what happens," Gordon said. He had a different kind of expression on his face — more serious, more urgent — but he didn't say anything to give his thoughts away.

I went down to the clinic again, scene of so many rejections, and spoke to the secretary. "My therapist said I must find out why I haven't been interviewed for the clinical masters selection." Elsewhere, I wouldn't begin a sentence like that, but therapists, of course, held the most sway in these circles.

"I'll go ask Ronnie," the secretary said, getting up and disappearing into Ronnie's office. She came back looking flustered. "He says to organize as many interviews as I can." She made a flurry of calls, "I can't get hold of everyone," she said. "It's such late notice, but Dr. Walsh is expecting you at one and Dr. Richards will see you at three." She was avoiding eye contact with me.

I knew these two interviewers. Dr. Walsh was the head of Psychology at Groote Schuur Hospital and Dr. Richards had been my very first piano teacher when I was ten. Dr. Walsh asked me straight out, "Do you know why you didn't get in the first time?"

Bless Gordon, he knew this game. "Yes," I said, "that was the first thing I found out when I decided to reapply." Dr. Walsh had been a member of the first selection panel I'd been through. It was possible that she remembered me and why I hadn't got in. I was careful not to complain, careful not to tell tales. I repeated what I was told, then shut up.

Dr. Walsh raised an eyebrow, waiting for me to continue, waiting for me to defend myself. I kept quiet, so she asked, "And your point of view?"

"I don't think I laughed differently from everyone else. I didn't feel that and I didn't mean that. And I didn't drop the case. It was a bad time of year, for everybody. I was as careful as I could be, but I didn't think it was my place to check up on a senior therapist." Then I shut up again.

Dr. Walsh waited again, to see if I would say more. After all, she was a therapist, she knew about pregnant silences, the silence before you say what you're really thinking and feeling, launch into your inner-most rantings and ravings. I knew about those silences too, and I knew she was testing me, see if I'd fall for it, or if I had *learned to be tactful* in the two years since my last selection interview.

I held my peace. The tone of her next question was softer, warmer. "What have you been doing for the past two years?" she asked. She seemed genuinely interested, not merely going through the motions.

The secretary from the clinic called me later that afternoon. "Both Dr. Walsh and Dr. Richards have put you forward for the final selection. You need to come at nine tomorrow morning for the panel interview."

I called Gordon. "I'm in the final selection," I said.

"That's better," he said, "well done." I could hear the relief in his voice.

"I'll say it's better. First nothing and then final selection. Thank you. Thank you for guiding me, it makes all the difference." It did make such a difference having Gordon in my life — the emotional support, the reason, the experienced professional advice.

I felt hopeful again, until I walked into the room. Then I knew I didn't stand a chance. The panel had grown in two years from six to fifteen, and only three knew me — Dr. Walsh, Dr. Richards and Mr. Ronnie Dickson. I was not accepted.

I phoned Gordon. "I didn't get in," I said, "Can I come up and see you?"

"Yes," he replied, "come this morning."

"Do you think I'll ever be a therapist? Do you think I'll get to work with people, help them heal?" I asked Gordon.

He nodded. "No question," he said, "you will help people heal."

We sat silently for a moment, pondering the future, then Gordon said, "Now you have to go speak to someone on the panel and find out *why* you didn't get in, how your interview went."

"Really? Who?"

"Who do you want to speak to?"

"Dr. Richards," I said, "I know him from before. He was my piano teacher when I was little."

I found Dr. Richards in the Psychology Department. "You were an unknown quantity," he said, "you couldn't compete against the other candidates who had been thoroughly interviewed by all the panel members. But Dr. Walsh favored your application and spoke very strongly for you. She was disappointed that you didn't get in." Interesting. Especially that last point. And helpful. It made me feel better, about myself, and not getting in. Gordon was right, it was important to finish the process, get answers to the nagging questions.

I couldn't get answers to all the questions, but time would take care of that. A decade later, the truth about Dr. Molloy would be splashed across the scandal pages of the Sunday newspapers. Dr. Molloy, the hottest psychotherapist in town, would turn out to be a fraud — he did not even have a school-leaving certificate. It was the down side of 'knowing the difference between cocoa and milo' — a fraud would not want me around. And a few years after the newspaper report, I'd hear a familiar voice behind me, saying, "Is that Vivien Singer, I see?" and I would turn around, knowing who was behind me, and we would talk, and he would ask me what I was doing, and I would tell him, and he would say, "Wait a second, are *you* the person I've been *hearing about*!" and his face would grow pale with respect, and then Ronnie Dickson would say, "You know, you were right about Dr. Molloy all along, did you see in the papers?" And I would nod, and turn my face away.

I wouldn't say, "I wasn't right. I didn't *know* anything. I didn't say anything," and I wouldn't say, "You used that to block me."

I would just keep my mouth shut, because, the only thing that mattered was that Ronnie Dickson had steered me away from the profession which called to me like a siren, and freed me to be carried by the current, toward my destiny.

PLAN B

Plan B, as I'd said to Shirley, was to do an academic masters. Little did I know that as far as the universe was concerned, Plan B had three facets, all to be set in motion in the first week of January, 1980.

First, I registered for an MA Psychology. I had to select an advisor from the staff in the Psychology Department. I chose Dr. Graham Saayman because he had published many times. I went to see him, with a book about Psychology and the body, my first area of interest. He looked at the book, "This isn't the kind of thing I'm into at the moment," he said, "I'm doing several projects on the dual-career family, its sociological relevance and psychological impact." Was this why the scene of the father in Oslo, holding up his baby, and the women pharmacists standing around, smiling, had made such an impression on me? Was it because I would be studying the dual-career family?

"O.K., I'll do that," I said.

Dr. Saayman gave me a funny look. "How can you decide so quickly that that's what you want to do?"

"My mother worked when I was growing up," I said. "She was the only one I knew of who worked full-time; and right now I look after two children in the afternoons because their mother works; and I intend to continue working even once I marry and have children."

"Oh!" he said, falling silent.

Second, Yvonne came back from her first visit to Walter and Dilys Carrington's Alexander training course in London. Yvonne's direct style was more mellow, yet even more direct. Her hands were soft and warm, able to communicate a powerful message of muscular release and up direction. She was more on the ground and reached higher to the sky, all at the same time. Joan and I sat on the edge of our seats, eager to hear a full report. Joyce brought out the china tea again, fluttering to and fro, "Mmm-hmmm," she said, "tell us all about it."

When I left Joyce's flat that morning, I felt odd. I couldn't put my finger on it. Yvonne had certainly begun telling us, but we hadn't heard any content. Yvonne knew something and I wanted to know it too. I looked Yvonne's number up in the telephone directory and called her, "Yvonne, this is Vivien," I said. I'd never phoned her before.

"Oh, Vivien, I wasn't expecting you to call."

"I want you to show me what you learned in London, but Joyce isn't giving you a chance."

There was a long silence. I realized I was being brash. "No-o-o," Yvonne faltered, "she isn't"

"You have to share this information with Joan and me."

"No, you're right," she said, sounding tired, "but I thought nobody cared."

"I care," I said. I was emphatic, "I care and I want to know."

"Do you want to come to my house, then I can show you."

"Yes, when?" We made a date for an afternoon in the week.

"They do things differently there," Yvonne said, "you might not feel anything." Yvonne put her hands on me. There was a rush of warmth through my abdomen, my neck opened, my feet connected with the floor, my breathing changed. Not feel anything? This was amazing. She wasn't doing anything with her hands, except placing one on my front, one on my back, and my body was going through a series of changes.

Yvonne mistook my thoughtful silence, "Is anything happening? Can you feel anything" she asked. She was anxious.

"Yes," I said, "there's a lot happening."

"I'm so relieved," Yvonne said, "I'm so relieved" It was the beginning of a new understanding of the Alexander Technique, and the beginning of my friendship with Yvonne.

Third, Gordon posed a big question. "What's your worst fear?" he asked.

"Oh," I said, "I know — that I won't meet someone to share my life with."

Gordon looked me squarely in the eyes, "Well, for you that's a realistic fear," he said. "It's quite possible that you won't meet someone." I had a suspicion that although I could find boyfriends, it would be hard to find a mate. I didn't want to put my destiny, and my potential, second to a relationship. My life's journey was too important to be given up in exchange for marrying and having children. I accepted that I might never marry, never find a life-long partner.

Later that week Terri 'phoned. "Has he called you yet?" she asked, "has he called you?"

"Who?" I asked, confused.

"Neil," she said, "Neil Schapera. I saw him last night, he asked for your number, he wanted to know how to get in touch." Five months since Neil and I had met in the bookstore, and Terri was telling me that I hadn't misread the situation. My bell was not wrong.

"This is it," I said, "I'm getting married."

"How can you say that?" Terri was taken aback. "You haven't even been out with him yet."

"I know," I replied, "I just know."

I put down the phone and it rang again, "Hello?" I said.

"I don't know if you remember me. My name is Neil, we met in the bookstore. I got your number from Terri Cohen."

"Of course I remember you," I said.

"I thought we could get together some time."

"Sure, when?"

"What about tomorrow evening," Neil said, "after I finish working at the bookstore."

"Sounds O.K.," I said, "where do you want to meet?"

"What about your place?" he suggested. I gave him directions.

He arrived at my flat a little after nine on Tuesday evening, "Have you eaten yet?" he asked.

"Yes," I said, "but we can still go somewhere. I'll come with you."

"What about *Umbles*?"

"That's fine, I eat there all the time." Umbles was a vegetarian restaurant in a converted Cape cottage. The lighting was low. We sat across from each other at the rough wooden table, too shy to look into each other's eyes, too magnetized to look away. We did a lot of swallowing. We were falling in love.

"Are you vegetarian?" I asked.

"Yes," he said, "and you?"

"Yes."

"Do you eat fish?"

"No."

"Me neither."

"What do you do?"

"I'm studying food technology, and you?"

"I've just started my Masters in Psychology."

"I have an Honors in Psychology."

"You do? Do you want to do Clinical Psychology?"

"I did, but I want to go to America, and you can't get in with Psychology. I already tried."

"You did?"

"Yes, I traveled for over a year. I just got back recently."

"Me too."

"Can I see you tomorrow?" Neil asked, "After work."

"Yes," I said, "but that's when I go for my run."

"I can wait. I'll read or something."

He arrived just as I was putting on my shoes, "I'll be about twenty minutes," I said, "maybe half an hour."

He looked around, his eye fell on my Time magazine, he made a grab for it. "I'll read this," he said, plonking himself on the couch. Woody, my pregnant cat, jumped on his lap, "Hello kitty," he said scratching behind her ears and under her chin. She started to purr.

When I got back Neil said, "I know a good place to run on the mountain. I'll bring my shoes tomorrow."

"O.K.," I said, "it's not too steep is it?"

"No, it's not steep. It's one of the lower tracks in Newlands Forest."

We parked the car at the top of Fernwood Estate, walked up a little path, through the trees, and there we were, on a wide track in the woods. We ran side-by-side. I could feel the cells of my body vibrating with the pulse of life. The blue of the sky became a vortex, sucking me upward. The pine trees parted like soldiers, moving aside to let us pass. The rocks rang out loudly, like bells, as the stream tinkled over them. The air was purer, the view across the Cape to the Indian Ocean, and the horizon beyond, stretched further than ever before. Through the ages the first flush of romance has inspired the talented song of artists in every language, but still, this was beyond anything I could have imagined.

I phoned Mom, "What do you think of having the Schaperas as in-laws?"

"The Schaperas? What are you talking about?"

"I'm going out with Neil," I said.

"They're very nice people," she said, "we've always liked them." Then she paused, "But you know he wants to go and live in America, don't you?"

"Yes," I said, "he told me."

"Are you ready for that?"

"Yes," I said, "I'd like to live in America."

At my next therapy session I sat down in the usual way, but for the first time I played with my hands, shuffled in my chair, then just admitted it, "I've met someone."

Gordon looked at me closely. "Do we hear wedding bells?"

"Yes," I answered, "But how can it be? Last week we were just agreeing that it was going to be hard for me to meet someone. I speak the words, I accept the possibility and within two days he walks into my life!"

Gordon shrugged, "That's the beauty of it," he said.

It was Tuesday again. Neil wanted to come by after working in the bookstore. I guessed what was going to happen. I called Jacky, "Give me the Venetian Rice recipe," I said, "I need to cook."

Sure enough, when Neil arrived he asked, "Have you eaten?"

"No," I said.

"Well, let's go to *Umbles* again."

"No," I said.

"Why not?"

"Because I cooked supper for us."

Neil's eyes flickered. When he tasted the food the flicker spread into a grin. "This is the first proper vegetarian meal anyone has ever cooked for me." He looked satisfied. He must have been, because the next day he brought a plastic bag with two cheeses, a gouda and a cheddar, and moved in.

"You're not going home?"

"No," he said, looking around, "I think I'll stay here."

"What do you think?" I asked, "what's going on?"

"Well, if we continue like this, then we should get married." It wasn't a proposal, it was a fact.

"O.K.," I said, "what's the time-line." It wasn't an acceptance, it was a schedule.

"A year. If this works out, in a year, we'll get married."

"You serious?"

"Yes." And that was it, we had an agreement.

Doing my masters was much harder than facing my worst fear. There were no courses, no class-mates, no exams. I had to create a two hundred page dissertation in a vacuum. There were too many steps. The ground-work dragged. I had to find the right measuring instruments for the statistical study. I researched possibilities, sent away for them, waited months for a response, then discovered they were false leads. At last everything was assembled, ready to go, except I didn't know how to access the dual-career and traditional families through random sampling. We came up with the idea of asking each member of the psychology class to hand out two or three flyers requesting volunteers."

"We shouldn't do it now," Dr. Saayman said, "students are busy with exams. We'll have to wait for the beginning of next year, when they're fresh and cooperative again." Next year? That was February. It was September now. September? Next year? If Neil and I were going to get married, we'd better make wedding plans.

"Wedding plans?" Neil balked, "Why don't we just carry on as we are?"

"No!" I said, "I'm not going to live with you for years and years, then have the relationship end. We either make a full commitment, or we can break up now."

"All right then," Neil said, "but let's get married on 1st August 1981."

"We agreed a year," I said, "why *that* date?"

"I like the numbers. They make a palindrome — 1.8.81." I didn't like the deviation from the original plan. I refrained from pointing out that It was only a palindrome in South Africa, and maybe in England, depending on how they wrote the date there, but in America — his would-be home — it wouldn't be, because they started with the month, not the day. But I left it at that, until I had something useful to say.

Two days later, we were driving in the car together, when it hit me. "I know," I said , "What about 18th January 1981? That's 18.1.81."

"Yes, that is an even better date," Neil conceded.

"Well, if its a Sunday, we'll get married, and if it isn't we won't," I gambled. When we got home, we checked the calendar. 18.1.81 was a Sunday. It felt like the date chose us. We told Miriam and Raphael, and we told Alec and Renée.

Neil and I got married on a sunny Sunday evening, January eighteenth, 1981. I wore a simple white satin sheath with an elaborate lace collar and lace gloves. The *chupah*, the canopy for the ceremony, was held outside on the patio of the sports club. Michael was best man and Terri was brides-maid. No flower girls, no entourage and no wedding cake. Mom organized a delicious menu, a vibrant band, giant bouquets of flowers and over two hundred guests who wished us well.

Afterwards, I couldn't find Neil. I drove myself home in my Fiat, wedding dress and all, and knocked on my neighbor's door. "I just got married," I announced.

"That's wonderful," said my neighbor, looking up and down the corridor, "but where's your husband?"

"Oh, I don't know," I said, "I couldn't find him. He'll be along shortly."

Neil arrived twenty minutes later. "Where were you?" I asked.

"Your mother collared me. We were talking in the kitchen."

"Oh," I said.

"She took all the presents to her house, something about putting them on display, but I've got all of these." He took a stack of envelopes out of his pocket. We sat on the floor, reading the cards and counting the checks. Once again, there was a substantial check from Uncle Harry, and once again, this money would open a door that would lead us step-by-step, toward our most elusive dream.

Just before I fell asleep, that night, I remembered something strange. When I was fourteen or fifteen years old I'd stood at the the bus stop, waiting for the bus that took me to school. I was pondering the world, thinking about the hundreds of people out there, with whom I would later cross paths. They didn't know me yet, I didn't know them, but they already existed, and one day we would meet and influence each others lives. Then I got more specific, I wondered where the man I would marry one day was right at that moment. "For all I know, he could live on this street," I had thought to myself. And he did. The bus stop was at the foot of Doris Road, the road where Neil grew up.

⁓

I didn't need to go to Gordon any more. I had seen him for a precious eighteen months. I hadn't resolved everything. "There will always be issues," Gordon said, and laughed, "but you can't come to therapy forever, you have to go out there and live.

Neil started work as a food technologist at Reckitt & Colman and I got a job as a secretary in a computer software company. I had my own office. Better yet, the headquarters were located in the suburban business district, close to home. Within three days the backlog of secretarial work dwindled. I had nothing to do. I tried to make it all right, doing nothing all day, but we moved to the city center.

I stood at the window, a prisoner in a high rise building, glaring at the sea, "How can you be so near, so far, so blue, so free?" I counted the hours to five o' clock, when I could go home, to my real life — change into my running clothes, pound the pavement, water our three hundred potted plants, cook our vegetarian dinner from our growing library of recipe books.

Friday afternoons, I would unwind a little, knowing that the weekend lay ahead. By Saturday I was already anxious, my spirits drooped, my temper flared. Neil and I got into a screaming match. "You need to go back for more therapy," he yelled at me, desperate.

"No, I don't. I don't need therapy," I shouted, "I need to resign from my job." The words hung in the air. I was feeling too bad to continue like this. I handed in my notice the next day. I planned to alternate working on my masters with temporary jobs. Instead I lay around all day. How could I work on a thesis? I couldn't even make the bed. The temp agency kept offering me jobs. I took them, no matter how awful I felt. I had to. I couldn't be sure when the next one was coming.

I was going nowhere fast. Neil was gainfully employed at Reckitt and Colman. His colleagues included young women, whose careers were flowering. I felt embarrassed. I hated my work life. My thesis was stuck, my Alexander course was just a hobby. Should I get myself a proper occupation? Neil and I discussed the options. I threw the question out to the universe: What am I supposed to do with my life? The answer came back, true as a boomerang.

Yvonne was going to London again for another visit to the Carringtons' course. "Can you give me a ride to the airport," she asked.

"Sure," I said. As we neared the airport I felt a ball of envy, bouncing around, hitting against my stomach and my throat and my rib-cage, calling for attention. What's this? I want to go to London, too? I want to finish my Alexander training? I never knew. I never even thought of that.

I parked the car and turned to face Yvonne, "I must go next year and finish my training."

"Yes," she replied, "I think you must."

"Will you help me write a letter when you come back?"

"Yes, of course I will."

And there it was. Plain and clear. Suddenly.

The more I analyzed my desire to become an Alexander teacher, the more I realized that this could equally meet all my motives for becoming a psychologist. I wanted to work one-on-one with people, I wanted to facilitate personal growth. Better still, all my reservations against becoming a psychologist did not apply. I knew my personality. I knew it would be hard to sit passively, that listening would drain me. Teaching, on the other hand, guiding the new experience, would energize me. Teaching was my first love, my first choice. And my special interest in psychology had always been the field of human potential, the exact territory of the Alexander Technique.

"Do you think you can earn a living as an Alexander teacher?" Neil asked me.

"Oh yes," I replied, "of course I can."

"Then it's worthwhile."

When Yvonne came back she helped me write a letter to the Carringtons. They responded immediately. They said I could come for six months, from February to July, 1983.

The Alexander Technique And More

PRELUDE

As soon as the letter from Walter arrived, confirming a space for me on his course, Yvonne and I spent more and more time together, practicing, and talking about the technique. Now that there was light shining on the path ahead, I allowed myself to be led into adventure. Jeffrey was forced into leadership by a mysterious condition — his skin broke out in stinging bumps, which didn't respond to medical treatment. Usually a 'my-doctor-says' kind of guy, he surrendered to alternative methods of healing. Like a traveler, he came back to regale us with reports of another culture.

He went to a spiritual healer. "Ooh," he said enthusiastically, "you've got to see this one. Her voice was so deep and gruff, I couldn't tell on the phone whether she was a man or a woman. We sat in her dining-room, around the table, and she talked and talked. She said I had a rabbi for a spirit-guide — that's a spirit that guides you through life. The part that most amazed me, was that she said I had something important written in a green book, which I kept at the bottom of my bookshelf — and she was right! I don't know how she could have known that."

"What was the healing like? Did it work?" Neil asked.

Jeffrey shrugged. The laying on of hands had diminished to a bit part in a big show. "She put her hands on me and prayed. I didn't notice anything in particular, but she was certainly right about a lot of the other things she said."

What's her name?" we asked.

"Esmé Butler. She lives down the road from you."

"When are you going again?"

"Next week," Jeffrey replied.

"We're coming too," we said.

Esmé's voice did boom like a man's, but her appearance was full and womanly. Her hair was swept up in a lacquered bun and she wore glasses with rhinestone frames. We sat round the table, as Jeffrey had described, and she relayed messages for each of us from the spirit world. "I'm only a channel," she said, "I don't really know. I'm like a hose-pipe, and hose-pipes can get dirty."

Sometimes her eyes closed and her voice adopted a foreign lilt. She'd push her hands together and point her index fingers at the intended recipient. Pointing at me, she said, "I see you working with people, using your hands, teaching them, helping them. You have healing hands. And your husband will be doing the same work as you. He will join you in a few years." What nonsense! Neil was safely ensconced at *Reckitt and Colman*. He showed no hint of wanting to leave, nor of being interested in training as an Alexander Teacher.

Esmé looked at the doubt on our faces, grabbed a fistful of lace and said, "I am so certain of this that I promise you — here and now — that I will eat this table-cloth, if it doesn't happen."

Back at our flat, we reviewed the evening with a light-hearted approach, treating Esmé's words like a visit to the theater — food for thought — not real life. We talked and laughed about it, but I did have a confession to make. Since I was a child, sometimes words got added onto the end of my sentence — like at the Alexander training course meeting with Joyce, Yvonne and Joan. I could see Jeffrey and Neil's reaction. They were thinking, "There goes Vivien again, always got to be able to do everything."

We moved onto the next subject. I complained to Neil, "Have you seen the mail-box key?" He shook his head. "I can't find it anywhere," I continued, "I've looked for it, everywhere . . . unless it's in the sock drawer."

"There," I said, "that was an example. I wasn't thinking that last part, about the sock-drawer. It came out by itself."

"Well, let's check," said Jeffrey. We ran to the bed-room, opened the drawer — nothing. On impulse, I reached across, randomly picked up one sock and revealed the missing key. We looked at each other questioningly, then broke into smiles. We were good psychology students. This was chance, or unconscious memory.

Jeffrey was preparing my mind for possibilities. One Saturday morning, in class, Joyce told us about something she had tried, on the recommendation of a pupil. "This week I went to see the Meggersees," she began.

"The Meggersees? What's that?"

"That's their name," Joyce explained, "Gail and Ewald, a husband and wife team. They're chiropractors, but they use a different method — its very gentle. I could barely feel anything they were doing. They lightly touched me alongside my spine. That was it. When I stood up, I was all different." She waved her hands in an abracadabra motion, "Ye-e-es," she said, "ye-e-es, very interesting."

My bell started to chime. "I think I should go," I said.

Yvonne and Joan turned to look at me. "Yes," they agreed, "that's a good idea." None of us knew why. It just seemed the right thing for me to do.

I thought I was going to find out more about Gail and Ewald's method. I wasn't expecting much more than that. Lying face down on their table, Ewald held my feet, Gail pressed points on my spine. One glance at my back and Gail said, "It looks like you get headaches."

"Mmm," I said, "I do."

After a few more seconds of assessment Ewald added, "Frequent headaches, quite severe."

"Yes," I admitted, "I get headaches every day, migraines two or three times a week."

"How long has this been going on?" they asked.

"Oh, as long as I can remember," I said, "but it's getting worse as I get older."

"Did you have a fall?" Ewald asked.

"No," I said, "I don't remember a fall."

"Well, the misalignment of your spine indicates that you fell on your back, at some point, disturbing the arrangement of the vertebrae."

My fifteen minutes were up. "Be careful," Gail warned, "you will have discomfort, because our work will have unmasked underlying inflammation." She stayed with me to explain what they had found, what they had done and what I needed to do, while Ewald went to get the next patient. Walking away, my back felt decidedly different. Lighter? More mobile? Energized? I couldn't put it into words.

As predicted, the greater ease was short-lived. Pain and stiffness settled in. But I didn't get a headache that day, nor the next and not even the day after that ... I went for a whole week without a headache. It was a miracle. Free of headaches, I didn't need to numb myself daily with headache pills. The whole world looked different, felt different.

I scoured my memory for the fall I must have had. After days, it came to me — that morning at nursery school when I'd stayed outside to hang upside down from the jungle gym.* I recalled how the shock had rumbled through my body. The trauma which had disorganized my spine, backbone of my body, had organized my life — sent me in search of the Alexander Technique — backbone of my existence. Now that I was safely en route to becoming a teacher, the disorder could be undone.

The insight made me think of Esmé Butler, and the spirit guides. It did feel like someone was watching over me. Perhaps I could get these watchers to help me with another problem. I had lost half the contents of my purse, including my passport and other travel documents. I was searching everywhere, like a dog running round in circles, looking again and again in the same place. I asked the spirits, "Tell me what's happened to my passport." Immediately an image formed in my mind — *my purse is lying unzipped on the seat beside me. I brake and the contents slide out of the purse, through the gap between the backrest and the seat, to lie on the floor of the back seat.* I ran down the stairs, looked through the window, into the back of the car. All there! My passport, my documents, everything.

WONDERLAND

February. Exactly five years since I'd gone to Israel, and I was on another solo journey. Neil and I couldn't both go to London. He would have to stay home and work.

This time, Tanya met me at the airport. She had moved to England, to study an advanced social work degree in London. It was a steel gray day. The air felt wet. The residue of my first attempt to find hospitality in London tainted my mood. "I don't know if I really want to be here," I said, "it's just that I have to finish this course."

"It's not so bad," she said, "you'll get used to it." She was referring mostly to the weather, which by our South African standards, was dismal. I was looking at the traffic, the soot and the thickness of the overcoats. "In summer it gets quite hot," Tanya continued, "you get to walk around in short sleeves." I was feigning disinterest. Outside it was colorless, but inside I was vibrant with the wonder of coming to London to become an Alexander Teacher.

"Here's my flat," Tanya said, showing me one big room, with a fireplace, and a kitchen, "and here's the bathroom," she said, leading me down the stairs.

"That's a big bath," I said, eying the tub, which squatted on four paws, like a thirsty beast.

See Childhood, page 5

"To get gas, we have to feed coins in this meter. That heats the bath water and the fireplace," Tanya explained.

She led me back up the stairs, to the kitchen, "You can sleep here." The kitchen was also a large room. A sink, stove and kitchen table lined three of the walls, and a bed lined the fourth. I put my bags down.

"What would you like to do?" Tanya asked.

"Go to a market," I said, not having to think. Five years before, Kenny had driven me past a market on the way to the airport. I'd wanted him to stop, let me out, so I could mingle with the crowds, see outlandish clothes and spiky hairstyles, look through stalls stacked high with bags and boxes.

"O.K.," said Tanya, "we'll go to Camden."

Camden Market was exactly what I'd hoped. I suspect it was the place I'd seen from the car. It had the same look and feel — the possibility of treasure. The only ethnic goods available at home were black market cotton skirts and dresses from India. Sanctions prevented access to the colorful wares of Asia, South America and the rest of Africa. I stared at the people. A girl dressed in black leather, chains around her neck, safety pins piercing her body and a live, white rat clinging to her shaved head, walked past me. I squeezed Tanya's hand. The sky was still gray, but so what? "I love it here," I said.

Monday morning the sun peeped through the grimy kitchen window, not gray anymore, a clear blue day. The day unfolded in slow-motion. A trudge to the first tube station, a wait for the train, a changeover, and then at last, Holland Park tube, at the foot of Lansdowne Road. I was Neil Armstrong walking on the moon — alone, far from home, taking a giant step. Then, I was standing in front of a white house, number eighteen Lansdowne Road. I took the stairs, opened the door and walked inside. I could hear a rushing in my head, a waterfall of white noise. How to begin? What should I say?

"Hi, my name is Vivien Schapera and I'm here to finish my training," I announced, to the secretary. Her nose and mouth twitched faintly in surprise. "Oh, I was expecting someone much older," she said, then, "Welcome!"

She glanced down at her watch. "Well, you're too early for class, so I'll introduce you to Dilys. Walter is teaching a private lesson and Dilys is teaching the first years. And my name is Judith."

She led me to the back porch. All the students, under Dilys' guidance, were standing with their hands up in the air, alongside their ears. "Now thinking about what you're doing, bring your hands down to your sides, letting your fingertips lead," Dilys directed. Her white hair was combed back into a loose bun, her fine skin gently framed her dark, mobile eyes. Then she turned to me and said in a soft voice, "Well, yes, hello then, I'm pleased to meet you. I'll see you in class with the second and third years." Turning to Judith she suggested, "Take Vivien upstairs until class starts."

Judith and I began our friendship over herbal tea. "This is what they mean by a creamy complexion," I thought, looking at her skin. She had blond hair, blue eyes and a sharp expression. She was not only the secretary, she was also one of the students on the course.

Judith was having her own thoughts about me and how I looked. "Are you a veggie?" she asked, "You look like a veggie."

"Yes," I said, surmising her meaning, "I've been a vegetarian for just over three years now."

"Good," she said, nodding with approval, "I've just become one." We'd established common ground. She looked at her watch again, "Let's go down now." I followed her.

Nothing much was happening in the general teaching-room, originally the living-room of the Carringtons' four storey house. Everyone was just hanging around. Their backs were straight, remarkably so, but nobody was doing anything. A redhead, named Ruth, was holding someone's head and neck and reporting the events of her week-end. There were several tables in the room. At one, a person stood, waiting, looking ahead, at nothing. On another, someone else was lying down. There was a skeleton, several bookshelves, numerous chairs and about twenty people, all doing nothing. Some turned to glance at me, then went back to doing nothing. I sat in one of the chairs and watched the people doing nothing.

After ten to fifteen minutes someone ambled over to me and asked if I wanted a turn. Yes, I certainly wanted a turn to do nothing. I felt like Alice in Wonderland again, like the first time I met Joyce. Except now I wasn't following the rabbit down the hole, I was at the Mad Hatter's tea-party. I was so busy, busy, busy on the inside, with nothing to do on the outside. Trapped by my internal busy-ness, nothing to do, but stop being busy.

Getting a turn helped. The clamor inside my head softened at the edges, the chatter of my muscles, the rushing of my blood, began to slow. I drank some long, deep breaths.

At eleven-thirty Walter came into the room. We could all feel him, before we saw him or heard his sonorous voice. The tone in the room deepened, the air freshened, the students and teachers expanded. Judith introduced me, and Walter said, "Well, hello then, very nice to have you here," with a congenial nod.

We sat for the daily lecture, a reading from one of Alexander's books. When Walter spoke, even a simple sentence, his measured words indicated a train of investigation and reflection, extending over years. He specialized in the craft of consciousness. After the lecture, we went back to doing nothing. Three lucky people went with Walter to learn how to "put hands on," which is to say, to learn how to teach. The rest of us stayed in the teaching-room, receiving turns — mini-Alexander lessons — from the faculty.

A one-hour lunch-break, then we all gathered in the school-room again, where Walter would choose someone and take them through a movement, or series of movements, explaining what he wanted, what we should look for and why. After the demonstration he divided us into groups of three, so we could be guided through the experience by one of the teachers. Then of course, we went back to doing nothing, until class ended at three thirty. I went home to Tanya's flat feeling empty. The day had been quite a let-down.

The next day was the same. A few more people offered to give me turns, but mostly I sat around doing nothing, watching others doing nothing. By the third day, my expectations were sadly reduced. I'd got used to doing nothing. On the fourth day, I glimpsed that all this doing nothing was leading to something. Something different. Was there more space inside me? Or was there more of me? Or was I a space in the room? It was hard to put my finger on it, but it was something to do with me. I was different.

By Friday, I began to distinguish between doing nothing, and non-doing. I was learning the skill of non-doing — consciously choosing not to do what I habitually do, choosing not to do what interferes with what I really want. By Friday, I knew that non-doing is serious magic. My limbs were long and loose, my head turned smoothly on my neck, my back was wide and strong. The clamor in my head had hushed, my blood pulsed smoothly and the chattering of my muscles had fallen into peaceful accord. I could sit quietly in a chair, no longer busy with nothing. I couldn't wait for more. I wanted more turns, I wanted more non-doing and I wanted to learn more from Walter.

Walter was one of five master teachers, in the world, who represented Alexander's legacy. He had dedicated himself to Alexander's work from the age of eighteen, only interrupting this during the war, to be a pilot for the RAF. He had been at Alexander's side, until his death in 1955, and then had taken over Alexander's training course.

Day after day Walter revealed to us how instinct programs us to respond with the fight or flight pattern, how our civilized world over-stimulates this reflex, and how we can overcome this reflex with conscious inhibition. He taught us how to use this technique of conscious inhibition to stop any unwanted pattern or reaction which interferes with our functioning. He showed us the truth. If we want change, we don't need to do something else — we must *stop doing* what we don't want. He demonstrated how straightforward the principles are, yet how compli-cated the practice is, because our tangled muscles and faulty thinking stand in our own way.

Walter's wife, Dilys, was no less accomplished. I stood next to Dilys watching. "There it comes," she said, "look." Seconds skipped by, the usual nothing happening. Then a minute later the student took in a long deep breath — the breathing release, which signified the deep reorgani-zation of all the layers of muscles.

"How did you know? What did you see?" I asked. All she'd done was place two fingers on either side of the head. How had she managed such far-reaching effect? Dilys shrugged lightly. It's impossible to explain fifty years of experience.

Walter and Dilys' school was a Mecca to Alexander teachers. Every day, there were visitors, at least once a week a well-known personality from another country. We met senior teachers from Germany, Israel, Switzerland and America. But the other faculty, who had two to ten years' experience, were also skilled teachers. I was a member of a fine lineage! If this had been the sum total of my trip to London, it would have been enough, but there was a lot more. London was a playground of opportunities. I grabbed the chance to experiment, advised by Judith.

"You should go to Aleph," she said.

"Who's Aleph?" I asked.

"Aleph's the psychic I go to. He's really good. Spot on."

Aleph's office was in the basement, decorated in black, the shades pulled down. He was of indeterminate nationality and indeterminate accent. His complexion reminded me of Gordon, as did his severity. We sat on black chairs. A coffee table supported a few mystical aids, including a crystal ball. I liked the exercise bicycle propped against the wall — comic relief, reminder of ordinary human needs.

Aleph followed the formula, telling me about my health, my wealth and my love-life. "You are basically very healthy, but you suffer from bad headaches. You are lucky with money. Whenever you need it, it comes your way, and you usually have as much as you need. You are married, happily. Who is the Pisces?"

"I don't know," I said. Nowhere to go on that one.

He looked into his crystal ball. "Who is the old woman, with white hair, who is having trouble walking?"

"That's my Alexander teacher in Cape Town, Joyce Roberts," I replied, reluctantly impressed that he could see Joyce and her painful hip.

"She will be all right," he reassured me.

"Will I graduate as an Alexander Teacher?" I asked. This was my true mission to London, this was the answer I most wanted to hear.

Aleph dismissed the question as insignificant, looking further into the future. "Yes, yes, you will. But I see here that you're going to America."

"Yes," I said, "I'm going in the Easter break." He looked at me, like Gordon would have, not clarifying. He wasn't talking about a vacation.

"You are a healer," he said, then for emphasis, not wanting me to confuse this information, "You have healing hands — you have important work to do."

"Well, I'm training as an Alexander teacher. That's why I'm here in London at the moment, to finish my training."

"Good," he said, "that's a start. Alexander Technique is good, it suits you. But remember, you have healing hands." He was a making a big thing of it, and I didn't know why. It was the second time I was hearing this message. Then he told me I would have two children and the session was over.

Aleph was right. I was still getting headaches. I wanted to continue the work the Meggersees had done with me, but there were virtually no chiropractors in London. Judith told me, "No, no, we have osteopaths here and the best are the cranio-sacral osteopaths. I know a good one."

Jack Taylor was a thin, balding Australian with a white face, black hair and an appropriately restrained manner. I sat on the edge of the table, while Jack traced the length of my spine with his index finger, holding it two inches away from my body. Every now and then I gave a little shudder, corresponding to the times he hit a block in the energy flow. "Lie down on your front," he said, then he shoved hard and precisely against my right sacroiliac joint and I felt a warm rush shoot up my spine, turning my ears red-hot.

"O.K., you can turn over," he said, and I turned over and lay on my back. He spent approximately ten minutes with his hand resting quietly under my sacrum, ten minutes with his hands holding my head. I could feel a slow pulse expanding through my body, until I became the pulse, unable to tell where I ended and Jack's hands began. I was very mellow by the time the half-hour appointment ended.

"You should try to come twice a week," Jack recommended.

I made appointments for the following week and drifted down the road in a soft dream. I enjoyed the therapy, but even more important, my headaches diminished in frequency again.

I heard Ruth, the redhead teacher at school, talking about someone called Edith. "Who's Edith?" I asked Judith.

"Edith Just," Judith said, "she's an iridologist."

"What's an iridologist?"

"Someone who diagnoses your health by looking at your iris," she replied.

"Does it work?" I asked.

"Oh yes," she said, "I go to Edith myself. She's quite a character."

Edith was a round, blond, Swiss woman in her fifties, at least. She shook her head at me and pronounced, "Loose weave." This was as good, or rather as bad, as the death knell, because it meant going on a stringent dietary regime — no wheat, no sugar, no dairy, no citrus, no strawberries, no tomatoes, no tea, no coffee, no rhubarb. I didn't care about the rhubarb.

Edith wrote out the list while sipping her coffee. I felt like a dog, watching his master eat dinner, waiting for something to drop from the fork.

"How come you can drink coffee?" I asked suspiciously.

"Aaah," she replied, "I have tight weave. I can eat what I like."

"How convenient," I grumbled to myself.

"Every cell in your body is inflamed," she told me, "it's a wonder you can walk around. Next week you must come and do the needle-test."

"What's the needle-test?"

"That's where I drain all the tension out of your body, using acupuncture needles and we see if you have more or less energy without the tension. Some people use tension to keep themselves going when they are exhausted, others are exhausted by their tension. We can only tell with the needle-test."

"O.K.," I said warily, "I'll come for the needle-test."

"In the meantime, I want you to drink this special cough mixture which will help your cells to expel the toxins. Follow the diet and do everything you can to relax. I have never seen so much tension in anyone's body and you are only in your twenties!" She gave me a recipe combining honey, vinegar and tissue salts.

"And this is after six years of Alexander Technique," I thought to myself, "you should have seen me before."

"Next time, if you come with Judith, I'll teach you to do moxabustion. That will speed up the healing process."

Moxabustion? I was on overload. How many therapies, treatments, diets, tests and techniques were there in London? How was I going to get through them all? My head was reeling as I left Edith Just's house.

I got back to the apartment. "How was it?" asked Tanya, who was keeping track of my experiments.

"She saved my life!" I responded dramatically. "This is the first person to recognize how much pain I've been in. She said that every cell in my body is inflamed, and I know she's right."

I followed the diet faithfully, and for the second time in my life, I didn't have a headache for a whole week. It was another miracle.

The following week I went back for the needle test and Edith drained all the tension from my body, as promised. "I had to do it for twice the usual amount of time," she said, despairing of my sad condition. I was just relieved to know that my tense and anxious state was not normal. At last I had found someone who was not perceiving me as cool, calm and collected, and I could get help. I felt great when I left, but even better the next day. Without tension I was buoyant with energy, walking from Notting Hill Gate to Holland Park, at three times my usual speed. Unfortunately the results of the needle-test only lasted three days.

"Its not a therapy," Edith said, "only a test."

Judith wasn't just a source of referrals, she had talents of her own. She was an astrologer. "Oh yes, I can do your astrological chart for you. I just need your date, place and time of birth," she explained.

Mom supplied my time of birth and Judith did my chart. We sat in her tiny little flat and I listened entranced, like a child, to the story of my life. It was all there, depicted in the configuration of the stars and planets at the time of my birth — my personality, my foibles, and even the way I liked to dress.

"You'll have three styles of dressing," said Judith, "a more anonymous style like jeans and t-shirt, a romantic style like Victorian dresses and a practical style that's also fairly fashionable."

"That's true," I said. "I thought I was a nut-case because I couldn't decide what I wanted, but now I see I was just following what's in my chart. I'm glad to have that explained."

She illuminated my relationship with my mother. "You were born on your mother's Saturn return. The exact date," she emphasized. "Saturn represents our shadow, the part of us we keep hidden, the part of ourselves we haven't been able to successfully integrate into our personalities. What this means is that you went through life triggering all the unresolved aspects of your mother that she couldn't deal with in herself."

"Hmm," I responded dryly, "that sounds right." Judith looked at me sympathetically.

"Your mother's a Scorpio, isn't she?"

"My father also," I said, "they both are."

"Both your parents!"

"And my brother is also a Leo," I added. Judith was giving me a funny look. "Why?" I asked, "what does that mean?"

"A difficult household, a lot of fighting. All chiefs, and no Indians. Four strong personalities, all wanting to do things their own way. Must have been fierce. And even though your Sun sign is only one degree into Leo, three other planets are also in Leo — so you are Leo, through and through. Leo and Scorpio are not a harmonious combination, but Leo and Sagittarius is excellent. "

"You've got that right, too," I said, resolving to minimize my future involvements with Scorpios, "*all* my serious boyfriends have been Sagittarius, including Neil."

"Every chart has a pattern in it," Judith continued. "Your's shows a three-legged table, with the missing leg being the physical body. That means your weakest area is your physical body."

"It's a strange truth," I agreed, "I've always been fit and strong at sport, yet I've also always felt weak in my body."

"It's very good that you're training as an Alexander Teacher because that means you are addressing this weakness. Remember, an astrological chart is only a map, describing the terrain. Its up to you to work with it however you want. From what I see here, you will get stronger as you get older. Knowing you, you will probably spend your life seeking what is missing in your chart, turning your weakness into a strength. It would be wise for you to delay having children until you are about thirty, by which time you will be strong enough," she concluded. This was practical information. I intended to take all this counsel to heart.

I got up to leave, shaking out my legs, taking a moment to look at the books on her shelf. "This looks interesting," I said, holding up a book entitled *Bodymind* by Ken Dychtwald.

"Mmm," said Judith, "it is good. You can borrow it if you want."

I skimmed the first few pages. I needed a book to read on the train. I was going to visit my friend Julia from the kibbutz, the next weekend. "I'll take it," I said.

The train journey, including the wait at the station, was about four hours long. Dychtwald's book drew me in from the first page. He described how a professor was able to give him an accurate, detailed emotional history by looking at his body. By the time I got to Sheffield, I'd read more than half the book. My mind was chewing away at the information.

Julia had finished her undergraduate degree in Wales and was now living in Sheffield. She shared a house with some other young people. Julia's friends were delighted when they discovered that I had some entertaining abilities. They'd heard about the Alexander Technique and were eager to have a turn. The next day Julia took me sightseeing. On the bus, we fell into conversation.

"What do you think of my roommates?" she asked tentatively. She didn't want to gossip, she had something on her mind.

"Oh, they seem very nice," I replied, waiting to hear her real question.

"Well, I mean John, what do you think of John? I'm not sure about him."

"Yes," I agreed, "he's quiet and withdrawn, perhaps even depressed. He seems to be very wounded and carrying a deep anger. I would watch out for that. I think he's one to be quiet and then lash out suddenly. But he has a good heart. He just can't tolerate too many demands, as if he can't even cope with himself, never mind other people."

Julia looked at me, "How do you know all this? You've only met him briefly, once. It's not like he did anything you're describing in front of you."

"Well, I've put my hands on him, I gave him a turn last night." There it was. I didn't even know I could "read" people, didn't even realize I was doing it. Dychtwald's book had given me permission to express this secret gift.

"Anything else?" Julia asked. I continued in similar vein. "Everything you're saying is true," she said. We both felt a little uncomfortable, not with each other, with ourselves. After we'd digested the afternoon's surprise, Julia said, "I can't wait for you to meet Peter. I'm really interested to hear what you've got to say about him." I didn't know if I could do it again, especially if I were trying.

Peter joined us for dinner. Julia revealed that I had a party trick. "Vivien can read your personality from your body," she announced to everyone at the table with a gleam in her eye. "I want her to read Peter's."

"Really?" Everyone was agog. "Come on Peter, give it a go," they urged.

Peter was game. "Sure," he said, "what do I have to do?"

"Come with me, let me put my hands on you and then I'll do the reading."

"Put your hands on me? That doesn't sound too bad," he quipped.

I worked with him for fifteen to twenty minutes on the living-room floor. The others waited for us in the dining-room. I was quite nervous, not sure I would succeed.

"Peter's biggest issue is authority figures," I began. I looked carefully at the people. No-one moved a muscle, they weren't going to give anything away. "I can tell this because of the shape of his haircut and the slope of his neck. This issue would have begun with his relationship with his father, but now it extends to all authority figures. Even someone who isn't an authority figure to him, but might resemble one, say someone in a uniform." For twenty minutes, I listened to myself describing the ins and outs of Peter's personality, not knowing when I had processed this information. It just flowed out of my mouth. When I was done, I dared to look at the faces again.

A babble burst out. "You're right, exactly right. Especially that bit about authority figures and people in uniform. He's even making up stuff about the postman these days!"

"How did you do it?" they asked. I didn't know how to answer. It seemed obvious to me, like reading a traffic sign. How could they not do it?

Peter was thoughtful. "It's true," he said, "you picked up on things I never admit to anyone. What you said was true."

On the way home, I concluded that I would not use my gift again, except for healing. I didn't want to know everybody's business. I didn't want to invade other people's privacy. I didn't want to burden myself with all this information. Like books on the shelf, I would only break open the covers and read the contents, on request and with specific intent.

AMERICA

I'd been in England six weeks. School was breaking for Easter and I was going on my first visit to America, the country that Neil aspired to make our home. First stop Manhattan, to visit my step-cousins, Maxine and David.

Saturday morning I woke up at four, and made my way to Victoria Station, to stand in line for a standby ticket to New York. Look at all the people! The queue stretched out of view. This was London. This was the Easter weekend, of course there were lots of people.

The early flights were sold out. A few tickets remained for the afternoon plane. I was on! Two more people behind me got tickets and that was it for the day. I felt really lucky. It didn't make sense to hang around for hours, so I went back to Tanya's by bus. The stop was far from her flat. I dragged my suitcase behind me.

"What's going on?" Tanya asked resentfully, "Haven't you gone yet?" The din of suitcase wheels drumming against the sidewalk had woken her up.

"No, I'm on the later flight, I was lucky to get on that. You should have seen the queue."

"Told you," she said, stuffing her head in the pillow, making it clear she'd been looking forward to having the flat to herself. We'd been having too good a time together. Tanya was concerned that she'd neglect her other friendships, lose her independence, miss me too much when I was gone.

The phone rang. It was Maxine calling from New York. We could hear her talking into the answering machine, "I'm trying to find out what's going on? When's Vivien arriving?"

I dashed to the phone, "I couldn't get a ticket for the morning flight. I'll be there this evening." I told Maxine the flight number and she explained how to get to her apartment from the airport.

I thought the seven-hour transatlantic flight would feel short compared to the fourteen-hour flights from South Africa, but flying into never-ending daylight played tricks on my mind. Following Maxine's directions, I found the train station. "Trains are on strike today," a cab driver told me. I'd heard that the cab-drivers feed off innocent tourists. I turned my back. Twenty minutes later enough of us had gathered on the platform to establish that the rumor was true. Not a train in sight. I had to take a cab. The driver kept combing his hair, looking at himself in the rear-view mirror. He switched off the meter and drove me back and forth across Manhattan. I knew he was ripping me off, but there was nothing I could do about it. I sat silently in the back seat, just wanting to get to Maxine's address safely.

The longest day of my life, had at last given way to evening. Maxine lived on the upper East side, in a plush building, with marbled entrance and a helpful doorman, who had an envelope for me, with a key in it. I flopped across the threshold into Maxine's apartment. David was home, he greeted me with a big smile.

I'd gotten up at four in the morning in London and added seven hours to my day by flying across the Atlantic. For most people from the small, dozy cities of the world, Manhattan is a shock. For me it was combined with visiting my two cousins who didn't need to sleep. They were excited to have me there. I was excited to be there. The chemistry was overwhelming. Out we went.

Manhattan mutated into a long smudge of lights, cabs, people, museums, restaurants, corner-grocers, donut shops and tours. Maxine was eager to have as many Alexander lessons as I was willing to give, and equally eager that her friends from upstairs should try it too. Everyone thought I was cute, especially my accent — "You're from England, aren't you?" Maxine and I just giggled. We weren't going to admit to being South Africans, pariahs of the world.

In a quiet morning moment, while Maxine and David were actually sleeping, I sat at the dining-room table, flipping through the Wholistic Times. I burned with envy. All my interests were represented here, in New York. The saliva wanted to drip from my mouth, onto the newsprint, leave big wet stains, like tears of longing.

I bought a plane ticket to go to Cincinnati to visit Neil's brother, Tony, his wife, Lois, and his uncle, Herby. Lois met me at the airport on crutches. She'd just torn her knee in a skiing accident. "You know you're in Kentucky?" she asked.

"Kentucky? I thought Cincinnati is in Ohio," I responded, unwittingly following the standard script.

"It is," she said, "but the airport is in Kentucky, across the river."

"Well, good, then I can say I've been to Kentucky *and* Ohio." It was an obligatory conversation for first time visitors to Cincinnati.

"Let's go to the railway station," Lois said.

"Why?" I asked, "what's there?"

"Not trains. It's been converted into a shopping mall, but it has interesting architecture. It's my favorite building."

"Sure," I said, "sounds fine to me." I'd only met Lois briefly two or three times before, but we were more like sisters than sisters-in-law. We knew each other instantly, wished we could live in the same city. It was cruel that we could be so close, married to brothers, yet so far apart. For the first time, we would be able to spend a couple of days together. We went to the railway station and then to her house.

It was April — spring in the mid-west. The tips of each twig and branch were dipped in fresh green. The blooming bulbs and blossoming trees impressed themselves on my two-season mind. I looked out the window and saw an exquisite red bird. *I'd* never seen one before — it must be rare. I gestured to Lois, "Look, look."

"Yes, it's a cardinal," she said, blasé. She was preoccupied, talking on the phone, calling her friends, telling them to come over immediately and experience the Alexander Technique. As far as she was concerned, I was the rare bird. Lois had had lessons when she and Tony were living in London. She'd also wanted to train, but they'd moved to Cincinnati, where there wasn't even one teacher, let alone a training course. A series of friends arrived and obediently received their demonstration Alexander lessons.

That night we had dinner at Herby's house. A gaggle of Schaperas came together to eat, and welcome me to Cincinnati. "How long are you here?" Herby asked.

"Three days," I said.

"Three days? That's all?" Lois asked, "I wish you'd stay longer."

"No, I promised Neil I'd visit Les and Louise in Boston." Everyone looked sad, including me. I went on to Boston, and then back to the insanity of New York. Maxine introduced me to more of her friends. "Aren't you staying, aren't you coming to live here?" It was a refrain, and so was the reply. "No. I'm going back to London. But we **want** to come and live here."

Maybe one day I could stay in America . . . I could only hope.

THE LOOKING GLASS

I was really happy to get back to the training course and unravel the New York knots. A young American, Ted Dimon, who had done most of his training in Boston, had come to London to do his final term. "When's your birthday?" I asked him.

"March," he said.

"Pisces?"

"I don't know. I don't pay much attention to astrology."

"That's O.K., I'll ask Judith."

"Yes," Judith confirmed, "that's Pisces." Was Ted the Pisces that Aleph had seen? Was he going to be significant in my life? It was hard to tell. Ted was very formal with me, viewing me with a skeptical eye. I guessed that he was wondering whether I understood the Alexander Technique — really appreciated it — like he did. Our situations were so similar and we were in the same stage of training. We had to rely on each other. It was a natural alliance.

After school, I rode over to Ted's flat on a borrowed bicycle and we practiced teaching each other, wallowing in deep discussions on the Technique. During the two weeks of Wimbledon, we sat on the couch, watching the tennis on TV, drinking beers, eating salad and beans, becoming good friends.

Yvonne arrived from South Africa, to do her final stint of training. She introduced me to her friends Carol and Hilmar, who were trained in energy healing, which meant they could affect people by working on their energy field, or aura. Hilmar, an Austrian, had given up his career as an architect to set himself up as a healer. He spoke very slowly, with long gaps between words, longer gaps between sentences, as if he were pulling the information from another source, other than his mind.

Hilmar was offering weekend workshops. I decided to attend. He taught us how to move energy through our bodies, using our minds, then how to direct this energy toward another. Sitting in the room, listening to his words, I could see shadows of light around everyone and everything, even the furnishings. I squinted my eyes. Shadows should be darker, not lighter. Was this glow of light the aura, suddenly visible to me?

"Vivien," Hilmar said, "you must do healing work. Your energy changes the moment you work with others."

What was he seeing? What exactly were the distinctions between healing work, healing hands and Alexander teaching? How was I supposed to train as a healer, and why did I keep getting this same message? I had private healing sessions with Hilmar, to see what it was. I lay on the table, eyes closed, relaxed, while he moved his hands over me. He didn't touch my body, but deep inside, it felt as though I were being massaged.

My last month in London. Yvonne and I went to The Mind, Body, Spirit Festival, held at the *Olympiad*, a huge exhibition center in London. Soozi Holbeche was giving a workshop on healing with gems and crystals.

Yvonne had told me about Soozi after one of her previous visits to London. "Its like my second birthday," she glowed, her face alight with the memory.

Yvonne introduced me to Soozi. I'd imagined a hippy or a gypsy, but Soozi was an elegant blond, with finely sculpted jaw and nose, flawless make-up and soft, feminine attire. She was preparing mentally for her upcoming talk. Our conversation was polite and brief, but her smile was warm and genuine.

Soozi's presentation was bold. "Since I was a child I have been able to read minds. I always wondered why grown-ups lied all the time. There was such a discrepancy between what they were thinking and what they were saying. Because of my claims I was taken to numerous psychologists and psychiatrists. They separately verified that I was telling the truth. That I really could accurately pick up on people's thoughts. When I looked at houses I could see inside them, as though the façades were cut away. I had X-ray vision. I saw terrible things happening inside the houses. I was very disturbed."

Such claims — I didn't know what to think. I looked searchingly at the upturned faces beside me. The others in the audience seemed to expect nothing less. Yvonne was quietly enjoying herself, the edges of her mouth curling with pleasure.

Soozi displayed beautiful crystals on the table alongside her. She talked of their healing powers, but I couldn't retain any details, except that crystals choose you, and not the other way round.

After the talk I stood at Soozi's booth. *Should I ask Soozi for an appointment, or shouldn't I? I'm already having healing sessions with Hilmar — do I need more healing? I can't really afford to spend more money . . . but Yvonne seemed to get so much out of it . . . I should jump at the opportunity. I only have three weeks left before I go home . . . I don't really have time . . . when will I do it?*

Soozi glanced over at me, and broke away from the group which surrounded her. "If you want an appointment with me before you go home, write your name and number on that list, as well as the date you leave, and I'll give you an appointment before then." *She had read my mind.* I hadn't heard of 'signs,' but I could respond to one. I wrote my name on the list.

True to her word, Soozi called me. "I'm coming to London next week for one night, and I can see you early the next morning." My breath caught between my teeth, under my tongue, in the back of my throat — the great Soozi Holbeche was making such effort for little insignificant me. I accepted.

I arrived early, unable to estimate the time I needed for the three-change bus-ride all across London. I was asked to wait downstairs. "Sorry," Soozi said, coming downstairs at last, "you had to wait a long time. Are you ready to begin?"

"Yes," I said.

I expected a version of what Hilmar did. I lay down on the floor and Soozi began by waving a huge crystal over me. I could feel the air swishing around. The crystal mesmerized me with its power and beauty. How did she know what to do with it?

Soozi started to guide me verbally through a journey, back in time, back to before I was born. What kind of healing session was this? Nobody told me about this part. I accepted the unexpected, went along for the ride. I was floating among the stars, seeing the Milky Way from a new angle, then arrived, feet first in a different place, a different time — a past life.

"Where are you? Describe your surroundings."

The imagery was compelling. "Somewhere in South America," I replied. I don't know how I knew that, but I'm still certain that I was correct, even though I was seeing pyramid-shaped, glass buildings.

"What is happening?" Soozi asked.

I was lying on a block of stone, above me stood a man with a knife. "I am about fourteen years old and I'm being sacrificed," was my answer. The priest conducting the ceremony, my executioner, held a dagger poised above my neck. In the last seconds of my lifetime, I saw that my sacrifice would be in vain. Looking into his eyes, instead of spiritual purity and human regret, I saw the beady anticipation of blood.

"Do you recognize your executioner?"

"Yes," I wheezed, very frightened, very shocked, "it's my mother." There was a long silence.

Soozi drew a deep breath. "You are holding something in your hand," she said, "it's a gift, from your mother. What is it?"

"It's a pearl," I replied.

"Yes," Soozi said, "a pearl. Something of beauty, something of value, which grows around a foreign body, an irritation."

Soozi waved and swung her crystal around me, reorganizing my aura to assimilate the lessons and insights, allowing me to float among the stars again, then asking me to come back down to earth.

"And now where are you?" she asked.

"England, I think."

"Who are you?"

"I'm a wizard, a well-versed Celtic wizard. I know a lot of magic. I am very powerful."

"What's happening?" Soozi asked.

I shuddered. I didn't like what I was remembering. I was remembering loving magic so much that I cared about it more than my own flesh and blood. "I have a daughter," I said, "and she's dying. She's three years old. Her mother died in childbirth, and because I could only pass my magic on down the male line, I have neglected her, fatally. I was too disappointed. I wanted a son, an apprentice. I didn't want a daughter. I have killed her."

Soozi resumed working on my aura with the crystal. "I see you were very powerful," Soozi commented, "and that you have mostly been very powerful men, and physically big too, in your previous lifetimes." She said it very pointedly, making sure I was getting it.

I was getting it — not just the boy/girl issue but also the pearl. For my Bat-Mitzvah Mom had given me a ring — my first piece of jewelry — a ring with pearls and citrines in it. Then, after a bitter mother-daughter battle, in reconciliation, she gave me a double string of pearls.

At the end of the session, Soozi said, "Vivien, you have healing hands, a lot of healing. You must put your hands on people as much as you can."

"Soozi," I asked, puzzled, frustrated, "I'm going to be an Alexander teacher, isn't that enough?"

"No," she said, "that isn't enough. There's more." It wasn't what I wanted to hear just then — not on the eve of my accomplishment.

I made my way back to the training course, still in a daze. I couldn't tell whether I had generated strange stories from my unconscious and called them memories. Did it matter? I was the author, and whether this was past life recall or unconscious mythology, it was still a valid aspect of my psychology. I understood my past differently, I understood my future differently. Like Yvonne said, I was reborn.

GRADUATION

The weeks had tumbled by. July 22nd, 1983, the day before I turned twenty-seven years old, the impossible happened and both Yvonne and I were certified as Teachers of the F. Matthias Alexander Technique. There was a fumbling in the room, and then out came a fellow trainee, bearing a cake with candles, and the course joined in song, singing "Happy Birthday" to me. The next day, I returned home with a profession.

After the confined inner spaces of London, our flat was large and spacious, but my eyes saw "barren and deserted." I longed for the Alexander world in London. It had become more real than my own life back home. I looked at Neil with alien eyes, wondering who he was, and whether he could ever know who I was — especially now that I'd changed so much. I tried to avoid him.

"Sooner or later we have to spend time together," he commented with a hint of exasperation.

"You're right," I said, "I'm sorry." I didn't want to repeat the crash I'd experienced the last time I'd come back from extended travels. I had to reconnect the pieces of my life; and I had to teach lessons and complete my thesis.

My plan was to work on my dissertation in the mornings and teach the Alexander Technique in the afternoons. As Aleph had seen, Miss Roberts' hip was giving her trouble, so she referred new prospects on to Yvonne and me. Quite a few of my former practice students chose to continue. Help also came from an unexpected source.

The phone rang. I picked it up, "Hello, can I speak to Vivien please?"

"This is Vivien."

"My name is Diana Wemyss and I'm a freelance journalist. I hear you are an Alexander teacher. I've been wanting to write an article on the Technique for years. Can I interview you?"

"Of course," I said.

"Can we meet on Friday, day after tomorrow. I'd like to get it in next week's edition." The article turned into a full page report, with photos, on the back page of the weekly suburban newspaper. The phone didn't stop ringing. It felt like everyone wanted Alexander lessons.

"I want to expand the article, send it to Cosmopolitan," Diana said, "can I interview some of your students, tell their story?"

"I'll ask," I said. That turned into a four page magazine article. I got calls from all over the country. I went to see Gordon. "Look," I said, "I'm in this magazine," opening Cosmopolitan at the article. He beamed at me. I showed Dr. Saayman, "I'm in this magazine," I said.

"You are?" he held it in his hand, flipping through the pages, "I didn't realize. You should have told me."

"Didn't realize what?"

"That you were doing this training and everything. My daughter has Alexander lessons with someone called Miss Roberts. Do you think this would help my ankle?" Suddenly I was a professional, someone to be consulted.

We started a second training group in September. I was busy teaching all day long. Writing my dissertation was cutting into earning time. I no longer needed a Masters in Psychology. How was this degree going to serve me? I couldn't answer the question, but I knew that there are very few circumstances in which it is wiser to quit, and this wasn't one of them. Energy leaks through the threads of unfinished business. I decided to finish my thesis.

Within a few months, with the success of my practice, Neil and I could afford to move. "I think you should see this house," Neil said. He stopped the car outside a gray roofed, ranch with an open aspect, a blooming frangipani tree, an ancient oak, orange cannas and a hedge of pink and white hibiscus.

"*We* can afford *this* house?" I asked.

"Yes," he nodded, "we can afford this house!" Inside, the house was perfect — an L-shaped lounge/dining room, a farmhouse kitchen, three bedrooms and a creeper-covered patio, surrounded by a genuine fairy garden. The owner, a Mr. Forrest, had recently died, and the executors of the estate were eager to close a deal. Two other couples had put in bids. We stayed at the phone, waiting to hear if we got it.

The phone rang. "They chose our bid!" Neil shouted. "They chose our bid. The house is ours."

Two hours later our jubilation turned to dismay. We discovered that Mr. Forrest was deceased, because he had been murdered in the house, by an intruder. Neil and I looked at each other. What had we done? We lay on the bed, staring at the ceiling, contemplating our situation. After ten minutes we simultaneously came out of our paralysis and sighed to cast off our doubts. "The murder has nothing to do with us," Neil said.

"No," I agreed, "and it's a very nice house, I still want it."

"Me too," Neil said, "the danger isn't in the house. Mr. Forrest was gay, he probably brought the stranger in himself." We knew about the proclivities of gay men. Michael had educated us.

When we moved in, we saw a stain on the bedroom carpet, where Mr. Forrest had bled to death from a blow to the head. We covered it with a little mat that my childhood friend, Phillippa, had given us as a wedding gift. We pushed the stain, and the murder, under the carpet and back, into the recesses of our minds.

Neil and I cleared out the room behind the garage and turned it into a study. Content in my work, I was able to summon the discipline to write. Each morning, I forced myself out of the warm house, through the overgrown vegetable patch, under the washing line, to the back room, to sit at my desk for the allotted time. Once sitting, I pushed and pulled at my pen, until, I grudgingly began.

This was different from creative writing at school — no story, no melody and no rhythm. I rustled through my notes, taken from various references, scrawled haphazardly with different inks on different papers. I tried to synthesize the material, hobbled by the academic conventions of writing a Psychology document. I sat isolated in the back room, with only my resistance for company. Was this part of the training? How could it be so hard? Months of discipline, then the thesis gained momentum. I found myself writing in every spare moment, pouring my energy into it. Now that the thesis had a life of its own, it made demands, "Finish me!" It pushed me into unusual behavior, pushed me through the statistics chapter.

No-one in the department was willing or able to help me. "You need Lester, but he left two years ago," was the best they could say.

"Well then, who?"

"Ask Prof. Du Preez."

"Ask Charles, but you better hurry. He's about to leave the country."

"What's his number?"

"Ask the secretary."

I called Charles. "He isn't here. He's at his parents. He's about to leave."

"Give me the number."

Finally I got hold of Charles. "I can't help you," he said, "I'm emigrating to America in two weeks."

"Where are you now?"

"I'm at my parents in Kenilworth."

"I'm coming over. Tell me how to get there."

I arrived, list of questions in hand. Charles, eyed me like a hunted animal, even though I was the one in a corner and he was the the one escaping the coop. He led me to the dining-room to sit at the mahogany table. He placed his elbows on the polished surface, rested his hands in his chin, exhaled loudly, looked at his watch and shifted from cheek to cheek in his seat.

I fixed a dark eye on him. "Charles, there isn't anyone else who knows a dammed thing about this. You *have* to help me. I *have* to get this done — so let's just do it." I began methodically at the top of my list. He saw that I wasn't leaving until I was totally clear on each and every answer. He saw that I'd written the chapter, except for the blanks, where I couldn't figure the statistics or didn't know how to write the interpretation. He gave in, and helped me, in detail.

I left the house in Kenilworth with a load off my shoulders. Only two more steps — typing and binding. Sunday morning I announced to Neil, "I think I'll go spend the day with the typist, and be on hand if there's anything she can't read or know how to lay out. It's imperative that we get this done today." At seven in the evening, we pressed "print" and two hundred pages of thesis peeled forth, like so many chicks hatching from their eggs. Our faces were sunken, our bodies were limp and our hair was mussed. We looked at each other and smiled, "We did it!"

The next day, I dropped the copies off at the binders. "Pick-up on Thursday," they said. Thursday afternoon. Three blue-bound copies in hand, I skipped up the stairs of the Psychology Department and handed my dissertation to Dr. Saayman. "Looks good," he said, his serious face conceding a grin. Unexpectedly, he put his arm around my shoulders, and squeezed me, in acknowledgement.

In December 1984, I graduated with an M.A. Psychology. I had come a long way from the days, only a few years earlier, when I was casting around, seeking a viable career. My faith paid off. My masters degree — nothing to do with my niche in life — was going to prove vital to securing our place in the world.

Milestones

HEALING

I settled into a rhythm of seeing eight people in the morning and seven in the afternoon. Three evenings a week I assisted with the new training course. Word of my skill was out. I was no longer a reject from the Clinical Psychology course. Doors were flung wide in invitation.

At a party, I recognized a man. Where had I seen him before? He came up to me, "You're Vivien, aren't you — the Alexander teacher? I wonder if you can help me. You see, I hurt my neck, quite badly, and its hard for me to turn it now."

"I see it's very shortened, and your is head pulled down at an angle. Are you in a lot of pain?" I asked.

"Yes," he said, "constant."

"What happened?" I asked.

"I was swimming in the sea, and I dived in, but the water was only a foot deep, and actually I broke my neck. But the vertebra cracked transversely, which is why I'm not paralyzed." I looked at the pinkness of his eyes, behind his glasses, and understood how much he had lost that day.

"Well, from the look of things, I'm almost certain I can help you," I said. His shoulders fell a notch, indicating how important my answer had been.

"Would you be interested in an exchange?" he asked, "I'm a yoga teacher. My name is John Evans."

"You're John Evans!" I exclaimed, hardly believing that the famous yoga teacher himself, was standing in front of me, wondering whether I would be interested in an exchange *with him*. "Of course, I said, of course I'll be interested in an exchange."

"Well actually," John said, when we started my first lesson, "I'm an anti-yoga teacher."

"What does that mean?"

"Well, it means that I don't teach the way other yoga teachers do. I have a different method. I like to give my students a chance to discover the yoga from the inside, rather than force their bodies into positions.

Come and lie down on the floor here and put your legs up the wall," John invited. The whole lesson was done with me lying on my back. "I like to use the floor as a reference point, let the student feel the length of the back against the floor. That way they know when they're tightening — pulling away, instead of getting support."

In my yoga lessons, we began the process of restoring flexibility to my back and hamstrings, uncovering the damage done by my fall off the jungle gym. In John's Alexander lessons, we began the process of restoring length and ease to his neck, helping him recover the part of himself that *he* lost in *his* accident.

Working with people back-to-back, hour-after-hour, day-after-day, my skills were gaining dimension. I was becoming adept at sensing energy and my intuition was also developing. One day, while I was holding a client's head, I wanted to ask, "Why does it feel like your legs have been cut off at the knees?" It didn't make sense, I could see my client's feet. I decided not to say anything. Within minutes he took a deep breath and said, "You know, when I was five years old the doctors wanted to amputate both my legs at the knees."

"Really?" I said.

"My legs were infected. They said I wouldn't get better."

"But you still have your legs. What happened next?"

"My uncle came to get me from the hospital. He told them, 'there's no way you're cutting this boy's legs off, I'm going to heal him.'" He slung me over his shoulder, took me out of there and nursed me back to health."

I fell silent, mulling over this strange coincidence, wondering whether it would sound like I was making it up. "That's odd," I ventured, "just a minute before you told me that, I was asking myself why it feels like your legs are cut off at the knees." I expected my client to doubt me, infer that I was trying to impress him.

"That's good," he said, "you're intuitive. That's good. I like that."

I still wished I'd said something before he had, for the sake of credibility. From then on, again and again, I would have a thought pattern and seconds or minutes later the client would speak words, or share a story revealing my accuracy. The regularity of these incidents challenged me. I had to make a rule — the three time rule — if the same thought came three times, I forced myself to speak it out loud.

It was as though there was an unseen force, demanding that I extend myself beyond the conventional limits. A couple of months after I returned from London, Dolores Krieger, a nurse who wrote *Therapeutic*

Touch, a book about energy healing, came to South Africa. Yvonne, my friend Pam and I enrolled to do her weekend workshop. Inspired, Pam and I arranged to meet once a week, to practice working on auras.

I was also being asked to expand my understanding of the Alexander Technique. A twenty-one year old, Russell, came to me when he was dying, diagnosed with secondary cancer. He'd already fought one round with chemotherapy. Now he was choosing not to go through the process again. "I'd rather die," he said. Russell's mother, Andrea, five foot tall with auburn hair, was a stick of dynamite, standing in support of her son. Together, they wanted to extract every last drop of meaning from Russell's life, and they were asking me to help Russell die. I didn't know if my training in the Alexander Technique had anything to do with death. I had to look more deeply into why my students came to me. I had to learn to use the Alexander Technique to touch the spirit.

Russell had an unusual presence, short and dark, with olive skin and almost black hair. There was a lot of light around him. At first, his lessons were ordinary enough, following the usual routine of sitting and standing, lying on the table. I couldn't imagine why anyone who was dying would care how they stood, sat and lay on a table, but I began to understand that that was just the format — an Alexander lesson is really about one's relationship with one's self, a relationship that becomes even more charged if we know we are about to die. Perhaps it is even less important to make peace with our maker, than it is to make peace with ourselves.

One day, when I called Russell to come from the living-room to the teaching-room, I heard a distinct sound, like taffeta swishing down the aisle, or cicadas singing their summer-song. Energy rushed into the room, pushing like the tide. The air became thick and strong, crowding the room. I couldn't deny there were forces in the teaching-room with us.

We started at the chair. Once Russell was on the table, I dared to glance to my left. Standing against the closet doors, I could clearly see three figures, hands linked, like a paper cut-out. In haste I looked away, not wanting to see, even though the feeling in the room was so supportive and benevolent. A short while later, I steeled myself to look again. The vibrating etheric forms remained constant.

"You have a lot of company," I said to Russell.

"I know," he said. When he left the room, a crescendo of rustling followed him, as his retinue departed, leaving the room empty as a wine glass at the end of a party.

At that time, I belonged to a group of holistic practitioners. We met once a week. Our most memorable meeting was the one when Russell addressed us, relating his story and sharing his feelings on his impending death. He looked us in the eye and said, "I have something none of you have. In six weeks I will be dead." The inner chatter fell mute, the room breathed as one. Russell commanded total attention. Some of the most celebrated healers in Cape Town were in that room. Our collective energy, bigger than a bomb, was dwarfed by the awesome power of a small, sick youth, who stared death in the face with the resolution of a highly trained super-warrior.

When I got home that night, I discovered my cat, Ocelot, dead on the garden path. I was sad, but Russell had so diminished death, that grief was a tolerable visitor.

"That talk you gave was quite something," I said to Russell, when he came for his lesson the next week.

"Really?" he said, flushing with pleasure, wanting to be remembered, wanting to leave his mark on the world.

"No-one could forget your words, you were amazing," I elaborated, knowing how inadequate I was at conveying to Russell the depth to which he had touched our souls, educated our healers' hearts. "But, you know what happened, when I got home? I found my cat dead on the path," I continued.

"Ooh!" he said sadly, "that's too bad, I'm sorry".

I was taken by surprise at his generosity, his humanness, his lack of self-centeredness. I was expecting some kind of superior and wise response about death, something that included his special insight. What I got was commiseration at the loss of a beloved pet. Wise indeed!

A few weeks later Russell was too sick to leave home. "Will you come to the house?" Andrea asked. I hesitated. I still didn't really understand how I fitted into these last intimate days. I looked at Andrea and saw in her eyes that it had nothing to do me with me. It didn't matter if *I* understood, *she* wanted me to come. "Yes," I said, "of course I will."

Drugged with morphine, Russell was drifting in and out of consciousness. We laid him on the floor of his bedroom, and as I worked with him, I could feel his spirit coming and going, leaving and reentering his dying body. Through the resonant connection of the Alexander Technique, I could go with him, keep him company. That was the last time I saw Russell.

When he was still up and about, Russell agreed to make contact with me from the other side, but I didn't expect anything to come of it. After a few months, Andrea resumed her regular weekly appointments. At the beginning of one of her lessons, in a natural way, the words, "So what do you hear from Russell?" framed themselves in my mind. In the nick of time I managed to censor the question. What was I thinking? Russell hadn't gone overseas, on interesting travels!

In the next second, Andrea said, "I dreamt about Russell last night." My skin chilled, my heart bumped against my chest.

"You know, I just stopped myself from asking you how Russell is."

"You felt it," she said, "you felt his energy." Andrea glowed.

"So how is he?" I continued, now free to ask the question.

"He's doing well," she said, "his energy was good, very good."

"Thank you, Russell," I spoke inside my head, "thank you for keeping our agreement."

TWO JOURNEYS, THREE DECISIONS

Neil and I needed a vacation. We went to a guest farm on the other side of Knysna, a six-hour drive from Cape Town, along the Garden route.

The guest farm was owned and run by the Crawfords, a family who'd followed a dream. They gave up their executive lifestyle in Johannesburg, and bought a farm in Nature's Valley, named for the wooded hills and open pastures, steep ravines and winding waterfalls, salty ocean vistas and white, undisturbed beaches.

As we pulled into the drive, Paul Crawford, a tall, strong man with sad eyes, and his son Robert, a rumpled youth in his twenties, came to greet us. My gaze was continually drawn to Robert. He leaned on one leg. His back was slightly twisted, his left arm bent at an awkward angle, not wrong, but not right. Paul and Robert led us into the main farmhouse, gave us our cottage keys, explained the farm layout and told us what time to be back for dinner, "And by the way, we have other guests from Cape Town, in the neighboring cottage. They've been here for the week-end and are leaving early tomorrow," they said.

The other guests from Cape Town turned out to be Jeffrey's younger brother and his new wife. We hadn't met before, but that didn't stop us from feeling we already knew each other. Jeffrey's stories had carried both ways, mingled our energies, long ago.

"Its great here," they said, "we've had a wonderful time, this is a special place." Special? Looking across the valley, thick with the ancient forests, vapor rising from the trees, 'special' seemed obvious. Even so, hidden surprises lay waiting to glide into our lives, make nests, prepare us for our future.

At dinner we met Gina Crawford, a blue-eyed blond, with an easy smile and warm-honey voice. Gina was the visionary who had driven the move. Gina had a son, with a Celtic name we'd never heard before — Aidan. "It means little fire, or fiery one," she said, puffing with pride at her blond powerhouse of a three-year-old.

"I saw baboons today," Aidan said, "they had teeth like this," he made hooks with his index fingers to describe the canines. The baboons had raided the vegetable patch, earlier in the day.

Gina was a networker. "What do you do?" she asked.

"I'm an Alexander Teacher," I said. "I help people with the way they move and think, their posture."

"Can you help Robert," she asked, "he had meningitis when he was two and he has cerebral palsy on his right side."

"It's worth a try," I said, "But I can't be sure."

"I'll speak to my dad," Gina said firmly. The Crawfords were always looking for something to help their son. Their interest was piqued. They asked me to give each of them a lesson.

"It will be my pleasure," I said, grateful that I had something to offer these fine people who opened their home and hearts to strangers, providing an invisible healing experience.

"You'll want to see the Magic Forest while you're here," Gina continued. "It's a part of the old, indigenous woods which are protected now and its right on our land."

Of course we wanted to see the Magic Forest. As we walked its twisting path, I said to Neil, "Aidan, now that's a nice name. Perhaps, if we have a son, we could call him Aidan."

"Yes," said Neil, "it *is* a nice name, I like it too."

The week passed easily. We went to the beach, walked in the woods, and in the evenings we ate dinner with the Crawfords. As arranged, I gave them each an Alexander lesson. When we were saying our final farewells, Gina rushed out, "Wait!" She handed me an envelope. "Thank you," she said, "we want to pay you for the lessons."

"I didn't expect payment." I tried to stop her, but she closed my hand over the gift, not taking 'No' for an answer.

On our way home, Neil and I stopped off in Knysna, one of the tourist towns on the coast. In a junk shop, I discovered two mineral specimens — a cluster of citrine crystals and a large milky quartz point. Ever since I'd met Soozi Holbeche, in London, I had been on the lookout for crystals. These seemed to embody the spirit of the gift from the Crawfords. I didn't know what I would *do* with them, but I wanted them. So what if they were going to lie dormant on the shelf?

The morning after we got home, as Neil was getting dressed for work, doing his tie in the mirror behind the closet door, he announced: "I think I'll start on the Alexander training course next term."

That was it — a decision, without discussion, without warning. Was it meeting the Crawfords, who'd given themselves permission to follow their dream? Was it the time away from hum-drum routine? Was it the magic energy of Nature's Valley? Whatever it was, it looked like Esmé Butler would not have to eat the table-cloth!

Neil was now as motivated as I, to go to London. We planned a two month trip — one month in the U.S. visiting friends and family, and one month in London, at the Carringtons' training course.

We landed in New York and visited Maxine, then flew on to Boston to visit Les and Louise. It was almost a replay of my trip two years earlier, except that we had additional connections — another friend in Boston — Ted.

I was a little anxious, wanting Neil and Ted to like each other, strike a chord. I was almost sure that Ted was the Pisces Aleph had seen in the psychic reading, and I was still waiting to find out why he was so important that he'd turned up in the cards.

We met at Ted's apartment. "What do you guys like to eat?" Ted asked.

"Oh anything," we said, "we love all the food in America, as long as it's vegetarian."

"Well let's go to Christopher's, the Tex-Mex restaurant around the corner." That was a good move. Burritos delighted Neil. We ate nachos, and beans, and melted cheese and laughed a lot. It turned out to be an easy threesome.

"I like Neil," Ted whispered to me, as Neil walked down the road ahead of us.

"I'm glad," I said.

"You didn't tell me that much about him when we were in London."

"It's hard to describe someone else, especially Neil."

"I guess that's true," Ted said. "Are you still thinking of coming to live here."

"Oh yes! We just don't know how," I replied.

Next stop was San Francisco, where Neil's brother, Tony, now lived. Tanya flew over to join us. Our food obsession annoyed her. "Stop it," she pouted, "stop talking about food all the time. Can't we think about something else? I didn't travel all this way just to eat. This is a cultured city with all kinds of things to offer besides food!"

She was right, but she was living in London. She didn't understand what it was like for us vegetarians, trapped in no-choice South Africa, suddenly able to order mouth-watering selections in restaurants. We tagged along to museums and art galleries, knowing we'd be rewarded with lunch afterwards.

In any case, the food *was* significant. While we were in the U.S., going from restaurant to restaurant, I came to a momentous insight. "I like Japanese food best," I said, "I just have to find the whole-foods equivalent."

Tanya, Neil and I drove down the coast from San Francisco to Los Angeles. The first part of the drive, as forewarned by the guide books, was shrouded in fog, but once the mist lifted, round about Monterey, we fell in love with the rugged strength and beauty of the land.

Our last night, sitting in a Chinese restaurant in Anaheim, after a day at Disneyland, Neil picked at his food, then less than half-eaten, pushed the plate away, "Too salty," he said. It was, but so were his uncried tears — too salty and too bitter. Every cell in Neil's body wanted to live in America. I turned my eyes away, hoping that Neil would cheer up enough to make the most of his experience in London.

As we walked up Lansdowne Road, to the Carringtons' school, I said, "Don't expect anything. It seems like nothing. There won't be much happening, but by the end of the week you'll feel the magic."

I introduced Neil to Walter and Dilys, who each said, "Yes, very nice to meet you," on cue and then there we were, back in the school-room, doing nothing again. And by the end of the week, Neil agreed with me. He *had* found the magic.

We had a whole month in London. A whole month of Alexander school, book stores, Neal's Yard, Covent Garden, Hampstead Heath, Portobello Road, cruising on the Thames, Hampton Court, Tanya and Kenny and Barbara. Then we had to return home to the empty roads of South Africa. We put our green non-passport passports in the safe and forced ourselves back into our lives.

"We must remember how bad this feels," I said to Neil. "We must remember how much we want to live in America. We must remember how free we felt there. We're going to adjust, get used to it here again, but we mustn't forget how much we really want to go."

"Yes," Neil said, "we must remember."

It was November, 1985 and we had been married for almost five years. We had a house, we'd traveled, we'd got used to each other — our thoughts turned to babies. Immersed as I was in nutrition and its effect on constitution and health, I wanted to give my offspring whatever good start was under my control. In London, we identified the whole-foods version of Japanese cooking as *Macrobiotics*. Neil and I graduated from mashed potatoes with cheese to the brown rice, wholefoods diet. I went on a dedicated cleansing regime, following a modified brown rice fast for two weeks and then a one-week stay at the naturopathic health spa, in Stellenbosch, to scrub lurking toxins from each and every cell of my body.

Our plan was to conceive in February and have a Sagittarius baby at the end of November. Whatever happened, I didn't want to have a Scorpio. Judith's reading of my chart convinced me that I'd had enough Scorpio intensity to last me through many lifetimes. I knew I could get on with easy-going Sagittarians.

"You can't plan it like that!" Mom said scornfully, "you can't decide exactly when you're going to conceive. It doesn't work like that."

"Well, then, how does it work?" I questioned, "I can at least try for what I want." I had an inner certainty. Besides, using science and intuition, I was aligning the energies.

February came and went, bringing with it the four-week wait, am I or aren't I? At the same time, I had decided I should learn to sew and I wanted a machine. I asked Mom to help me choose, and we went to the Goodwood Trade Show together — a rare mother-daughter moment. On the way to the show, I said, "I think I'm pregnant."

"That's the best news I've had all day, all week, in a very long time!" Mom said. We floated into the show together, suddenly united in the bond of motherhood.

"When you buy a sewing machine, you buy one for life," Mom advised me, with a finger-wag. Mom noticed me glancing at the more expensive models, the brand-new, computerized machines. "How much *can* you spend?" she asked.

"Whatever I want," I answered. Neil and I were riding a wave of success, we had disposable income. Mom's excitement barometer went up — free choice! This was even better than the vague possibility of a first grandchild.

I fell in love with the new computerized Pfaff. At the mere push of a button it performed every function, including the extremely necessary ninety-nine embroidery stitches. The machine cost thousands. "If you like it, you must get it. Look at the savings," Mom said, pointing to the special show discount.

There was only one problem. If the machine was 'for life' and I was going to live in America, I would need to purchase a one hundred and ten volt machine, instead of the South African two hundred and twenty. All Neil and I had was our dream. Would we really be going to live there one day? It felt like this sewing machine would decide our fate, like a Roman Emperor at a gladiatorial fight — thumbs up or thumbs down.

"She might be going to live in America," Mom announced to the salesman.

The technician, a German immigrant, wanted the sale. "You can buy a hundred and ten volt machine and use a transformer."

I looked at him dubiously. "Will it affect the machine adversely? What difference would it make?"

"No," he said, "the machine will run fine."

"So what's the catch?" I asked. "What are the drawbacks?"

"The transformer is heavy and you have to drag it around with your machine. If you plug it in without the transformer, you'll blow all the circuits. We don't carry the parts for one hundred and ten volt machines, so we'd have to special order them."

I pictured myself with this anomaly. A lone hundred and ten volt sewing machine in a two twenty volt country. Far away from spare parts and repairs, all because of a pipe-dream. The technician interrupted the scene in my mind, "But, if you think you're really going to America, it's still the best thing to do."

The future sucked the fun out of the purchase. "Let's walk around a bit," I said to Mom, "I need to think."

"Of course," said Mom, "let's go get something to eat."

Walking through the milling crowd, I remembered our last night in America. I remembered Neil's face. Besides, what about all the psychic predictions, the hopes and desires? And what about faith? "I really do think we're going to live in America," I said.

"Well, then," said Mom, "you must go with that. You must get the hundred and ten volt machine."

I wanted to rush through the transaction, then speed home to think slowly about what I had done. "You won't be sorry," said the technician, "your machine will work just fine here and when you get to America, you'll just disconnect the transformer, and plug it in there!" Congratulations, a sewing machine for life.

By the time we left the show, it was late and we were tired. Mom remembered how the evening began. "So," she said, "I keep meaning to ask you — but we've been busy with other things — how overdue are you?"

"One day," I responded, suppressing a giggle.

"Uh please," she said impatiently, flinging her hand into the air with annoyance, "and there I was all excited for a moment. You really can be silly sometimes."

I sat quietly. Sensitized by my Alexander training, careful nutrition, and attunement to energy, I was aware that something was very different. Two weeks later the blood test came back positive. We'd done it. We'd conceived our baby in February, as planned.

There was only one flaw. In my ignorance I had calculated the date of birth as forty weeks from conception, not knowing that counting begins from first day of last period. I had to subtract two weeks, and thirty-eight weeks placed me fairly and squarely in the wrong part of November. I was going to have a Scorpio, after all. Correctly calculated the baby was due November ninth. With meticulous planning, I had controlled the details and fallen heavily, into the hands of fate.

At four in the morning, November ninth, 1986, I woke up with a start. After lying in bed, listening, waiting for something to happen, I heaved onto my feet, to go to the bathroom — and a flood broke loose. "Call Denise," I said to Neil, "my waters have broken." Denise, the midwife, said to wait for contractions that were regular and intense, and then to call her again. We were planning to have our baby at home.

We ambled through the morning. Neil's sister, Janis, a trained midwife, came over at about ten to visit. "You're doing really well," she said, as I showed her the jacket I'd just sewed on my sewing machine, explaining the technicalities of sticky-taping shiny faux leather, because pins would have left holes. I paused now and then to acknowledge a contraction, to give my Alexander directions, free my neck, lengthen my back, manage the pain.

I wasn't so dapper by four in the afternoon. Denise had arrived a few hours before, and I was tired — tired of waiting, tired from being awake for twelve hours, tired of trying to connect these bad feelings with the joy of having a baby. Neil was watching me out the corner of one eye, putting a supportive hand on my back, his other eye reading *Active Birth*, the book on birthing. He hadn't "had time" to read until now. Denise was observing me, measuring my behavior on her scale of experience.

Checking me again, Denise said, "You aren't dilating, but these are very intense contractions. We need to do something." She called the obstetrician, who prescribed *demerol*, and Janis went to get it. "I feel better now," Janis said. "I was worried about you doing this without any help."

"You know, Denise," I said, "I haven't had any drugs, not even a head-ache pill, in my bloodstream for over a year now, and I'm really sensitive to medication."

Denise looked at me carefully. "I think we'll do half the dose then, and see how that goes." She administered the injection and within minutes the action began. Neil dropped the book and held me as the contractions, which I'd considered already painful enough, tore at my insides with savage-animal fierceness. I lost all sense of time. Seconds of intense pain became minutes, minutes of pausing, between contractions, became seconds. The longer the time between pains meant the longer to go, the shorter the time between pains, the less to go — pain meant better, relief meant worse — I let my mind drift to the outside world. It was still light outside. Other people were out and about, walking on the mountain, walking on the beach. I was here in a darkened room, sweating in pain, supported by my husband, monitored by a mid-wife. More than an hour passed.

"You must lie down," Denise said, "so that I can check you again." It was unbearable to lie down, it was helpless to lie down. The pain overwhelmed me and I felt like I couldn't ever get up again. "How much longer is this going to go on?" I asked myself. I just wanted the misery to stop. The image of a soft new-born, had long been chased out of my mind by the immediacy of pain.

"Almost there," Denise said, "eight inches now." I'd been watching her face for cues all afternoon. At last I was getting the one I wanted. She looked confident. I could hang in there, see it through. It was almost over.

And then it was over. The contractions stopped. "You're fully dilated," Denise said triumphantly. Transition — a lull. Denise went to call her husband. I heard the air forced out of my lungs, heard myself groan, involuntarily, and Denise said, "Got to go now," dropping the 'phone and came, telling me to push and I didn't know how, and a life depended on it. Why was it all so hard? Why couldn't someone do it for me? And why, even with Neil and Denise in the room, did it seem like I was alone?

Neil held my weight as I hung there, holding onto the burglar bars. Denise coached me, encouraged me, until I could feel the hard reality of a baby's crown, holding me open. "Lots of hair," Denise said with a proud smile. Then one push and the head was free and another and the baby slid out with the whoosh of the waters, and the yell of a warrior, and I said, "It's a boy, that's Aidan!" and melted into a puddle on the floor.

I watched. After the initial yell the baby lay still, ash-blue, eyes closed. Neil was transfixed, speechless. He couldn't have reached that part of the book in his hasty scan of the day. He didn't know fresh-born babies are purple, until the blood oxygenates. He thought the baby was dead. Then the baby's ribs sprung open, sucking in air, eyes opened, face pinked and Dad could breathe again. Denise clipped the cord, wrapped the baby in a towel and handed him to me. I held him listlessly. Too flooded by all the emotions of the day, I couldn't find the quiet love to connect with my baby. "Let Neil hold him," I said, "give him to Neil."

"Mom always wants to hold the baby," Denise said gently, puzzled by my unusual behavior, but handing the baby to Neil.

Now that it was all over, I lay on the bed and surveyed the room. It was a war-zone, a field hospital. A saline drip stood ready in one corner. Denise's open bag spilled its contents in the middle of the room. Black garbage bags lined the carpet. When did this happen?

Despite the mess and mayhem, there was a stillness in the room, a prayer, the presence of spirit. Denise and I turned our heads, to see Neil, kneeling on the bed, holding his baby on a pillow — faces close, entranced, a father and son in sacred union. Denise looked at me, acknowledging Neil's special energy, understanding why, in this house, Mom wanted Dad to hold the baby.

Denise showed us how to dress the baby, wrapped him in his receiving blanket, and said, "Goodbye, I'll be back tomorrow. Remember who's boss," leaving us alone with this terrifying object — a new-born.

"Does Baby have a name yet?" Denise asked, when she came the next day.

"Yes," I said, "Aidan. But Neil isn't ready to commit, so I'm just giving him time to psyche himself up."

We did settle on 'Aidan.' We looked at our infant son, with his full head of hair, and knew, as every parent knows, that there is no more beautiful sight in the universe. How can love be so instant? We watched in awe as he slept, feeling the blessing of an angel.

Aidan was a blessing in our lives, and upon our house. Where the waters of his birth had whooshed onto the floor, there was a new stain on the carpet. "Eileen," I said to our maid, "See if you can wash out that stain with these new detergents I bought, they're supposed to clean everything, and while you're about it . . ."

"Yes," she interrupted me, "I'll see about the other stain* as well. I was thinking the same thing." She walked over to the little mat which hid the mark of the murder and picked it up. Her dark skin turned white. She looked at me, her lip quivering, "It's gone," she said hoarsely, unable to believe her eyes. The stain had disappeared. Death in the room, melted away by birth in the room.

THE CALL

The reality of caring for a baby was hard for me. Why hadn't all those mothers who'd gone before me, warned me how it would feel to have this tiny, dependent tyrant overtake my existence? I looked enviously at all the other people in the world. They were chatting freely, eating and drinking, their existence intact. They didn't know what it felt like to carry this second-by-second responsibility for another life. Besides, I was used to a rapid pace and lively conversation with a variety of people.

After two months, I couldn't stand it any more. "I'm going back to work," I said, "before I go crazy." I understood why Mom wasn't all goo-goo about babies. Clearly I wasn't either. There was only one way out — call Jacky. "Jacky, will you come look after Aidan in the afternoons, so I can teach?"

"Yes," she said, "the Lord told me I must come take care of your child. When do you want me to start?"

"Beginning of February," I said with a grateful sigh of thanks, to Jacky and the Lord.

"Gosh, back to work so soon," my clients said, "that's very impressive."

"You don't understand," I felt obliged to explain, "I **admire** those moms who **can stay** with their kids. I just can't do it. I'm doing this for my sanity."

Eileen, our regular maid, took care of Aidan in the mornings, and Jacky, my beloved nanny, took care of Aidan in the afternoons, and I went back to work. But even though I worked, Aidan never took even one sip from a bottle, and I was always there if he needed me. Mom was right. I needed a career where I could work at home.

A few months later, Neil went back to London to finish his training on the Carringtons' course. After he came back, life pretty much rolled along, in the groove. I taught the *Alexander Technique* and Neil continued to work as manager of Quality Control at Reckitt's. Our desire to move to America was as strong as ever. We **were** remembering, but we didn't have a plan.

A year later, I got a phone call. "Is that Vivien Schapera?"

"Yes," I replied.

"I'm calling long-distance from Johannesburg. I hear you're an Alexander teacher and I'm wondering whether you can refer me to someone here."

"I'm sorry," I said, "there are no teachers in Johannesburg."

"Oh, that's too bad," said the caller, "I really wanted to have Alexander lessons." I could tell that was the truth because long-distance calls are exorbitant in South Africa.

A day later I received another call, "Hello, is that Vivien Schapera?"

"Yes," I replied.

"I'm calling long-distance from Johannesburg. I hear you're an Alexander teacher and I wondered if you could refer me to anyone here?"

"I'm sorry," I said, "there are no teachers in Johannesburg, but what's going on up there, I got a similar call yesterday?"

"I don't know," said the caller, "I just wanted to have Alexander lessons." There was something odd about getting two calls in two days. After I put the phone down, I realized that I should have taken their names.

The next week it happened again, "Hello, is that Vivien Schapera?"

"Yes," I replied.

"I'm calling long-distance from Johannesburg, I hear you're an Alexander teacher and I wondered whether you can refer me to someone here?"

This time I was prepared, "I'm sorry," I said, "there are no teachers in Johannesburg. But I tell you what, something funny's going on, because suddenly I'm getting a rash of calls from Johannesburg. Let me take your name and number, and if more people call, perhaps I'll come up there to give a course of lessons."

"Lewis," said the caller, "my name is Lewis, and if you come I want my daughter to have lessons, too." He gave me his details.

Sure enough another call came in the next day, "Hello, is that Vivien Schapera?"

"Yes," I replied, knowing what was coming next, because I could hear the long-distance whine of the phone.

"I'm calling from Johannesburg. I'm looking for an Alexander teacher here. Do you know who I could go to?"

"Well, there aren't any Alexander teachers in Johannesburg," I replied, "but for some reason I'm getting a lot of calls from Johannesburg at the moment and I'm making a list. If ten people will commit to having a course of ten lessons each, I will come to Johannesburg for two weeks to teach you."

"Are you serious?" asked the caller, "because I belong to a meditation group and I know at least two other people who are also interested."

"Yes, I'm serious," I said, and in no time at all the list of ten was compiled.

Where was I going to stay? How was I going to get around? Who was going to take care of Aidan? The logistics seemed insurmountable. Everyone in Cape Town, including me, was baffled. "Why on earth are you going to Johannesburg, with all these difficulties, when you have more than enough work in Cape Town?"

"I don't know," I replied, "but I'm being called to Johannesburg. I'll only find out why when I get there." I surprised myself. It was one of those answers that just came out my mouth.

At the eleventh hour, one of the prospective students, called to say that her neighbors would be out of town, and they had agreed to let us stay in their house in Saxonwold. The name of the suburb conjured up rolling lawns and mature, leafy trees. It sounded ideal. Not only that, to our other questions, Fiona replied, "Yes, you can work from the house," and "Yes, they do have a live-in maid and she will be happy to look after Aidan." Once everything had fallen into place, Neil decided to come too.

The suburb was aptly named. Saxonwold is one of the lush, established areas of Johannesburg. The house was gently decorated with gleaming wood and nubby textiles, surrounded by lawns and flower-gardens. Built in the 1920's, it had good, solid walls, spacious rooms, a generous floor plan and a strong, old feeling. Maggie, the maid, a noble Zulu, took one look at Aidan and was besotted. We had no idea what spell this house was about to cast on us, what influences were at work. Generous strangers, who didn't know us, or the Alexander Technique, had inexplicably opened their home to us. They didn't want anything from us, "Just pay Maggie a decent sum for taking care of you and your child." they said.

Now that Neil was along for the ride, I tweaked my plans. "You take the ten people," I said, "I'll take the two stragglers who just want one lesson each, then I can spend some time with Aidan and have a little break." The first morning, I put Aidan in the stroller, waved a cheery goodbye to Neil as he was showing his first client into the house, and walked Aidan down to Zoo Lake. My leisure lasted exactly one day. The grapevine had already begun to hum, word spread like flowing water, "Alexander teachers in town." The phone rang continually. By the end of the first week, we were teaching more than twenty-five people per day.

It was Easter, traditionally a time of renewal, even in the southern hemisphere where it is fall, not spring. Friday night, tired from all the teaching, I lay on the bed, alternately gazing out the window at the perfectly framed whiteness of the rising full moon in the indigo sky, and staring at the ceiling, enjoying a light state of altered consciousness. A vision formed itself in my mind, of another city in another country. Like Johannesburg, it was a city built on hills, without mountains, without oceans, without the Alexander Technique — the city of Cincinnati. I saw a red carpet unfurling toward us, summoning us, with an assurance of peace, safety and prosperity. The vision broke into words, and I turned to Neil and said, "If we can come to Johannesburg and get so busy, so quickly, why can't we do this in a city in America?" I paused. "Let's do this in Cincinnati. We can ask your uncle, Herby, to employ us as Alexander teachers in his medical practice, and get into America that way."

Neil looked at me. Up until now we had assumed that our only way in was on his Food Technology ticket. Usually quick to find holes and slow to commit, this time he said, "Yes, I can't see why that wouldn't work. Let's do that."

We had got the answer to why we needed to go to Johannesburg! The willingness to hear the call, take the risk and let the pieces fall into place; the generosity of strangers, the appreciation of the people of Johannesburg and the financial success of this venture; the magic of this house, the full moon and Easter, had conspired to birth this plan.

More was to come. We returned to Cape Town and on Monday morning Neil went off to work. That was the last usual Monday morning we were ever going to have. Before nine-thirty in the morning the phone rang. "I've had it," he said, "I'm leaving. I've resigned. I'm going to be a full-time Alexander Teacher."

"What happened?" I asked, my body flushing hot and cold all over as relief flooded through me.

"As soon as I walked in, my boss wanted to know why I hadn't completed the assignment he'd given me — like he didn't know I'd been away for two weeks. I realized I didn't need to take it anymore, so I resigned on the spot. I'll be home in an hour."

So much was changing, so rapidly. It was hard to know what were the big steps and what were the little steps. Neil and Raphael called Herby, in Cincinnati. "Of course I'll help," said Herby, "just tell me what to do."

"Well, we're going to England in July, for an international Alexander Congress, so I'll come to America after that and we can get the ball rolling," Neil said.

While Neil was in Cincinnati he and Herby engaged the services of an immigration lawyer, Mike, to guide us through the bureaucratic steps. Neil phoned home with big news. "We need to choose between applying for permanent residence visas and a temporary work permit. Permanent residence will take two plus years to complete and the temporary work permit will take three months to come through."

"What do you think?" I asked Neil, suspecting he would choose the quick route.

"Let's do the temporary visa," he said, "and then we can change our status once we're here."

"O.K.," I agreed, eager to get on with the rest of our lives, "let's do that."

I couldn't resist going to see a tarot card reader, Marie-Claire, to find out what the outcome would be. Marie-Claire laid out the cards, looked at them and took a deep breath, "I see you are emigrating to America." This was good. This was exactly what I wanted to hear.

"You have a whole new life ahead of you," she said, "I see you meeting someone, a man, who is presently overseas. You will be very happy."

I frowned, this didn't sound right. "I'm married," I said, "I'm not looking to meet someone else."

She looked at the cards again, "Then this could mean that the man you are married to is going to change, become different, but there is definitely the sign of a 'new man' here."

"That makes sense," I responded, relieved, "my husband is overseas at the moment. He has always wanted to live in America and I expect he will change when his wish is granted."

"I see you do healing work," she continued, looking at the cards, "a cross between a nurse and a teacher." I didn't say anything, this was a pretty accurate way to depict my style.

"I smell oranges," she said, sniffing the air repeatedly, "perhaps you are going to live in California, or Florida."

I frowned again. This didn't sound right either, "I think we'll be going to Cincinnati," I said.

"I don't know," Marie-Claire answered, "I definitely smell oranges."

"I have a question," I said, "My husband is currently in America, and he has been offered two jobs. Which opportunity will work better for us?" Neil was not only investigating the Alexander angle, he was looking into Food Technology, as well.

Marie-Claire couldn't squeeze guidance out of the cards. "It doesn't matter," she said, "it makes no difference which one you choose." It was a puzzling response. The choice to pursue Food Technology or Alexander Technique as a career, seemed to me to make a big difference.

Marie-Claire had one more intriguing thing to say. "I see you taking a vacation first before you go to America."

"That's interesting," I replied, "we were considering going to England by sea, and then flying to America from London."

"Yes," she said, "I see a small suitcase in front of a large suitcase — first a small trip then a big trip."

"Thank you," I said, "thank you. You've told me everything I wanted to hear." I left Marie-Claire's house with a buoyant step. As far as I was concerned, with news like that, we were in America already!

Neil came home and it was all we could do to sit out the time waiting for our papers to be processed. One morning, the phone rang at five. It was Herby, "Are you ready?" he asked, voice full of the pleasure of good news. "Congratulations, all the paperwork has been approved on this side. Now all you have to do is get your passports stamped by the immigration officer in South Africa."

The day of our interview arrived. We went to the U.S. Consulate in Cape Town, stilling ourselves with anxious reassurances that all was done and sealed in America. This was just a rubber stamp process. We passed the unflinching Marines in the hallway, hearts filling with advance patriotic pride, and took our seats, waiting our turn to hear the words "open sesame," to gain admittance to the rest of our lives. The bullet-proof window, equipped with microphones, startled us. We'd expected a cozy interview in a room with a desk, and a sitting area — a friendly exchange with an understanding immigration officer, a welcome to a new country. Our big moment was being reduced to buying bus tickets in a dangerous neighborhood.

We listened in dismay, to each supplicant's life story. We were hearing contention, pleading. We were watching hopeful faces shrink with dejection as they trailed away from the window. A horrible truth leered at us, hovering in the air of that waiting room — this *was not* a rubber stamp process. The word "No!" permeated every tuft of the new beige carpet, every stroke of the freshly painted walls, lived in every breath of the stale indoor air. "We're different," I told myself, "our papers are all in order, we're different."

We stepped up to the window. I searched the immigration officer for signs of compassion, and saw that all humanness had been trained out of him. He listened to us, cold as black steel. He looked at our papers, looked at his papers and said, "I'm not going to give you a temporary visa, because I believe you are planning to live in the United States permanently. I recommend that you apply for permanent residence. Good luck." That was it. Our turn was over. No desk, no interview, no chat — just "No!" We stood, gasping like dying fish, looking at our worthless papers, looking at the worthless 'approved' stamp, looking at the dust of our crushed plans.

We slunk away from the window, crept past the unforgiving Marines, guarding their country against the likes of us, down the stairs, back to our car, and just sat. I couldn't look at Neil. I couldn't make sense of what had happened. We were angry. We knew many people who had gone into the United States on temporary work permits and had converted their status once there. Why were we being blocked? We even knew people who'd won green cards in the *lottery*. All the predictions, all the energies, all the intuition indicated we were going to America. Why were we being blocked?

We couldn't leave it at that. We called Herby. We called our lawyer. We made a second attempt, but we couldn't change the result. "Apply for permanent residence," said the immigration officer, "I wish you good luck." It was December 1988.

With both of us teaching at home, and the arrival of Aidan, our house had become too small. It was time to move. Miriam and Raphael enjoyed buying homes, remodeling the kitchens and bathrooms, and then selling them again. "We saw a really nice house today," Raphael reported to us. "You two should come and look at it. It would really suit you."

The house was in upper Claremont, two minutes' walk from where we grew up. I walked through the wooden gate and felt at home. A mature pecan tree sheltered the front yard. The pathway to the front door was lined with old, established white and pink camellias, feathery stre-litzias, white arum lilies, pink abelia and a multitude of orange clivia. A rolling lawn led down to the gently curved swimming pool, carefully bricked, landscaped with palms and roses and bougainvillea in shades of white, pink, lilac and magenta. Inside, the house was generous, solid. The huge kitchen, with adjoining breakfast and utility room, equaled half of our entire current home. There were three bathrooms, side entrances, a fully-contained suite, three more bed-rooms, a study, a family room with anthracite heater and a large glass-enclosed porch, offering a spectacular view of the mountain. I wanted this house — if I couldn't be in America, I wanted to at least live in this home.

We thought it would be easy to sell our house, so we put in an unconditional bid, which was accepted. But we hit a snag. The stain on the carpet wasn't the last hint of Mr. Forrest, the deceased previous owner — he seemed to be hanging around, influencing decisions about his former property. We suspected Mr. Forrest because the realtor told us how a serious prospect suddenly lost interest in buying the house: "Oh he was ready to buy, but he strolled down the street, to get a feel for the neighborhood, and one of your neighbors stepped out and told him it's the house where Mr. Forrest was murdered." The timing was uncanny.

We'd noticed Mr. Forrest before. Aidan used to point to the air at the height of a medium built man and say "The man, the man," and Jacky claimed she could feel his presence sometimes. I'd had one incident which had made the hair on my arms stand up and the skin on my neck tingle and itch. I'd noticed an empty spot under the oak tree and had decided to plant a camellia. I'd thought camellias came in white and pink and it would be a straightforward choice, but when I got to the nursery I was faced with a range of forty varieties. I kept coming back to a pink and white double bloom, labelled 'Albert Schweitzer.'

At home, I hauled it over to the empty spot and when I got there, I noticed a dry stick, protruding from the earth, with a nursery tag at its base. I bent to look. 'Albert Schweitzer camellia,' it said. Did Mr. Forrest guide my choice? It seemed an unlikely coincidence.

Now, we were under pressure to sell our house. One night, after working late on a project, not wanting to disturb Neil and Aidan, I rolled out the futon and went to sleep on the floor of my teaching room. Lying in the dark, I felt a breeze touch my face. I knew this wasn't a draft from the windows — the windows were closed. Besides, the breeze was coming and going. "Is that you Mr. Forrest," I asked, not out loud, inside my head.

"Yes," offered itself.

"Mr. Forrest," I asked, "why won't you let the house sell?"

"I don't want you to move," came the inside reply, "how will I know that the next owners will take proper care of the garden? You must stay and take care of this home."

"But, Mr. Forrest," I said, "we've already bought another house. We have to move. We won't sell the house to just anybody, only to a family who'll take care of it, appreciate it, the way we do. I promise. Please don't stop us from selling the house anymore."

The breeze evaporated and all was still in the room, too still. I ran back to the bedroom, back to my snoring, sighing, out-loud family. Within the week, we sold the house.

After we had moved, I realized that the move to this house, was the small move, the small suitcase that Marie-Claire had seen. The big suitcase, the big move across the ocean, lay sometime ahead, in the future. No wonder Marie-Claire had said Neil's choice of job didn't matter.

"This is a beautiful house," Pam said, when she came to visit. "You must stay here and populate it!"

"No," I laughed, "we will populate it, but we are still going to emigrate."

"What's next?" Pam asked.

"Well, we have to apply for labor certification."

"What's that?" Pam asked.

"Oh, it's a mountain of paperwork. Herby needs to apply to employ one of us in his practice, and he has to demonstrate that there isn't an American citizen who wants the job and has the qualifications."

"Who's helping you?" Pam asked. Pam understood how things worked in layers. I didn't have to explain how hard it was to get into America. I told her about Mike, our lawyer, and Ted, our friend in Boston, that I'd met at the Carringtons'. Ted had become the president of the North American Society of Teachers of the Alexander Technique and he was supplying all the documentation about the Alexander Technique.

Pam was interested in seeing how the energies were lining up, over time, to produce the intended result. "It sounds like a long process."

"It will take years," I said, "it's a bureaucratic nightmare. The application has to go from office to office, department to department. We have no idea how long. It depends on the bottlenecks."

"What exactly is the job?" Pam asked.

"An Alexander teacher, with an M.A. in Psychology to work in a doctor's practice."

"Why the Psychology part?"

"Because labor certification is only for professionals and a profession is defined as a career which requires a college degree."

"Lucky you finished your masters!" Pam said.

"And I didn't expect to ever need it!"

We sat together, contemplating the future. Pam looked down at the ground. It would be very hard to say goodbye. Pam looked up again. "Well, what about populating the house?" she asked, returning to the first subject.

"It is time for another baby. One thing's for sure — it's easier to have babies here in South Africa, where we have Jacky, and grandparents. Maybe waiting won't be such a bad thing after all." There were other ways to get on with our lives, besides going to America. And it was important to have a good attitude about waiting.

As soon as I was pregnant, I sought out a new prenatal teacher, Meloma, because John, my yoga teacher, had gone to England to train as an Alexander teacher. Meloma had gathered around her all kinds of alternative style mothers-to-be. She gave us plenty of time to talk about our fears and expectations, especially those of us who'd already had children and wanted to talk about what we wanted to do differently this time.

Listening to stories of Caesarean sections and long, miserable labors in hospitals, I realized that I had done well with my home-birth. Still, when Meloma heard my story, she looked at me squarely and commented, "I wonder what it was that you couldn't manage, that you needed the *demerol*?" What did she mean, that I couldn't manage? I'd managed fine, I simply hadn't dilated, that's why I'd needed the drug. I put the question on the shelf, where it could wait out its answer.

The question was waiting, we were waiting and even Aidan was waiting. "When *is* this baby coming, I'm waiting and waiting!" Aidan demanded.

"I'm waiting too," I replied.

"How can *you* be waiting," he questioned, his eyes widening in shock at my terrible lie, "*you're* the one who's got it!"

The full moon announced the end of his wait. Nine months had come and gone. While I was sewing a ninja turtle outfit for Aidan, my contractions started. Denise came over at about six in the evening, very tired from delivering babies all through the night, several nights in a row, and went to call her stepdaughter to report my progress. "Labor's moving along," I heard her saying. Jacky put Aidan to bed and went back to the kitchen. We were all sure that this labor would be straightforward. After all, it was the second one, and Denise, Neil and I were a practiced team.

By midnight we were feeling miffed. Aidan woke up and spoke for all of us. "Where's the baby? Hasn't it arrived yet?" He refused to go back to sleep. His patience was all used up, so Jacky took him to the family room to be out of the way.

Trouble was, I wasn't dilating again. Meloma's question rang in my ears. Denise got impatient, too. "These are very intense contractions. There should be more happening. I should have got a supply of *demerol*." The only place we were going to get *demerol* at this time of night was in the hospital itself.

Denise made me lie down on the bed in Aidan's room, took a long needle and deliberately broke the waters. The severity of the contractions incremented and after fifteen or twenty minutes Denise checked me again, both of us hoping that something must have changed by now. Denise shook her head, "You've dilated a little more, but not nearly enough, I think we'll have to go to hospital."

"I **want** to go to hospital," I said, stamping my foot. "I **want** to have an epidural, I'm sick of this." I was feeling cheated of my easy second labor. It wasn't supposed to be like this. I wanted to tear at my hair, and shout at Neil and shout at Denise, and shout so loud that the neighbors would hear and come running to see who was torturing the nice woman next-door and rescue me from this horrible fate. I was tired of being a lady and coping with the pain and putting up with this misery in such a sweet, understanding way. Neil watched in dismay as I raged up and down, crying and cussing, and Denise got salty, throwing all her equipment into her bag. She called the obstetrician to say we were on our way.

Then Denise came back in the bathroom and said, "I have to check you one more time before we get into the car," and Denise and I knew what the outcome would be, because we'd both felt the energies change and knew that now that I'd given up control — controlling my behavior, controlling the pain — I would have started to dilate. "You aren't going anywhere," she said, self-satisfied, "there isn't enough time, you're too far dilated now."

Neil watched in confusion as the equipment rolled back out of the bag. He'd missed the swing of the pendulum. He'd believed the charade that I was going to hospital. And then I gave into the pain and told myself, "This is good pain, not bad. It's not damaging me, it's opening me up. Let it be, let it be," and it was such a terrible pain that I couldn't stand it, but I had to give in to it, and allow it to rip open my body, so that a baby could get out. Within twenty minutes I was fully dilated and into transition and in ten minutes, because now I knew how to push, a baby boy was born, and when he cried, Aidan heard him and said to Jacky, "At last, there's the baby!"

"That was a difficult labor," said Denise, wiping her brow, wiping away the dynamics of the night.

"I can't go through this again," said Neil, " I didn't know what was going on, first we were never going to hospital, then we were going, then we weren't going. I couldn't keep up."

I just smiled. I had an answer for Meloma, I had an answer for myself. The thing that I couldn't manage, on my own, the first time around, was the principle that lies at the heart of the Alexander Technique, the principle that I teach every day of my life. I needed to learn how to allow. I had to give up being in control, I had to learn how to let the right thing happen.

Denise got us all cleaned up and Jacky went to her room. Aidan, Jason, Neil and I got into bed, at five in the morning, with the full moon setting and the sun rising. We went to sleep — all together — we were a whole family now.

Death

I'd watched Russell face death and I'd met the spirit of Mr. Forrest. I
didn't expect to be glad of these experiences, but then I didn't know
that death was coming, in her diaphanous gown, a beautiful
temptress, calling a loved one away, asking us to let go.

Pam and her husband, Neil and I, were sitting around the table, eating
dinner, on a Monday night, glad for the public holiday the next day. We
were talking about facing our fears, when I came up with one of my
annoying observations: "If we don't face our fears, they will happen to us."

"Don't talk like that," Neil said, "it's scary."

I shrugged, grinning at him, but then a tremor rippled inside me. "So
what are you afraid of? What fear do you have to face?" It came to me, so
huge, it turned my legs to water — that Mom would turn into Becky, my
grandmother, getting more and more difficult as she got older. She would
get sick, unable to breathe, and I would have to take care of her — have
her living in my house, sitting next to me, sighing noisily, when I watched
TV. That she would call me to her bedroom in the middle of the morning,
in the middle of the night, tell me how to bring up my children, check for
dust on the top of the pictures, turn her nose up at dinner and make me
cry in my own home when I was a grown-up. I wanted to shrug it off —
oh, Michael will take care of Mom.

The phone rang just after nine thirty that night. Neil answered the
phone, "Yes, Alec . . . o-o-oh! . . . I see . . . yes . . . when did it happen. . .
I'm sorry to hear that . . . and where are you now?" I could tell from his
voice, and what he was saying that something bad had happened.
Something bad had happened to Michael. It was the call in the night, the
call we had been expecting, as the years had ticked by, numbering the
minutes.

Neil handed the phone to me, to speak to Dad. Dad's voice was calm
— too calm, too measured. "Michael is in surgery," he said, "he was
stabbed behind the ear."

"What do you mean, 'surgery?'" I asked, trying not to visualize the
stab wound, not to imagine the blood dripping from my brother, trying to
keep my mind clean. "Don't you mean being stitched?"

"No," explained Dad, "the knife is embedded in the bone." We both paused, then Dad continued. "The neurologist checked him and he was able to answer all the questions, follow all the commands. Just his speech was a little slurred. Mom and I are at Constantiaberg Clinic, we'll be waiting here."

"Well, let me know what happens." I said. I lay back down, arranging myself in bed. At first I was blank, but as I lay there, thoughts rushed in, pushing the puzzle pieces together. Dad had been deliberately obscure. The knife "behind the ear" must actually be a knife penetrating the brain. Michael must be undergoing serious brain surgery. I leapt out of bed knowing that this was the end.

Michael had been assaulted, stabbed with knives, throttled many times. He would arrive at the house in Mountain Road, bleeding from the head, the neck, wherever, and Mom or Dad would take him to the doctor.

Michael's life was threatened because the fun, the dancing, the transvestism, wasn't enough. Michael was a sex addict with a taste for 'rough trade' — the sleazy, criminal element who for want of any other way to earn money, sell themselves as male prostitutes, padding their earnings by stealing from their customers. Then just because — just because — they've been treated like dirt and life is worthless, beating their customers, murdering them.

It was as if there was a script and Michael was rehearsing, seeing what worked, seeing what didn't, doing variations on the performance, improvising. We all knew the last line. We'd tell him, "Michael, you must be more careful, you're going to get killed."

"I've always known I would die young," he'd say, from time to time, in an even voice, smoothly looking toward the future. I knew this was true. I could tell from his favorite movies that he strongly identified with offbeat romantic figures who lived passionate, misunderstood lives and did die young. A palm reader told Michael, when he was in his twenties, that he would die in his early thirties.

Six weeks earlier, soon after he turned thirty-seven, he said to Mom: "I thought I'd be dead by now, but it looks like I was wrong. It seems like I need to make provision for my future." He was opening a second business, an interior decorating store. This was the day he signed the lease for the new premises.

Now I was on my way to the hospital, my blood turning to ice in my veins, explaining the cliche. The roads, completely familiar, took on a surreal quality — ghost scenes — scenes of desertion. I felt like I wasn't traveling, time had slowed to a standstill. Then, all changed. The scenery traveled past me. Time was moving forward, but I was in stillness.

I parked the car, ran into the hospital and located Mom and Dad. Sitting together in the dimly lit waiting area, Mom nodded when she saw me. "What happened? Tell me!"

Dad spoke deliberately, in a grocery-list voice. "Just after seven we got a 'phone call from Michael's maid. She was very upset, distressed. She said there was a lot of banging and crashing in the house and the panic alarm had been set off. She said we must come immediately because she was too scared to go inside. We rushed over to Michael's house. All the doors were locked, but there was a hole smashed through the front door. We called to him from outside, 'Michael are you in there? Are you all right?' He answered, 'Mommy, Mommy I'm dead.' We used our keys to get inside, but the bedroom door was locked. We had to persuade him to open the door. His room was a mess. You could see he'd fought for his life. He told me how to switch off the burglar alarm. He made us promise 'no police.' He asked me to pull the knife out, but I couldn't. Your mom came here with him in the ambulance and I drove the car. Aunt Alicia's in there with him."

I looked at them, wondering how they had managed to take in the scene. The broken lamp, knocked down beside the broken table. Blood spattered on the closet doors, pooling on the carpet. Bloody fingerprints where grasping hands slid down the wall. How did they look at their son, beaten and bleeding, hilt of a knife wedged up against his head? How did they hear the words "Mommy, Mommy I'm dead," and how did they wait here, an ordinary couple, sitting together on the couch?

I sat alongside them. At the very moment, seven that evening, when I was thinking "Oh, Michael will take care of Mom," this was happening to him.

Then I thought about Michael with severe brain damage, Michael in a wheelchair or something even worse for Michael. I turned to Mom and asked, "Could Michael see?"

"I don't know," she said. "I didn't ask that."

"What did he say? What were his last words?"

Dad responded, "He told Mom that he loved her. He couldn't stop telling her, he wouldn't stop calling her. She had to leave, so they could operate."

We fell silent, holding the same thought. We wouldn't say it out loud. These weren't the words of a common prayer — let Michael die, rather than live a severely handicapped life. An ugly calm settled upon us.

Aunt Alicia's footsteps came down the hall. The hollow sound of falling feet, the dejected shadow knocking along the wall, carried the urgent warning, "Bad news coming." The gray somberness of her face, the lankness of her hair, the one hundred-years-old-seen-too-much-now expression, left no room for doubt. "There's no hope," Aunt Alicia said, "no hope at all. It wasn't a knife, it was a bayonet, an army bayonet. We were sick, we couldn't look. It cut through the mid-line of the brain, it was embedded in the other side of the skull. We took the knife out, but now the brain-tissue will swell and he will die." How hard it must have been for her to discover the fatal wound of her best friend's son, to be the one to break the news, to tell her best friend the worst words a mother can hear.

"It's just a matter of time. Because Michael's young and strong he will continue through the night, his organs will gradually fail and the hospital will be able to call you in good time. You may as well go home and get some sleep."

Sleep? How can one sleep at a time like this? I couldn't imagine the possibility. I got home at midnight. I went straight to the phone and called Jacky. "Jacky," I said, "you must pray for Michael, he's been stabbed in the head. Pray for him to die peacefully, pray for his soul." Jacky was our direct line to God.

"I knew it," she said, "I knew this would happen." She sighed deeply, pushing against the heavy weight on her heart, "All right Viv, I'll pray. I'll pray for his immortal soul." I put down the phone and fell into a deep sleep.

Waking at seven, we called the hospital. Michael was still strong and it would be a while — a few hours — before he died. We arranged for Aidan to go to Miriam and Raphael, but we took five-month-old Jason with us. We didn't know how long we would be. Jason would probably need to nurse at least once or twice.

We went up to see Michael, as soon as we arrived at the hospital. He lay quietly, patiently, eyes closed, eyelids flickering. His breathing was strong and even, regulated by the suck and hiss of the ventilator. His vital signs were monitored and displayed on a battery of screens. This was a scene from a movie. A familiar scene, the ho-hum melodrama — the tears, the heart-wrenching death-bed scene, where crying family members, fists clenched, surround the dying relative — except, pinch me, poke me, this wasn't a movie. Head wrapped in clean white bandages, chest bare, a beautiful thirty-seven year old tennis-playing, dancing, lover's body — my childhood companion, my mentor, my old-age companion — about to die.

Eat? Who can eat at a time like this? But we had a hearty appetite. We went down to the cafeteria to eat scrambled eggs and toast, drink coffee, tea and orange juice, talk about the coming week. Moments of forgetting that upstairs, Michael lay dying.

As we chewed our last mouthfuls, Jason unexpectedly fell into a deep sleep. Within the minute the phone rang to summon us to Michael's side. His blood pressure was dropping, he was dying.

I was certain that Jason would waken as we wheeled him into the elevator. It was nine-fifteen, not at all his usual sleeping time. Through the hallways, into the intensive care unit, through the changes in atmosphere and lighting — all the triggers that would normally wake him — he sank into a deeper and deeper sleep.

While the nurses drew the curtains around Michael's bed, we stationed Jason's stroller against the wall. Mom, Dad, Neil and I sat around Michael, watching as he took his last breaths. Mom cried out, "My heart is breaking." Unnecessary words, squeezed from her lips, from emotions too hard to contain. Her big, strong body was too small to hold the pressure of a mother's pain. We reached out for each other's hands, something to hold, something to anchor us in life, lest death should blow on us like a cold wind and take us too, and Mom and Dad willed themselves to release their beloved only son.

As I watched, this most painful thing I'd ever witnessed became the most encouraging, enlightening, sustaining experience of my life. I saw Michael's spirit withdraw from his body, a hand from a glove, hovering half in, half out, glowing a series of pink, green and gold translucent colors. Breathing his last, his spirit flew upward, like a fountain, bursting into a shower of radiant light, falling back into the room, billions of holograms so bright, dazzling me. I had to close my eyes. Michael — restless, fidgety Michael; jiggling, jangling, limb-drumming Michael; constantly moving, head-rolling, neck-popping Michael — lay tranquil and serene. His spirit free, escaped from his body, Michael was truly at peace.

We exhaled, unhooking ourselves from the chairs, shaking our numb bodies. Mom's face was too bright, Dad's too ashen — shock had stolen the color from his lips, and eyes, painting him putty-gray.

"Someone must call Uncle Harry," Mom said.

"I will," I said. Something to do, no matter how horrible. A nurse showed me the phone.

"Uncle Harry, Michael died at ten o' clock this morning."

"All right my lovey, we'll come down to the hospital now. I'll see you there."

"But there's nothing to do, it's over," I said.

"No, Viv, I want to see him, and someone must sit with the body. I want to sit with him."

Two more calls. Harold, Michael's best friend deserved to be told, as soon as possible. Harold was angry, "I told him. I told him he'll get killed. You know Michael, he just wouldn't listen, always knew better. Have you called the police?"

"Why the police?" I was confused.

"Well, Vivien, it's murder." The point had passed me by. I thought of it as suicide.

Jacky was next. "I prayed for him," she said, "was it peaceful?"

"Oh, Jacky, it was beautiful. I'll tell you all about it. His spirit is free, he's at peace now." Jacky sighed with pain — pain and acceptance.

The nurse came to tell me that Michael was off the ventilator and I went to see him for the last time. Perfect. Perfectly still, angelic, true to his name, Mi - cha - el, he who is like God. In the busy ward, the bustling intensive care unit, Michael's body lay on a bed, a big empty space, infinite.

It was a time of speaking the truth. The next day, as we sat waiting for the rabbi, Dad, a self-proclaimed atheist, turned to me and said, "Viv, I know you felt it, and I felt it too. I felt the peace."

Later Neil said, "I think Jason went with Michael."

"Yes," I said, "I wondered if Jason would wake up at a crucial moment, so I tuned to him, but it felt like the stroller was empty. It felt like he was far away, like his spirit went to greet Michael and show him the way." We nodded our heads. Jason had fallen asleep so strangely, exactly when the nurses saw the pressure falling, the organs failing, and stayed asleep, through the transition, waking two hours after it was all over — sleeping for five whole hours in the morning, when he normally slept an hour-and-a-half, when we were lucky. Our simple agreement gave us complex comfort.

It seemed like Michael stayed close, for the days immediately after his death. I could feel his energy around me, suggesting thoughts to my mind. Looking at my face in the mirror, I'd see more than the subtle family resemblance. I'd see a push and a pull, enlarging my nose, lengthening my forehead, filling my lips, so that I looked like him, his face urging itself through my skin. Kariem, Michael's friend came to the door, and doubled over when he saw me. "Oh my God, you look just like him. What is going on here!" We needed the release of melodrama, we needed to know that the end of the physical incarnation, was not the end of Michael. He could still make himself felt, make himself heard and even make himself seen.

At the public seance, held at the spiritual church, Thursday evening, two days after his death, a comet of light danced through the auditorium, landing on the stage alongside the medium, who announced: "There is a young man here, a soul who has just passed over, a man who died a violent death. He wants everyone to know that he didn't believe in this place, but now he's here and he wants his mother to know that he's all right."

"It's Michael Singer!" the audience sang.

It was a time of seeing the truth. There was great public outrage, "A man killed in the prime of his life! This shouldn't be." But I couldn't see it that way. I saw a soul with a plan for a shorter life, a debt fulfilled, a release. I spent many hours thinking about Michael's life. I knew so much detail, I could see his life as a perfect whole, and the pattern of his life indicated the time to die.

Michael had strained forty-eight hours to be born. He arrived in the world battered, bruised, slightly brain damaged. His life see-sawed, as he struggled to balance incongruent aspects of his personality. He was a shy loner, at six years old, standing isolated on the sidelines, watching the other children playing together. As an adult, under cover of night he took center stage, the life and soul of the night club. On the court, he was a robust sportsman, playing a vigorous game of tennis. At home, he was a sensitive aesthete, surrounding himself with fine antiques, magnificent canvasses and exquisite *objéts d'arts*. Socially, he was a sharp-tongued critic, a harsh judge, filled with generosity and compassion. His efforts to harmonize and blend polarities, was most fully expressed, in being a man who dressed as a woman.

Behind the gourmet cooking and fine dining, the fancy outfits and passionate dancing, the impeccable taste and stately decor, loomed the darkness of depression. Michael's life was a bitter contest between upright character and wayward personality. A raw, raging addiction seethed at the edges of refinement. He knew it would be better to die, than face the slow decay, as this untamable craving gnawed at him, dissolving the fabric of his being. He left, as he came in — bruised, beaten and brain-damaged.

Michael couldn't have planned a better farewell. Once he confided in me, "I wish I could show people who I really am, and that they would still accept me. I wish I could take my boyfriend to Uncle Harry, and say, 'this is my partner.' That's what I really want." So sensational was the nature of his life and death, that the newspapers fanfared his truth across the nation in headlines. The radio broadcast his tale for all to hear, to stand up and listen, to take heed. Stylish as always, Michael exited with a grand flourish, leaving us gasping for more, a standing ovation.

The temple wasn't big enough for all the people pouring into the memorial service, Black and White, Christian, Muslim and Jewish. Dividing doors were folded away, extra chairs provided, so that all these people could pay homage to the truth, show their love and acceptance of the character, the personality, the tragic hero, that was Michael Singer. Then, a black pall fell over Cape Town. The foods in the restaurants lost their juice, fabrics lost their color, the nightclubs stood empty. No music, no dancing, no glitter. Without Michael's big smile, the whole city mourned.

After months of investigation the police filed the case for lack of any leads. "Will you call me first, when you've finished with the house?" I asked the case detective, "I don't want my mother to have to deal with all the women's clothes, the shoes, the photos, the wigs. Please call me first." Dutifully, he'd searched the house for clues. Of all the priceless art, the gorgeous antiques, the museum pieces, only two items were missing — two pairs of Rayban sunglasses, exchangeable for drugs on the black market. No clues to the identity of the murderer, no leads to follow. Michael had been unwilling to reveal the name of his attacker before succumbing to the general anesthetic.

I never considered thoughts of revenge, or justice, toward my brother's murderer. Whoever it was, was merely another actor in Michael's script. But suddenly, a year later, a man was heard boasting at a party, that he was the one who killed Michael Singer. A young man, barely eighteen, who wanted some credit, some acknowledgement for being the mystery man, the one who killed an almost celebrity.

The police arrested a youth who had a reputation, dating from childhood. A young man who knew that life is cheap — a South African man, a product of the system — his family, unable to afford him, had sold him, when he was four.

The case made legal history — the first gay murder where the judge did not find extenuating circumstances for the accused. Instead, the judge expressed outrage at the scourge of society who thought it fitting to prey on their fellow men, considering it justified because they were homosexual. Not a slap on the hand, nor a suspended sentence — twenty years — a breakthrough.

Dad, who had to stand in court, describe Michael's condition, the way he found him in his bedroom that night, had to look at his son's bisected brain, preserved in a jar, shook his head sadly and said, "Another life wasted." And, during all the fuss and attention, cards of condolence and tears of loss, immediately after Michael's death, Mom commented, "This week's news will soon be replaced by next week's seven-day wonder."

But Michael's life wasn't wasted. And Cape Town did not forget Michael, the man who gave his share to the soul of his city. Seven years later Michael's friend took Mom to see a play about homosexuality. The play ended with the construction of five memorial mounds, each in tribute to a man who had died because he was homosexual, and whose life and death had raised compassion and tolerance to the plight of homosexuals in the community. Mom listened as she watched the construction of the last mound, listened as she heard the final words of the play — the end of the script, culmination of all the improvising, all the rehearsals — "And this is for Michael Singer."

The New World

WORRIES

After Michael died, I sat on the steps, outside the sun-room, staring at the mountain. Time on my own, grieving. "Will you die, Mommy," Aidan asked, "promise me you won't die." I didn't want to lie — what if something happened, a car accident, a freak event?

"I don't plan to die, I'm going to live to ninety," I said, "but we all die some time."

"No, Mommy, you must never die. Promise me you'll never die," Aidan begged, throwing his body against me, unable to get close enough, not wanting to be separate from me.

I had no comfort to give, no false reassurance. We all had to get used to mortality, absorb it into our understanding of life. And we had to get used to being separated from each other. At prayers, the evening of Michael's memorial service, Mom had sidled up behind me, whispering in my ear, "Don't let this change your plans to emigrate."

There was a reason Mom supported our plans. Every morning we opened our newspapers to be confronted by the news of the day — who'd been burglarized, assaulted, raped, murdered or killed in a car crash. We had a breakfast ritual. Neil would look at me. I'd look at him. We'd shake our heads and say, "We've got to get out of here."

The threat wasn't just in the newspapers, in other people's lives. It was in our life. One Saturday afternoon, before Jason was born, Neil, groggy with a touch of flu, went to sleep in our bedroom. Aidan fell asleep on his bed, and I fell asleep on the futon at the fireplace in the family room. I woke with a start, to see a man standing behind the TV set, his hand poised over Neil's watch.

"What are you doing?" I asked.

"I'm looking for work."

"In here?" I stayed where I was, allowing him to back out. As soon as he was through the doorway, he turned and ran. I was scared, not of the man, but because the house was too quiet. Where were Neil and Aidan? Why couldn't I hear them? Had the man killed them in their sleep? I forced myself to get up and and look. Aidan was still fast asleep. Neil was snoring like a sick bear, sandwiched inside his stack of four pillows, his gun lying underneath his head, useless. The cupboard door stood ajar. The shelf, where we kept our cash, was empty.

"Neil," I said, "wake up. There was a burglar in the house."

"What?" he said, heaving upward, bringing the covers with him, rubbing his eyes, wondering why I was disturbing him.

"There was a burglar," I repeated. We walked disconsolately around the house. The pile of checks was still there, he'd just taken the cash — a petty thief. We called the police, did an identikit, and that was it. We knew we'd got off lightly — just a few hundred rands stolen in exchange for a reminder to keep our house more secure.

My insomnia, my stress reaction, which had first showed itself when I was ten, returned. I fell asleep, exhausted, at eight in the evening, only to wake at one or two in the morning, and spend the rest of the night with questions, images and arguments running through my head. South Africa just wasn't a safe place to live.

If only it weren't for the politics, then we wouldn't have to leave! But there wasn't any point in saying, "If it weren't for the politics. . ." To live in South Africa was to be political. All areas of our life were undermined by the acid of Apartheid, a philosophy inspired by the lowest rung of human nature — the instincts of fear, territoriality, and greed. Everyone's future — nine Black tribes, two White tribes, English and Afrikaans, Colored, Indian and Chinese — was filled with question marks. There was no apparent solution to the political, economic and social conundrums of this polyethnic nation. The answer lay unborn, still to be created, in the unfolding of time.

Any case, it wasn't only the political issues. It was also the frustration, the isolation. We borrowed our English-speaking culture from England and the U.S. But we didn't want to be borrowers — poor cousins in hand-me-downs from Carnaby Street wearing black eye-liner, platform shoes and bell-bottoms; nor imitation flower children preaching "Love not War," listening to recordings of *Jesus Christ Superstar* and *Hair*; having to be satisfied with the movie of *Woodstock*. We'd wanted to participate in the sixties and seventies. We wanted to march forward, side-by-side, into the Dawning of the Age of Aquarius. We were tired of being third worlders, our noses pressed up against the window of life in the West.

We were all caught in a never-ending conversation of what was best, where was best, when was best, searching for our window of opportunity. All our friends had left — David Stern, Ilana, Lesley, Les and Louise,

Tony and Lois, Kenny and Barbara, Tanya, Maxine and David. O.K., we'd made new friends, but then they left too.

Ever since I was five looking at the packed boxes in the Bleimans' house, I knew I would leave. When I was a teenager, Dad had said, "You don't go somewhere because you're leaving somewhere else. You go somewhere because there's something there that you want." Neil knew that he wanted to live in America. He appreciated the life there. I wanted to go where I could learn more, network, develop my potential. I didn't feel like I could fulfill my destiny at the tip of Africa.

I thought about how it felt when our friends and relatives came back to visit. How we'd fall silent, as they described their new lives in their new countries. It was a continual replay of that Christmas, so many years ago, when I was eight, when the Bleimans came back on their first visit. I remembered the feeling of sitting in the back yard of the Gingerbread House, on Mountain Road, having a cook-out. How the Chinese lanterns put out a soft, colored glow, pulled in a whirring multitude of rose-beetles and moths. How Mom and Dad, Jack and Rita, talked about life in England. How their English accents lent a bell-like quality to the Bleiman children's voices. Their adjustment was complete. They'd left us behind.

Then I thought about our char, Sylvia, who came in three days a week to clean the house and do the ironing. How I'd glimpsed Sylvia working her way through a mountain of ironing. Shirts, jeans, t-shirts, sheets, towels and underwear lay in a stiff pile on the left; ironed and folded items lay stacked, benignly, on the right. Sylvia was ironing a pair of panties.

In America I'd have to do all that myself. How would I manage? How would I find time to clean the house, do the shopping, take care of the children, do the ironing, do the cooking *and* work? What would I do without Mom and Dad and Raphael and Miriam? How could I survive without Jacky? It took three women, one gardener, and four grandparents to help us run our household. There was no way I could do it. No wonder there were people who turned a blind eye to the conditions of life in South Africa. The alternative was too difficult.

My questions ping-ponged back and forth. What if we didn't get our labor certification? What if we didn't get our visas? Then . . . what if we did? I would have to leave everything — my practice, my home, my support. I would have to go.

I turned over on my side. There's millions of people in America, and they manage. I can manage too. I turned over on my other side. Perhaps they just don't iron their underwear — that's probably how they save time.

THE LAST STRAW

Before we left the country, we wanted to indulge our favorite recreation — game viewing. We arranged to meet our friends, Margaret and Chris Snow, in Natal, to go to Hluhluwe Game Reserve.

When Sylvia arrived that morning, I explained to her, "Sylvia, we're catching an airplane this morning, we have to leave the house at exactly 11:45. Even if you haven't finished your work, we'll have to lock up and leave. Do you understand?"

"Yes, Madam," she said. I was unconvinced. Sylvia and I didn't share a language and in the African culture, one never said 'No', because this would displease.

"You really do understand, don't you?" I quizzed, looking searchingly into Sylvia's dark eyes. She nodded her head, which assured me she was willing to understand, but did nothing to quench my suspicion that she didn't. I had no choice. I couldn't speak her language, she had trouble with mine. I would just have to see what happened.

When Mom came to fetch us to take us to the airport, Sylvia refused to leave, because her work was unfinished. I flapped my arms to indicate flying, pointed to my watch, but she didn't want to go — she hadn't finished her work.

I did a quick calculation in my head. It was noon, and the housesitter would be arriving at about one thirty. "All right, then," I said, "you'll have to lock up. Here are the keys. Now when you leave, after you've locked the door, throw the keys through the burglar bars, into the kitchen." I mimed my way through the motions, an exaggerated charade, with key-turning and key-hurling. I didn't want someone to be able to reach through the burglar bars and grab the keys off the counter. With the beggars and prospective burglars, casing the neighborhood on a daily basis, this would be a big risk. "Make sure the keys land on the floor," I gesticulated, "not on the counter." I patted the floor, nodding my head to indicate yes, "Here," I said, and patting the kitchen counter and shaking my head, "not here."

Sylvia watched me carefully, taking in every word and every movement. Now she looked dubious, but she claimed to understand. Her ambiguous "Yes, Madam," punctuated each gestural phrase.

We jumped into Mom's car. We still had to pick Aidan up from her house. Suddenly our careful choreography of the morning was looking downright stupid.

"I think we'll go the top route," Mom said, "because of the traffic." There seemed to be some kind of game on, because the roads around the rugby grounds, access to her house, were choc-a-bloc. As soon as we rounded the corner, we saw that the traffic on the top route was also backed up. There must have been an accident. We kept looking at our watches, wanting the time to stand as still as the traffic, but the minutes were flying by. Mom was debating out loud, with herself, about the best way to handle the dilemma, expressing her frustration by alternately applying her foot to the gas and the brake, causing us to jerk along at snail's pace.

"I think we should turn down into Newlands, find a phone, call Dad and ask him to bring Aidan to the airport, because this is hopeless," I said.

"I think so too," said Neil.

"I think so too," said Mom.

I dashed into the Golden Spur steakhouse, called Dad, and jumped back in the car. We went back up to the highway, where the traffic was still stalled, to sit and wait. Suddenly the traffic opened, the way was clear, and we were free to drive on to the airport. Mom didn't stop jabbering all the way, venting her anxiety. "Next time, none of your hair-brained schemes. I knew all along this was a bad idea. We should have kept Aidan with us, we should have left on time, we should have taken the other route." Now that the road was open ahead, she treated herself to long depressions of the gas pedal, alternating with quick stabs at the brake, so that we could jerk along, at the speed limit.

"Yes, Mom," I said. Neil maintained a stoic silence.

Dad was waiting, arms folded, with Aidan, outside Departures. "You're O.K.," he said, "plane hasn't left yet." We rushed through ticketing and baggage, shouted hugs and thanks, and boarded the plane.

Jeffrey met us in Durban. He'd moved to Natal to continue his studies in Psychology. He hadn't met Jason yet. "That's another beautiful boy," he said enviously. "You know you must hold your children at all times, here," he added. "Don't let go of them, they can be stolen for *muti*.* I have a client whose child was taken. It's a terrible thing." Our eyes grew round with fright. We didn't want to hear more South African horror stories. We didn't believe that Black people made medicine with White children, but whatever the purpose, children did get kidnapped.

The next morning, we set off for Hluhluwe, a five-hour drive through the homeland of the Zulu nation, and Inkatha, their military arm, the fiercest tribe in southern Africa. Inkatha were the originators of

muti - Black Medicine

'necklaces,' tires, soaked in gasoline, placed around those who opposed them, then ignited.

We didn't see anything, other than the usual dismal poverty, the shoeless urchins, following our car with their hungry eyes, the skeletal dogs, sharing the misery of their masters. Each time we passed a group, we'd fear an onslaught of stones, the cheap and effective missiles of the disinherited. At last we were at the gates of the Game Reserve, passing from poor farmland, into the splendor of nature, unspoiled, honored and preserved. We drove over the river, past a crocodile basking on a rock, past the herd of impala standing on the hillside, up a winding road and on, to the camp.

Neil went to book us in and came back with a disgruntled expression. "The Snows left a message to say that they had car troubles and they won't be here until the day after tomorrow."

"Oh, no," I said, "what are we going to do about food? They were bringing all the groceries!" We were hundreds of miles from a supermarket. We were supposed to bring our own food, hand it over to the cooks for preparation and be served our dinner, colonial style, by the staff.

"I'll go ask," Neil said, going back into the office, returning after a short while. "There's a little shop here for the staff only, but they'll let us buy some things, seeing as we're stuck without any food."

We went to the store and looked at the slim pickings. Canned goods, peanut butter, hardly anything that we considered food. The best we could do was white rice and dried beans. We bought some bread and butter for Aidan. Jason was still nursing. Our host came over to pick up the ingredients for dinner and we handed him the box.

At first, in keeping with his training, he was suitably expressionless. When he felt the lightness of the box, he subtly twisted his head to peek inside, unable to stop a puzzled frown, as if to say, "Who are these strange White people who eat Black food."

That evening we sat down to a table carefully laid with silver cutlery and cloth napkins and our host and his helper carried our food in on silver platters. The covers were removed, with a flourish, to reveal — beans and rice. We all kept our faces straight, as we munched away. Truth was, we would have been perfectly happy, if only we'd had brown rice and perhaps a mushroom, or two.

In the middle of the night we heard hooves galloping, snorts and grunts, snuffles and bleats. We got up to look out of the window. There were giraffes and zebra and wart hogs, in the glow of the stars and moon, grazing on the lawn outside our bungalow. The next morning we saw white rhino, and even, miraculously, because of their extreme shyness, two black rhino, retreating into the trees.

Our mealtimes continued to follow the same farcical routine. Our host was clearly frustrated with us. Why wouldn't we give him a chance to show off his culinary skills? Where were we hiding our food, instead of handing it over to him to store in the refrigerator?

After two days of beans and rice, the Snows arrived, their car laden with supplies. They tumbled out and we shared our harrowing tales of getting to Hluhluwe. The mechanic had done a bum job on their car, and held them up for two days. They listened to our airport saga. "Did you fight," they asked, "did you kill each other?"

"No," we said, in unison, "that was the amazing part, we didn't."

"That's good," they said, "that's impressive. We would have killed each other."

"Hand over the food," we said. "All we've had is beans and rice for two days."

"Oh, no," Margaret said, "I'm sorry. I was so worried about you."

"Actually, it's been O.K. We're feeling good, like we've been on a cleansing diet. But our host is concerned about us. He thinks we're strange." We explained the system.

That night we all gathered in the bungalow for dinner. "No more beans and rice," our host beamed at us, stepping out of his butler role. Then he stepped back into it, to remove the silver lids, one after the other, revealing roast chicken, potatoes, green beans, carrots, mushrooms and salad. He was clearly relieved to find out the truth about our food and restore us to the correct categorization of White people.

We returned home, to be greeted by Jacky. "I have to tell you something," she said, in a confidential tone.

"What?" I said, alarmed.

"Something happened yesterday," she continued. "You know the whole time you were away, I felt like something was wrong with the house. Every night I prayed to the Lord, to keep the house safe. Every night I put a white light around the house. I felt the house needed protection. I couldn't get rid of the feeling.

"Then yesterday, when we were at the back, hanging up the washing, Sylvia locked us out, and there was food cooking on the stove. I was very worried — but then you know what she said?"

"I don't know," I said, "hurry Jacky, tell me what happened."

"She said, 'Don't worry, the keys are outside.' So I said, 'what do you mean the keys are outside?', so she said, 'the keys are outside where Madam told me to throw them.' And there they were, on a lily leaf, right next to the garden path, where every beggar could have seen them. They were left out in the rain, all rusty, but at least we could get back inside." Jacky was watching me to see how I would react.

"No!" I exclaimed, grabbing her arm, feeling like I was going to fall over from laughing. I remembered my instructions and gestures, and imagined Sylvia clambering up on the kitchen counter, aiming carefully, and throwing the keys through the burglar bars, into the garden outside the front door. This was beyond a language barrier, this was beyond the clashing of two cultures, this was beyond explanation. No wonder she had looked at me so dubiously. She must have thought I was off my head wanting my keys thrown into the yard.

"What's going on in here," Neil asked, walking into the kitchen, "what are you two laughing about?"

"You tell him Jacky," I stammered out between yelps, "I'm laughing too much."

Jacky told Neil. Neil's face grew dark. He wasn't so amused. "I'm going to fire her," he said, "that's not funny."

"No," I said, "don't. It's over now, and she didn't mean to do harm. She's honest and reliable. She does her work faithfully." Neil thought it over, and agreed. I thought it over too, in terms of the bigger picture, and it was another nail in the coffin of my relationship with South Africa. I didn't want to live in a country where there could be such a dangerous misunderstanding.

The next week, I made five routine 'phone calls. I put the phone down after the fifth call and a stone I didn't even know I'd swallowed, sank to the bottom of my stomach. I realized that each of the five people I had just spoken to, including myself, had had a close family member murdered.

I realized that Apartheid had brought murder into every South African home. It wasn't just out there in the Colored townships and the Black squatter camps. It wasn't even on the doorstep, it was *right inside* our homes. I looked through the porch windows at Table Mountain, an eternal joy in my life. The bright blue sky flickered, becoming dark and heavy. I blinked. The light over Cape Town had gone out. I wasn't going to wait for another member of my family to be claimed. It was no longer a matter of 'if your life and home were threatened,' it was simply a matter

of 'when,' and I wasn't hanging around for that black day. Fear of house-
work, fear of letting go of what I had, fear of the unknown, wasn't going
to stop me from getting a new life, a safe life, a peaceful life. I was ready
to follow my dream. I was ready to leave.

I was mentally ready, but nothing else was in place. The birth of a
new baby, Michael's death, the visa struggle, the thirty-three percent
inflation and the waiting game overwhelmed me. "I'm going back to
Gordon," I said. I wanted my therapist.

Gordon was surprised to see me, until he heard what was going on in
my life. "That is a lot," he affirmed, resting his chin in his hand.

After my second visit, Neil said, "I think I should come with you
next time."

"I'll ask Gordon."

Neil and I hadn't killed each other on the way to the airport, but that
was a miracle. With everything that was going on, we did need help.
Gordon agreed, but I couldn't help noticing the expression on his face, as
he listened to us — the look of someone who opens the box to find an
unwanted present. The therapists in South Africa were depleted, drained
dry by their attempts to shore us up against the situational stress driving
down from all directions.

We were beyond tense. We were about to find out the results of our
labor certification process. Our job had been advertised for almost a
month, only two more days to go. Neil called Mike. "Looks good,
nobody's applied," said Mike, "although it might have been better if at
least one person had."

"What do you think he meant?" I asked Neil. "Did we want someone
to apply for the job?"

"I'm not sure," Neil said. "Perhaps it would have been better, because
that would have shown that it was a legitimate grouping of qualifications.
But I don't know."

A day later, Mike called back. "Someone *has* applied for the job. An
Alexander teacher from Delaware who has a Masters in Movement
Therapy."

"How does that affect us?" Neil asked. "Do you think the Labor
Department will accept those qualifications as the same?"

"I don't know," Mike said, "shouldn't do, but can't say for certain.
Any case, she would still have to be interviewed by Herby and then she'd
have to want the job." Who would have thought that any of the five
hundred Alexander teachers in the U.S. would even have seen the ad, let

alone apply? Could this cause our entire application, our hope, our future to fall away?

"What's her name?" Neil asked. "We'll call Ted and see if he knows her."

Ted did know the applicant. "She probably saw the ad and decided to apply, just because she was so surprised to see a job opportunity advertised for an Alexander teacher, and her qualifications are close," Ted said. Then he added, "but a Masters in Movement Therapy is not considered the same as a Masters in Psychology." In the end, Ted was right. The Masters in Movement Therapy was not considered the same as a Masters in Psychology. Thank heavens I'd completed the masters degree that I thought I'd never need.

We were inching forward. We had our labor certification, but our application still had to go through several more twists and turns.

Easter 1991, exactly three years after the vision in Johannesburg, I was lying in bed, wakeful as ever, when I thought I saw something fly across the sky. But it wasn't in the sky, it was inside me. My stomach stopped churning, my restless spirit calmed — rough seas settling when the wind drops. I was certain that at that moment, across the Atlantic Ocean, where it was still daytime, our paperwork had just been approved.

Two weeks later Herby called. I could hear Neil talking on the phone in the hallway. I could hear the "Yes!" in his voice, and from my unconscious sprang the words, "I'm going home. I can go home now!" Neil came back to the bedroom, "Our permanent residence applications have gone through and the next step will be the issuing of our visas. Herby says he hopes we're ready."

All we needed were our visas. Except . . . there were no visa numbers available. We couldn't believe our ears. How long would this take? The embassy didn't know — there was nothing they could do. The immigration laws had changed. They didn't know what was happening. It was all guesswork. It could take another year. They were waiting too.

We decided to put the house on the market. It could take months to sell. Besides, we had to hope that our visas would come soon. It was the very beginning of winter. Pam said she could see us leaving in the summer. "Actually" she said, "what I see is short sleeves." I counted — June, July, August, September — four months and then we'd be in short sleeves again. We could be leaving in October — or months, years later — but we had to have faith.

Within weeks we got a bid on the house, more than double what we'd paid, less than two years before. It was only June. What if we let the house go and then didn't get our visas and didn't have a place to live? Neil and I looked at each other in despair. That brick and mortar, that solid construction with its flowing rooms and view of the mountain, was the pinnacle of our lives in South Africa. Could we give it up, could we let someone else have our space in the world? Could we trust that there was a space waiting for us somewhere else? We'd been approved on the American side before, only to have our application turned down in South Africa. This was supposed to be different, but how could we be sure?

We forced ourselves to gather our thoughts. After a few more sleepless nights, I said to Neil, "This is a really good offer. I think we must let the house go. At least it is a step forward." Neil's face was solemn. "Otherwise we could refuse this, get our visas and then be stuck here, unable to sell the house." Neil's face flickered. He didn't like the thought of not selling the house, getting stuck in South Africa, even once we had visas for America.

"Although this isn't the sequence we want, any step forward is a step nearer. Let's take it," I declared. Neil agreed. We had to commit to our future. It was time to pack and move. We no longer had a dream. We had the beginnings of a new reality.

Two weeks later I went to pick Aidan up from school, and when I came back I saw that Neil's car was still outside the house. He was supposed to go teach in town. Why was he still here? "Nothing's the same two minutes in a row. This is too hectic," I groaned to myself.

I crept into the house. I found Neil wandering around with a distracted expression on his face, his appointment book clutched under one arm. His hair looked particularly disheveled and his face seemed pale. "Uh-oh, the stress is getting to him, he's losing it," I thought to myself. He opened his book, unable to speak, and pointed to a day where he'd scrawled, "Go to Johannesburg for visa interview." He was over the edge — he'd taken to writing fantasy dates in his book.

"Will it be all right?" he stammered. "Can we manage it on that day?" I stared at him. This was his idea of a joke? I waited and waited, wondering how we were going to pull him back into sanity.

Finally he explained. "I called the embassy with some other question and the secretary said, 'Oh, Mr. Schapera, I'm so glad you called, you're going to be over the moon with me.' I didn't know what she meant, I thought she'd got her expressions confused, and then she said, 'I have your visa number!' Faith had served us, yet again. Even before we moved out of the house, our visa numbers had come.

Permanent residence visas could not be handled by the consulate in Cape Town, only by the embassy in Johannesburg. We stayed overnight with Margaret and Chris. "I'll take care of Aidan and Jason," Margaret said. "You two go on in alone, it will be easier." It was over an hour drive into the city. We could hardly talk to each other. All the years of longing, the discouragement, the conflict and doubt, the commitment and endurance, were about to climax . . . or dissolve. Could it be real? This time, could it be real?

We entered the embassy with tentative hearts. We eyed the Marines suspiciously, the clerks behind the counter, the interviewing officers. They were still our enemies, until they declared themselves our friends and handed over those cards, with our photos, labeling us resident aliens. We weren't going to believe until those visas were stamped in our passports, until the papers were in our hands, until the immigration officer said, "Welcome to the United States."

We watched another family filling in forms. We overheard a woman explaining that she'd grabbed the wrong passport on her mad dash to the airport — her South African passport, instead of her American passport. "One moment, Ma'am," the officer said, "what did you say your name and address is?" He looked her up in his massive binder, confirming her U.S. citizen status. "We'll sort that out for you right away," he added affably. So easy, once you were an insider. Such service, such friendliness.

It was our turn. A breeze, nothing to it. It was simply a matter of the final stamping of the passports. We had our green cards, we could enter the United States as permanent residents. And what do you know, the laws had just been changed. Professional people could now enter the U.S. on temporary work permits, even if their intention was to become permanent residents — but that wasn't going to spoil our accomplishment. After years of holding our breath, we exhaled the last drops of stale air and savored the pleasure of breathing in deeply. We walked out of the embassy, still unable to speak to each other. On the sidewalk, outside the building, we asked each other, "What should we do? How can we celebrate?"

"We can go and have a cup of coffee across the road," Neil said, pointing to the shopping center.

"O.K." I said, "let's do that." We were discovering that you can't celebrate the biggest moment of your life. No word, no action, no poem is big enough to honor the greatness. Worse, it is even harder when that moment is something that separates you from your loved ones, causes anxiety and envy, loss and fear, feelings of abandonment in your community. We gulped our coffee, it tasted bitter. It tasted sweet. It had no taste at all. We were numb.

Neil said, "You know, now that we have our green cards we can settle anywhere we want. We don't have to go to Cincinnati."

I tried to picture ourselves some place else. "No," I said, "the vision clearly indicated Cincinnati. That's the place calling us. That's the place we must go." I didn't want to meddle with the energies. I knew that in Cincinnati we would find our destined students, and our destined teachers. There was something there that we needed to teach and something there that we needed to learn. It felt important to honor and respect the integrity of the process. Besides, the other possible cities, the cities where we knew people, San Francisco, Boston and New York all had Alexander teachers. They didn't need us. We were being called to Cincinnati, specifically.

We arrived back at Margaret's house. "We got it," we shouted, "we got it."

"Come on," Margaret said, "I've got to get a photo of this!"

She arranged us into a tableau on the lawn, waving our papers, hugging Aidan and Jason. "That's great," she said, "just great." Then she ran inside to call Chris at work, tell him the good news.

Back in Cape Town, we called Herby, to set a date of arrival. October 31st seemed a good date for us. "I might have a bit of trouble picking you up at the airport," Herby said, "it's Halloween, so I have to let my staff off early from work."

"Halloween?" I said, "then we must arrive in time for Halloween. The boys would love that!" We'd read tantalizing poems, examined costumes in the two mail-order catalogs we thumbed, read stories, seen pictures, but we'd never experienced Halloween. We would arrive October 29th. That would give us enough time to get costumes, be ready to join the fun.

We called the movers. This was the big suitcase Marie-Claire saw, the big move. We began to dismantle our home. We walked from room to room, deciding what to take, and what to leave. Mom and Dad, Miriam and Raphael, took turns to come and walk behind us. They followed us from room to room, chattering, advising, lamenting. They blurted stories, inadvertently vocalizing their anxieties, their grief, their joy, their support. It was a spontaneous funeral procession, sending us off to the new world.

October 25th, 1991. Day of departure. Upstairs in the apartment, I hugged Jacky goodbye. "I promise you a trip to America," I said. "Don't worry, you'll be coming to see us." I was really promising myself that I would see Jacky again, soon. This time, we climbed into the car with Dad. We knew he'd be the most level-headed of all the parents, the most even.

Dad's face was the color of putty again, like when Michael died. "This isn't the same as last year," he said. "I keep telling myself this is different. That was forever." He swallowed with difficulty, then added, "I will be seeing you all again, this isn't the same." It was different. It was better, and it was just as bad — it was a terrible loss. It was the end of an era, the end of participating in the life of his only surviving child, and the end of participating in the life of his only grandchildren. It was the beginning of a long, empty road.

Mom and Dad, Miriam and Raphael, Janis, her husband and their two daughters, Pam and her husband, and their three sons, Jeffrey and Yvonne came to the airport to see us off. They all stood around us, a circle of love, imprinting us with their energy. They were giving us something that we could take with us into our future, establishing a cord that would connect us across time and space, cause us to remember, cause us to return, at least to visit.

Time to go through ticketing. Time to say goodbye, to hug and kiss one last time. Raphael broke down, "I can't believe it," he said, "I can't believe it." He stifled his cries. " I love you all so much. You're doing the right thing. It's just so hard." There was nowhere to cast our eyes, nowhere to hide. The emotion was all around. The emotion was inside, pushing through into white knuckles, bitten lips, fidgety feet.

As I hugged Pam I said, "You were right, we're wearing short sleeves."

"Yes," she grinned, "I noticed. Now just find out the points of the compass when you get there, know where North and South are and you'll find your way." Simple instructions, with layers of meaning.

Does anyone like goodbyes? We waved at the turnstiles and resolutely turned our bodies, turned our faces away from Cape Town, away from our families, away from our friends. We turned our faces toward Cincinnati, and as Gordon had said, in our last session with him, toward "a lot of hellos."

We had to fly via London. Due to sanctions, South African Airways had lost landing rights in the U.S. We would be staying with Tanya for three days, resting. Kenny and Barbara, and John Evans and his new wife and baby, came over. "How're you feeling?" they asked.

"Tired, but happy. It's such a relief to be out of South Africa, at last. I'm exhausted, but I don't want to sleep. I want to be awake to enjoy the relief," I replied. I looked at them carefully. These friends of mine, Tanya, Kenny, Barbara and John were all friends who had emigrated, settled in a new country. And here we were, together again, passing each other, like ants, greeting, kissing, then resuming our journeys.

Tanya arranged a cab to take us to Gatwick. We would be flying straight into Cincinnati on Delta. The driver was late. Didn't he know the significance of this trip to the airport? The car-ride to the airport went on and on, into the English countryside. We were sure we were lost. How could we be late for this flight? What if we missed the plane? After more than an hour, the cabbie said, "There it is, there's Gatwick." Dragging suit-cases, diaper bags, duvets and pillows, we made our way through ticketing and immigration on toward the gate, onto the plane and across the Atlantic, over the East coast, to the mid-West, to the Queen City, Cincinnati.

We wanted to announce, "Look at us, we're here at last. This isn't a visit, we've come to stay! We've got green cards!" But there wasn't anyone to tell. Cincinnati was not a usual port of entry for immigrants. We had to wait for over an hour while immigration officers were summoned and made their way to the airport.

THE NEW WORLD

Herby was waiting for us on the other side of the barrier. He guided us out of the building and left us on the sidewalk outside Arrivals, while he went to get his station wagon. Our body clocks said midnight, but it was still daylight. I looked at the sky. It was gray, low, sticky-looking. I looked at the cars. They were unrecognizable shapes, new and shiny, different colors and styles, lots of vans with pointy noses. I looked at the people. They dressed differently, owned the space, weren't apologetic. They spoke loudly with American accents.

Herby drove up in a giant blue Oldsmobile, with blue leather seats, and loaded us in. We were going to stay with him until we had a home of our own. He drove us past Spring Grove cemetery. "It's an arboretum," he said. I could see the tall trees, bare, standing on the other side of a stone wall. The wall was long, it seemed to go on forever. Then we were at Hilltop Lane. We drove up the drive. Two cars were parked side-by-side, outside the garage, a Toyota Tercel and a Chevy station wagon. "These are your cars," Herby said. "I got them for you at a good price."

He showed us into the house, into the kitchen and down to the base-ment where he had a guest suite. Everything was ready for us — beds for the boys, beds for us, a bathroom with little shampoos and soaps. We unpacked our pillows and duvets, laying them out, marking our territory. We went back upstairs and sat in the kitchen together, round the table.

Little spurts of conversation. What do you say when you start a new life? What do you say to the person who made it possible?

Next day, Herby took us down to his office and showed us the space on the top floor, where we would be working. Three little rooms and a waiting-room, only two with windows. The dark brown carpet was water-damaged, the faux paneling was from the sixties — we would have to do some serious remodeling. From there, Herby drove us up Winton Road, to Tri-County, for part two of our mission — to go to *Toys R Us*. We had shopping to do, costumes to buy, toys to acquire.

Aidan dashed across the parking lot, face pinched, fearful that they would not have what he wanted. We stepped inside the mega-store. We were accustomed to little toy stores in shopping malls. This was a warehouse. We grabbed a shopping cart and started walking the aisles. The fluorescent lighting, the magnitude, the choices tired us out before we began. This place, just for toys and kid equipment, was bigger, better stocked than a South African supermarket. We bought the obligatory Batman outfits for Halloween and a load of new toys.

On the way home, Herby said, "Our neighbors across the street have three boys. I told them you're coming. They said you can go trick or treating with them."

We walked across the road to meet them. "Yes," they said, "we go to Burns Ave, the Victorian part of Wyoming. That community puts in a lot of effort. We'll leave at six."

We drove down Compton Road, onto Springfield Pike and parked the van. Five boys sprang out, wielding their empty pillowcases and flashlights, ready for action. As darkness fell, the streets came alive with scurrying ghouls and goblins, ghosts and witches. The pathways and lawns were adorned with jack o' lanterns, coffins and bats, cauldrons and skeletons. Walking up the stairs to the porches, we heard creaking sounds, eerie music, bells tolling. Children in masks ran across the lawns, swinging buckets of candy. Fathers carried their little ones up to the door, telling them, "Say trick or treat." Grown-ups came to the door, all dressed up, bent down to hand out candy, a hundred times in one evening. Abundance, community, fun. Hearts joining in celebration. Not anything we were used to.

The next day Neil called Lois. "When can we see you?" she asked. "Can you come tomorrow? I can't believe it, family at last!" That was her way of letting us know that even though she was married to a new husband, Chris, she still thought of us as relatives.

"Lois has an American accent!" Neil said, putting down the phone. "We're going to visit tomorrow."

"How are we going to get there?"

"We'll have to drive," Neil said. "I got directions."

"Are you ready?" I asked. That was one of the worst challenges that faced us — learning to drive on the other side of the road.

To get to Lois, Neil had to negotiate three highways — the I75, the Norwood Lateral and the I71. I sat silently, biting my lip the whole way, and sighed with relief when we pulled up outside Lois' home. The street, and her house, looked like an illustration out of a children's book. On the way, we'd driven past a house that resembled a mushroom. What kind of houses were these? Where was the brick and mortar? Open lawns rolled between the homes, front doors were visible from the street. Where were the fences?

We stood nervously on the front steps and rang the bell. Lois came to the door with a big smile, ushered us into her white-carpeted living room and introduced us to her two children. "Come, let me show you around," she said. We toured the upstairs, the downstairs and the deck. "The basement's through there, but I don't go there unless I have to."

"The basement?" we queried.

"Oh yes, almost all the houses here have basements, not like South Africa. That's where we keep our washer and dryer."

"Washer and *dryer*?"

Lois laughed. "Yes, we tumble dry all our laundry. No-one has time to hang washing on the line and do ironing. Any case, you can't hang washing outside in the winter. It's too cold."

"No ironing?" I asked, close to getting an answer to one of the questions which had plagued me during my insomniac hours.

"Almost no ironing," Lois said. "We might iron a few special items, but in general we just tumble dry."

Lois was an ideal bridge for us between life in South Africa and life in Cincinnati. She knew how we thought. She told us about school districts and realtors, then wanted to move on to another topic. "What about the Alexander Technique?" she asked.

"What about the Alexander Technique?" we responded. "That's what we do. We're going to work in Herby's practice as Alexander teachers."

"What about a training course?" Lois pursued.

"A training course?" I echoed. We'd only just arrived. We hardly had plans in that direction.

"Yes. I still want to train and I know some others who are also interested."

"That's fine," I said, "I have the credentials to direct a training course, but we'd have to do it properly. I have to apply to the professional organization, get official approval."

"Will you do that?" Lois asked.

"Yes," I said, "once we're settled — if you're serious."

"I am serious," Lois said.

Neil followed Lois' advice and looked in the newspaper for a realtor. He struck gold — a realtor, named Tina. We spent the rest of our first week in Cincinnati driving around with her. She pointed out the different styles of houses to us. She could tell the floor plan by looking at the façade. "That's a Colonial," she said, "and that's a Cape Cod." We had to get used to the timber-frame construction, the lack of sound-proofing and the heating and cooling, which meant no open windows — these houses were sealed boxes! She oriented us to Cincinnati, taking us on a tour of Wyoming, Anderson, Symmes, Westchester, Blue Ash, Montgomery, Madeira and Kenwood.

"There's the main shopping center," Tina said, indicating a sprawling building situated in a gigantic parking lot.

"Look at all those parking spaces," I said. "Do they ever get filled?"

"Yes," laughed Tina, "another couple of weeks and every space will be taken. The day after Thanksgiving is the big shopping day of the year."

"When's Thanksgiving?" I asked.

Tina rolled her eyes, "You two really are fresh off the boat. Fourth Thursday in November, that's Thanksgiving."

"Oh," I said, "I always read about Thanksgiving. I do know you eat turkey."

As soon as Tina dropped us off at Herby's house, Neil said, "Let's go back to that shopping mall, I want to see inside."

"O.K.," I agreed. We didn't have anything else to do. *Kenwood Towne Centre* dazzled us. Stores with hardwood floors, indoor fountains and water features, filled with goods we dreamed of — Levi jeans, Nike shoes, Polo shirts, Noritake china, Ralph Lauren, Liz Claiborne, Laura Ashley — all the big names. Some of these goods were once available in South Africa, before sanctions, at elite boutiques carrying imported garments for the wealthy. Here they were in abundance, on sale, for a quarter of the original price. We sat at the Centre Cafe and the boys played on the patterned carpet, jumped on and off the stage, with the other kids who gathered there.

The next morning, we emerged from the basement, into the kitchen, to find Herby sitting at the table, reading the newspaper, a suppressed smile, tickling his face. "Look outside," he said nonchalantly. We looked.

"It snowed," we shouted, "it snowed, it snowed!" I'd been in snow once before, at age fourteen. An inch of it, when Dad had driven us, two hours, in the night, to where it had snowed on the mountain pass. I'd seen it from afar, capping the mountains of the Boland, and in Europe, on the Alps, pretty and untouchable as a bride on her wedding day — reserved for someone else.

We descended, back into the basement, dressed up in gloves, hats, boots and coats and ran outside to roll in the little white crystals. Herby took a roll of photographs to send back to snowless South Africa. Jason dipped a tentative finger into the icy frosting, and shook his hand, disbelievingly, a pained expression gripping his face. Our noses turned red, our hands turned white, our toes went numb. We lasted five minutes. Herby took us to Tri-County to buy proper winter coats, in time for our afternoon house-hunting with Tina.

Tina wanted to show us a house in Montgomery. "Now where is this in relation to that nice shopping mall?" I asked, a voice from the back seat.

"You mean *Kenwood Towne Centre*? It's two miles south of here," Tina said.

"Good, that's O.K. then. I don't want to be too far from that shopping mall." That's what I said out loud. To myself I was thinking, "Two miles *south?* Pam was right, I did need to get my bearings by the compass."

"This is a bi-level," Tina said, as we walked in through the front door, "that means there is an upstairs and a downstairs. The downstairs is considered a half-basement . . . What's the matter?" she interrupted herself. I was transfixed, staring at the piano.

"Look," I said, "there's a piano like ours."

"Oh," Tina shrugged, "that's a *Baldwin Acrosonic*. They're made here."

"No!" I said.

"Why? What's so special?"

"We have one of only two Baldwin Acrosonics imported into South Africa in the fifties. I always knew it came from America, and now you're telling me our piano was made here in Cincinnati?"

"Yes," Tina said.

"Well that means we brought our piano home!"

It was a sign. This house must be meant for us. We looked at the downstairs, we looked at the upstairs. Sure enough, it was perfectly suited to our needs. The layout was ideal, the room sizes were generous and the living room was the only one we'd seen which could accommodate the leather sectional couch I'd inherited from Michael. "This is it," we said to Tina, "we're ready to put in a bid."

The house was meant for us. The owner accepted our offer, even though she had already received a higher bid. To celebrate we went to a restaurant called *TGIF's*. The restaurant was dark and noisy. There were bunches of balloons everywhere. The waiter came over. His outfit was covered with badges and he was wearing pants with suspenders. "What do you want to drink?" he asked.

"We'll just have *worter* thanks."

"Please?"

"Sorry?"

"Please?" We didn't know why he was saying "please." We fell silent.

"What do you want to drink?" the waiter attempted, again.

"*Worter.*"

The server shook his head, walked away and came back with help — the manager.

"And what would you folk like to drink?" the would-be translator asked.

"We just want *worter* please, you know, in a glass, from the tap."

"From where?"

"The tap, I mean, the faucet."

"Oh, they want waah' duh!" the translator explained to the server.

"Oh! *Waah' duh!*"

We could speak English, but we couldn't speak American. 'Please' turned out to be a Cincinnati idiom, from the German 'Bitte.' Many words had different meanings: a scone was a biscuit, a biscuit was a cookie, a cookie was a cupcake. Taking a class did not mean being the teacher, it meant being the student and downright dangerously, the road was referred to as the pavement and the pavement was the sidewalk. There was different vocabulary. The lift was an elevator, the boot was the trunk, the bonnet was the hood, surnames were last names, and there was no such thing as a fortnight, nor 'just now.' Every time the cashier at *Krogers* asked me 'How are you?' I suffered an agony of indecision. How was I supposed to know that 'How are you?' meant hello and 'see you later' meant goodbye?

We'd been in Cincinnati two weeks. The days were too loose. It was time to start working. I wanted routine. I wanted clients. "I'm going to start teaching next week, on Thursday," I announced.

"But who will you teach?" asked Neil.

"I don't know," I said, "but I'll find someone."

It wasn't so hard. Herby had listed us in the phone book as Alexander Technique of Cincinnati and put our name on the board outside the office. Herby, and his significant other, Josy were interested — both in the Technique and in helping us. "Will you see my colleague, Kathy?" Josy asked. "She has a very bad neck which gives her lots of trouble. Do you think you can help?"

"Yes, of course I'll see her." I gave my first lesson in Cincinnati on Herby's living room floor. I was nervous. Kathy seemed nervous too, like she didn't know what she'd let herself in for, but she didn't seem to mind the less than professional setting. She was understanding and adventurous, and desperate enough to want help for her neck. The lesson must have gone well. She wanted to come again. Josy also recommended us to two massage therapists. The one wanted a course of lessons. Lois wanted a course of lessons, and Herby's staff of nurses and secretaries agreed to a course of lessons each.

As promised, four weeks after our arrival it was Thanksgiving. We already had a house, a school for Aidan, a sitter for Jason, and work. We had a lot to be thankful for. At dinner Josy's father filled our glasses with champagne and spoke of what it had meant to him, and his family, to come to America, from France. We drank a toast, to the United States of America, land of opportunity. The champagne poured from our glasses into our hearts, bubbles of celebration rising upward, into our grateful spirits.

The day after Thanksgiving we rushed off to Kenwood Towne Centre — I wanted to see how the parking lot looked when it was full. The mall was decorated for Christmas. When did that happen? I gaped at the two storey Christmas trees, the giant baubles hanging from the ceiling, the silver and gold lamé bows. Until Christmas, we could shop from early in the morning 'til midnight, seven days a week.

Driving back that evening, we discovered that the houses had also been decorated, with lights. Every night, we strapped the boys into the back of the station wagon, put the car heater on and drove around the neighborhoods, looking at the multitude of lights, white and green and blue and red, rippling in sequence. It seemed to us like the stars had come to earth. Either that, or we were in fairyland.

In the last week of December we closed on our new house. The night before our belongings were delivered we slept on the floor, on the new futon we'd bought. The next morning the van arrived, with our possessions, last seen many months before, under a different sky, under different circumstances. We watched the two movers roll the heavy beds, cabinets and bookcases down the ramp and carry them up the stairs, remembering the bevy of eight men who'd handled the same items in Cape Town.

We hung up our clothes, unpacked our cutlery and crockery, our glassware, our paintings, our fragile treasures. Not one thing was scratched or chipped, not one thing was broken. We'd all made it safely across the ocean.

We surveyed our new home. No clutter, no mess, no unwanted hand-me-downs — only what we'd selected to accompany us into our new lives. Shelves in the closets lay empty, spacious, inviting the future.

By the middle of January, the flush of excitement was used up. The Christmas lights were dismantled, the parties and dinners suddenly stopped.

People were friendly enough, welcoming, "Where you from? Africa? How interesting. What made you want to come to Cincinnati? What did you say you do? The Alexander Technique? What's that? How interesting! Well we'll have you over in the summer. We can sit outside, have a cook-out." In *The Summer?* What did that mean? Why was that the only time of year that we could come over? And what were we supposed to do in the meantime?

Sitting alone, with my won ton soup, almond chicken and fried wings, at Golden China, the restaurant around the corner from our office, a wave of helplessness engulfed me. The days were so short and dark, we only had enough money for six months and we were lonely. "Wait a second," I thought, taking charge of myself, "this really is the beginning of the rest of my life. For years we've been dreaming about this move. For years I've been working too hard, packing my days with students, beating off rising inflation, always busy, pressured. Here I am, with time to sit by myself, enjoy lunch, before picking up the boys. I should enjoy this, before it's over." I resolved not to cheat myself, of this time, with anxiety and fear. I would allow the future to come to me, trusting that all would fall into place, as it had done before. As I relaxed into this thought, another one followed: "We needn't wait passively, for clients to come our way. We can be systematic, pro-active, establish ourselves rapidly. We should get a public relations consultant."

As soon as I got home, I ran the idea by Neil. "Sure," he said, that sounds like the right way to go. We'll call Lois' friend, Cindy."

"Yes," Cindy said, "I'll help you get started, but you need to remodel your offices. That's urgent."

Neil and I examined the three small rooms and the waiting room, planning the changes. I remembered Lois' request — we needed to turn this into one big room, so that the space would work for a training course, and group workshops. We talked it over with Herby. "if that's what you need, then that's what you must have," he said, "fine with me." We hired a remodeler and told her what we wanted.

Outside, January became February, February became March and March became April. The earth was changing. We'd never seen spring before, never experienced this orchestration of color and life. First there was the forsythia, bright yellow sprays, then daffodils and papery narcissus, magnolias, white and pink, then tulips, freesias and hyacinths, followed by crabapple, pear, dogwood and redbud. We witnessed the new green shoots, the softness of the leaves, the rapid growth of the grass. Inside, the remodeler took down dry wall and changed the configuration of the rooms. Cindy designed a brochure and business cards, compiled a mailing list, set a date for an open house and sent out invitations.

The day of the open house came. Our schedule for demonstration lessons was fully booked. We secured fourteen new students in one day. Within six months we were self-sufficient, no longer needing to supplement our income.

In June, Jacky came for six months. We went to pick her up at the airport. Five-year-old Aidan tugged at my arm, so that he could whisper in my ear. "I know who she is," he said, "but I feel shy. I need to get used to her again." Two-year-old Jason had no such reservations, he fell into her arms, just like I wanted to.

We found out what *The Summer* meant. The summer was the time when people took time out of their overbooked schedules to catch up with friends. School, work and sporting commitments took up all the time the rest of the year. Everyone who'd threatened to do so, invited us over. It was also the time for vacation. We took advantage of an air-fare price war, buying tickets for the four of us, and Jacky, to visit Les and Louise, and Ted, in Boston and Tony in San Francisco.

Toward the middle of September, Mom arrived. I couldn't wait to show her our new life. I knew how much she would love the first world opportunities — of course there was the shopping, the sales — but also the museums, the library, the restaurants, coffee shops and bread stores. She did, but there was another treat in store for us, as well.

Gradually, innocently, the leaves were starting to turn. First a little hint of crimson, a flame burnishing the green leaves, creeping up on us, taking us by surprise. Rosy hues progressed into a blaze of yellow, red and gold. Mom, Jacky and I drove around exclaiming "Look there, look at that one," gasping at the colors of autumn, this proud peacock display of the American Fall.

Halloween again. Neil, Mom, Jacky, Aidan, Jason and I drove down to Wyoming, to the Victorian section on Springfield Pike to trick or treat. Mom watched the kids, just as I had done the year before. She viewed the festivities, the people, the ambience. She breathed in our new life. "It's amazing," she said, with a nod of satisfaction, "I can rest easy now that I know you're all safe. It is my first thought when I wake up in the morning, my last thought when I go to bed at night." I saw the pain of being a visitor in her daughter's life, and I saw also the relief in her heart, the blessing on her lips. I saw the deepest act of love a mother can express — the willingness to let her child go.

The following evening, when I came back from work, I made an announcement: "We have to perform a ceremony," I said.

"What ceremony?" Mom asked.

"The sewing machine ceremony," I answered.

I went to get my machine. Neil cut off the transformer and reconnected the cord with a new plug. I switched it on and sewed a seam, while Neil, Mom, Jacky, Aidan and Jason watched. "There!" I said, "A sewing machine for life."

Powers

BODY, MIND, SPIRIT AND EMOTIONS

Our practice was growing by word of mouth. The massage therapist that came to us on Josy's recommendation, referred a young man, Paul, a martial arts instructor, who suffered from chronic muscle tightness and back pain.

The first time he walked through my door, the words, "This is my teacher," dropped into my head, from nowhere.

The thought took me by surprise, because I had no intention of doing martial arts. I'd buried that wish when I was a teenager, reading *Modesty Blaise*. I wasn't flexible enough and I was hopeless at learning even simple sequences of movements — but I was keen that my children should train. I asked Paul about lessons for Aidan.

"How old is he?" Paul asked.

"Five," I replied.

"Of course," he said, "bring him along. We offer specialized classes for his age group." I took Aidan to his first lesson at the school on Wooster Pike. I watched, with Jason, now two, on my lap, as the instructor put the kids through their paces, teaching them the etiquette of bowing, and learning to kick and punch. At the end of the class, Aidan hung his tongue out his mouth, the signal that meant, "I love this!"

I watched the children learning how to control their limbs, coordinate body and mind. It was hard for them. They might be more flexible, but their nervous systems were undeveloped. I also noticed that all the black belts, whether they knew it or not, had a command of energy flow — better than any healer I'd seen. I wanted the command of energy, even more than the punching and kicking ability.

I reasoned with myself: "If the children could learn this, so could I. It would help my work." I asked Paul if he would teach me some basic moves, and he agreed. I was self-conscious and the movements were hard — but very satisfying. At last I could vent the physical tension, that had built up since childhood, twittering inside me, with no proper outlet. My Taekwondo lessons became a focal point of my week and my way of balancing constant output, with input.

One day Paul took me by surprise. "You're testing today," he said. "I'm wha-at?" I queried.

"You're testing today," he repeated. "You're testing for your yellow tip."

"Why? I just want to do Taekwondo. I don't care about testing. In fact I promised myself, after I finished my masters, 'no more tests.'"

"You have to," he said, "that's the system. You can't promote unless you test."

"I don't want to promote. Can't I just learn some moves. I've no intention of becoming a black belt or anything. I'm just doing this for fun."

"No," he said. "If you want to learn Taekwondo, you have to progress from belt to belt. Today you're testing for your yellow-tip. Don't worry you'll be fine. We give you the soft intro the first time — you test in class — but afterwards you have to come to the promotions."

Tests had spoiled my childhood, my teenage years and my young adulthood, making me tense and sick and miserable. Worse yet, whilst I was still competent at written exams, and could manage public-speaking, my greatest terror was to have to get up and perform in front of an audience. If I had known, I wouldn't have taken up Taekwondo. By sheer force of will, Paul put me through the paces and gave me my yellow tip. I went home feeling sick to my stomach. What had I got myself into? Unfortunately, my discomfort was undermined by the sneaky worm of pride in my yellow tip, on my formerly virginal white belt.

A few months later, I had to do my yellow belt test. This was my first contact with other members of the school. We had to perform in a group and I couldn't keep up. I was distracted by the crowded energy in the room, and intimidated by the small, watching eyes of the judges. My nerves got the better of me and I fluffed my form, the set sequence of stances, hand and foot techniques. "Do it again," came the order. My big nightmare came true — I had to perform in front of an audience, on my own. My voice deserted me, and I couldn't do the "kiyap," the yell which releases energy.

"I want to hear that young lady *kiyap*," the master said, picking me out, when we all lined up as a group. "Ha! He thinks I can't shout, but I can," I thought to myself, remembering how I could scream the house down, when I was a teenager. I roared out, from my heart, and Master Beasley's head jerked back, his eyes widening in surprise. "Oh, she can *kiya*p," he said.

What a relief, it was over. No longer drowning in anxiety, I noticed that the judges weren't really fierce — they were interested. They weren't telling me what to do — I was choosing to do Taekwondo, and they were supporting me. I left the test, yellow belt in hand, feeling high, on community.

Self-employed, in a new city, community was what I needed most. With pressure from Lois, I applied to NASTAT to become a training course director. The timing was uncanny. My application was the last to be processed before a moratorium on new courses. In September 1993, Neil and I opened our training course. We started with four trainees. Lois was unable to enroll — she was pregnant.

Being a training course director was a big responsibility, with a whole new learning curve. I couldn't face the struggle of learning new Taekwondo techniques, the stress of testing — I couldn't even manage the driving and trying to get there on time, especially now that the boys were both at a new school — I quit Taekwondo. Alexander Technique was enough for me, especially now that I could explore the deeper levels with my trainees. I would continue with racquetball instead. That was just a game, more in line with my natural abilities, didn't require so much discipline.

But Esmé, Aleph, Hilmar and Soozi had warned me . . . there was more. A current of air insisted on pushing me forward. If I wasn't going to deal with my resistance on one frontier, I would have to deal with it on another.

When we decorated our new teaching rooms in Cincinnati, I placed my few crystals in a prominent position on the glass rack, hoping they would positively energize the space. While I was giving Anne, a counselor, her weekly lesson, my attention was pulled by the milky quartz point that I had bought in Knysna in the old junk shop, with the money from the Crawfords. I turned to look at it, then looked back at Anne. Again I was drawn to the stone. I found myself walking over to the crystal, picking it up and walking back to Anne.

I held the crystal over her, focusing on her joints, sensing a magnetic pulsing. The crystal led me, like a dog owner, being taken for a walk, pulled by the dog. We were both hold-your-breath silent. When this spontaneous procedure was complete, I asked Anne, "Have your joints been painful? Do you have arthritis?"

"Yes," she replied, "I've been so stiff and sore, but I feel better now." We agreed that the crystal seemed to 'know' something, to have healing properties. It was too strange for us to discuss sensibly. We accepted what had happened and moved on to the next subject. From then on, when people needed pain relief, or they seemed low, I would get the crystal from the shelf and give them a dose of crystal energy.

Anne wasn't the only who was stiff and blocked. My legs were getting tighter and tighter from playing racqqetball. I couldn't sit on my heels, or touch my toes.

"You have to go back to Taekwondo," I told myself.

"I don't want to," I protested, "it's too hard and I don't like the testing."

"You have no choice. You can't let yourself get so stiff. You have to do something to help yourself. In any case, you're the one who wants to be able to move and focus energy. And you know that's the best training you can get."

"But I'm no good at it," I wailed to myself.

"So what?" I challenged myself. "It's good for you to be a beginner again, and it's good for you to be a member of a class, and it's good for you to do something you're not good at. You're the one who despises teachers who don't venture out of their safe zone."

It was no use arguing with myself — I knew how to get the better of me. It was time to make a commitment to the whole process. I thought I meant the process of promoting, the willingness to confront my fear of physical performance. I didn't yet apprehend the full picture — the consequence of coordinating body, mind, spirit and emotions.

A few weeks after returning to the school, Carole, one of the instructors, came up and whispered something in my ear. All I could hear was her distress. "What?" I asked, "I couldn't hear you."

"My husband has asked me for a divorce," she said. Her gaze held mine, searching my face for the kind of help I couldn't give her. "I'm really in a bad way and I know you do some kind of healing work. Can I come and see you?"

"Sure," I said, not knowing that I was being led down a path.

When I put my hand on Carole's neck, at the beginning of her lesson, I noticed that it was unusually tense. "Are you aware that your neck is very tight?"
I asked.

"Oh yes," she said, "I can never get comfortable."

"Do you know why?" I asked.

"In some ways I do, but also I don't. At the moment I'm trying to remember my childhood."

I left it at that, but when she was on the table, I heard myself saying, "What's this about a dog and a box?" I had no idea what I was talking about, it had just fallen out of my mouth. She startled, "Who told you?" she demanded, "Who told you? How did you know?"

I stepped backwards. "Nobody told me, it came out of your leg," I said, wanting to calm her, give her space.

"Can you see anything else?" she asked.

"No, that's all."

That incident led Carole to believe that I was psychic. Every time she came to see me she'd say, "Please tell me something Vivien. Please say something to make me feel better, give me hope." She was very fearful of the future.

One day the sound in her voice, opened something in my heart and something in my mind, and for the first time, I let myself look. It must have been my desire to help and to heal, that caused me to see a sequence of pictures — a movie — inside my head. I saw a man in his thirties, with John Lennon glasses, short hair that looked long, a carpenter or handyman, who would be coming into Carole's life on the count of three.

"It's not three weeks," I said, "and it's not three years, so it must be three months."

"Do I know him?" she asked.

"You have met him before, but he's not someone you see regularly, although you're in the same orbit."

"Orbit?" she queried, "What does that mean, in the same orbit."

"You go somewhere he goes, you frequent the same places."

Every time Carole came for a lesson, she'd press me for more information, but I didn't have any more to give.

Three months later, she walked in with a beam, tugging at a baseball cap on her head, practically yelling, "You were right, you were right. I met him yesterday, ninety days, to the day. Oh my God, Vivien, you've got to see, he's exactly, *exactly* how you described!"

"Come on in," I said, ushering her in to my teaching room, wanting to hear the full story.

"I go to *Stonemill Bakery* for coffee every morning," Carole said, "but yesterday I went at eleven instead of ten. He was there, he goes to *Stonemill* every morning at eleven. You were right, he was in my orbit. And I did know him from before. We met long ago. When he saw me he said, 'Aren't you Carole?'"

I assumed that Carole was exaggerating when she said Andy was exactly as I'd described, but nine months later, while I was having a lesson, a man walked into the Taekwondo school. I didn't need any introductions. What I needed to do was to sit down, and catch my breath. The man I'd seen in the movie, inside my head — a man I couldn't possibly have ever met in the flesh before — Andy, had just stepped into the school.

Three months later, I met Neil and the boys at Tri-County Mall for dinner at the Chinese buffet. After dinner, as I stepped through the doorway of the restaurant, into the mall, a strange trance-like sensation came over me, like I'd stepped through a portal into another dimension. I could see Neil and the boys, talk to them, but I was in another reality, behind a sheet of glass, where the air was different. "Neil," I said, "there's something here I'm supposed to buy."

"All right, I'll take the boys home," Neil said.

I wandered toward the main leg of the mall. This was absurd. What was I supposed to buy? And how was I going to find it? I shook myself, rubbed my face, but I couldn't chase the feeling away. I rounded the corner of the main leg of the mall — there was a craft expo. My hopes went up. Maybe I would find something unusual here, something to justify this madness.

The first few stalls weren't remotely interesting — knitted doll's clothes, painted wood. Then I saw a stall selling beads and semi-precious jewelry. Perhaps I could find a string of onyx beads to go with the rhodonite and onyx earrings Mom gave me. I walked up to the stall. My eye caught a jewelry tree with pendants hanging from it. My hand closed over a crystal pendant, wrapped in gold wire. This was what had called me.

The man behind the counter saw my hand close over the crystal. He cocked his head to look at me, but his gaze didn't settle on me. He was looking deep inside, and beyond. "That's a *something something* crystal from *somewhere somewhere* in Brazil," he said meaningfully. My head was buzzing and fluttering. The pendant seemed pricey, fifty dollars. Too expensive, but I couldn't let go. Just like Soozi had said, this one had chosen me. I looked at the onyx beads. I wanted them, but I didn't want to spend too much money. I bought the crystal pendant, and went home.

In the morning, I changed my mind. I went back for the onyx beads. When the vendor saw me he said, "I'm glad you're back. Do you mind if I ask you something?"

"Sure, go ahead," I responded, noting from his downcast gaze that he was about to enter a private space.

"I was wondering if you knew how I can help someone who is really struggling to overcome childhood abuse?" he looked up at me, searching my face. Why was he asking me? I did know an answer, but how did he know that I knew? Must be the crystal . . . he knew something about me, because I chose that crystal. It was a forewarning.

I loved my crystal pendant dearly. I wore it almost every day. It didn't make sense, but I felt lonely on the days when I didn't wear it. Once, I left home without it. I put my hand up to hold it, and my hand found nothing.

Where is it? Good question. It wasn't on the dressing table where it should have been. I felt urgent, anxious. What was this now? Just because I wasn't wearing my crystal I was having a panic attack? An image came to mind. I saw the cat knocking the crystal into the waste paper basket, under the dressing table and the crystal being covered by tissues and papers. My crystal's in the trash? What if it gets thrown out?

I had to wait the whole day. As soon as I got home I ran upstairs, sorted through the trash — nothing. Again, look again! There was shouting in my mind. I looked again, more carefully. Right in the corner of the bag, which lined the trash basket, lay my crystal. I could have sworn it called me. I could have sworn I'd felt its fear and anxiety.

I wasn't the only one who felt the pull. People would literally walk purposefully toward me, grasp the crystal and say, "I love your necklace." I was taken aback. This was definitely unusual behavior for polite Cincinnati, but it didn't matter where I was. All over America, wherever I traveled, whenever I wore it, my crystal attracted the same conversation, "That's a nice stone you're wearing."

"Thank you."

"Is it special? Does it have special significance?"

"I don't know."

"What is it?"

"It's quartz, but I can't remember the rest. I can't remember what the man I bought it from told me."

In the last week of April, the following year ('94), I read *The Celestine Prophecy* to see what all the hype was about. A clever allegory synthesizing popular New Age concepts pertaining to personal and spiritual growth. The material was familiar, but I was struck by one insight in particular — we need to draw energy from the universal source, not from other people.

I was lying in bed reading. I looked out the window at the soft-green leaves. That's what I needed, a source of energy. I was so busy with the training course, private lessons, two young children. Life was demanding, depleting. In spring it was easy to tune into the universal energy simply by looking at all the frothy blossoms, the bright buds and new shoots, but what would nourish me after spring? How would I access the source when the grass turned brown, the leaves aged, the heat of summer sucked us dry?

That Saturday night Herby and Josy came for dinner. Josy was in a spry mood. Her face twinkled, "I was at the gem show today," she said, "it was fascinating. Such interesting people, all gnarly, not at all what I would have expected. I was collecting beads, shells and stones for my artwork."

She caught me with the first part of the first sentence, I stopped listening, "You were at the what!" I spluttered, head turtling forward, my internal bell chiming out of control.

"Yes" she said "the Cincinnati Gem and Mineral Show. It's on today and tomorrow. You should see all the crystals . . ." She went on about how unusual the dealers were, but my mind, which had been stuck behind on the beginning words, was now racing ahead.

Next morning, first thing, I called my friend, Barbara, who also had a beginning interest in crystals. I was nervous about calling so early. I knew Barbara was a night owl, but I didn't want to leave her out, and I didn't want to wait too long.

"The Cincinnati Gem and Mineral Show is on. I've heard there are beautiful crystals for sale," I told her. "Do you want to come with me?"

There was a long pause, probably because she was still waking up. Then she responded, "Sure, that sounds good. I'll be ready in half an hour. I'll bring my book."

Which book? I didn't know anything about a book. Barbara came to pick me up in her big blue car. There was a book on the passenger seat. I eyed it cautiously. The book was an encyclopedia, a reference on the metaphysical properties of crystals, by someone called Melody, who didn't have a last name, and decorated the page numbers with musical notes — a signature tune. Every time I wanted to consult a book on metaphysical subjects I had intuitively felt something preventing me, telling me: "No, don't do that." I wondered if I would gain "permission" to use this reference, get a chance to read about crystals. The back of my throat felt dry, like thirst, but it wasn't for water.

We entered the gem show. We'd both made the same mistake — we'd skipped breakfast. The crystals made us hungry and spacy. Crowds of eager people, weary vendors and ready boy scouts bombarded our senses. We wandered from booth to booth, not knowing where or how to begin, awed, cowed, inspired by the sight of so many radiant crystals. We found the wholesale section. One large quartz crystal, with a sparkling green inclusion, beckoned me. "I like that one," I said, "it keeps calling me. I wonder what it is."

"I don't know what's in it," Barbara said, "but I do know its a channeling crystal."

"How do you know that?" I asked, mystified.

"It says in the book. I was reading about it last night." She opened

Melody's book and showed me the section on quartz. This was awesome. The crystals had a code, a language, a pedigree.

"That's chlorite inside," the man alongside us said, overhearing our conversation.

"Really?" we chorused, "Chlorite, Hmm,. let's look it up." We flipped through the book and cocked our heads over the page. Not bad, chlorite was one of the best healing minerals available, according to the encyclopedia.

"It's not chlorite," the vendor said, as soon as the man left. "He's mistaken. It's feldspar and mica — probably."

"Really?" we chorused, flipping the book open again. This was fun. Feldspar didn't have quite the impressive qualities of chlorite, but it wasn't bad. Point was, superior pedigree or no, this crystal seemed special to me. Too bad it was so expensive — one hundred and eighty dollars! "I'll think about it," I said to Barbara. "We can come back."

We decided that each time we were attracted to a crystal, we would consult the book, ascertain its properties. It was strange. The healing energies of the crystals which appealed to us, exactly matched our psychological and physical needs.

Next row over were long tables stacked high with boxes — or flats — as they are known in the trade. We perused the open display of polished Brazilian wands, obelisks, spheres, as well as mineral specimens. "Everything here is half the marked price," the woman next to me said.

"It is?" I questioned.

"Yeah, says so over there — keystone. That's what keystone means, half the marked price."

"Well, what am I waiting for then?" I asked her, "let's get on with it."

"Yeah, really!" she said, loading another ten minerals into her cardboard container. Barbara and I did likewise, but cautiously, not wanting to spend too much. We didn't know what we were doing. The dealer put our boxes under the table. We could collect them later.

We continued, trailing round and round the three sections of the show — the wholesale, the retail and the swap area — finally satisfying ourselves that we were done. Right at the end I said to Barbara, "You know, I still want that crystal, the one with the feldspar."

"Well, get it then," she said. "You'll only be sorry if you don't."

"But it's so expensive," I whined, "hundred and eighty dollars."

"Yes, but it'll be half of that. It's in the wholesale section."

"It will? Are you sure?"

"Yes," she said, "everything in the wholesale section is half what it's marked."

"Well then I'll definitely get it. To think I've spent all this time agonizing when, all along, it was half the marked price." I was thrilled with my new friend, who weighed at least three pounds and was proud of it.

We'd bought what we considered to be a boat-load of crystals. We packed them safely on the floor and back seat and climbed in the front. A short way into the journey home we looked at each other in dismay. "What's that?" we wondered. We were frowning. We could both feel this strong buzzing behind us. "It's the crystals!" we said in unison. Even without our conscious intent, the crystals were already working to increase our vibrational frequencies. Through the stones, we were accessing energy from the universal source. We could feel the effect, but the technique and mechanism were yet to be revealed. That information lay inscribed in Melody's green book. I wanted to read it. I wanted to own it. My intuition said "Yes, I could get *this* book — *Love Is In The Earth A Kaleidoscope Of Crystals.*" Great! A doorway to a whole new world.

I was curious about my pendant. Now I could consult the book, look it up in the section on quartz. There it was. The *"something something* crystal from *somewhere somewhere* in Brazil" was a red phantom quartz crystal which had come from Minas Gerais in Brazil. Among other things, I could use it, in meditation, to contact my spirit guides.

A few weeks later, on a Friday afternoon, I had unexpected time. My client didn't arrive. I was wearing my red phantom crystal. Why not do that meditation now, contact my guides?

I went into the smaller teaching room. Without windows, it had suitably dim lighting. I found the page, read the instructions and entered the meditation, one eye half open, to check the directions, as I went along. It was straightforward: I had to imagine myself in a garden and invite my guide to come and greet me.

I pictured myself sitting on a garden bench. It was easy. The scene popped into my mind, whole and colorful, trees and shrubs, sunlight and shadows. I saw two figures walking toward me, taking their places next to me, one on either side.

"Oh," I thought, this one is an Indian, as I looked at the tall brown figure to my right.

"Don't be so quick," he admonished me. "Look again."

I looked again, as ordered, and saw that he was a Tibetan Buddhist monk who wore a gold-orange turban. I asked him if he worked through me sometimes, and he nodded his head, his expression serious.

He was right to be serious. He'd scared me on more than one occasion. One afternoon, I'd felt two arms slip inside me, from between my shoulder blades, as though my arms were sleeves. Looking down I had seen an image of long brown fingers superimposed on my own hands and felt a healing energy passing through me and into my client, so strong that we both vibrated. Often, after that, I had felt this same healing energy being passed through me.

To my right sat an Indian woman. She was short and round, her eyes sang, she was filled with love and happiness. Even more striking than this unusual good cheer, was her sari — it was like butterfly wings, in shades of green through blue, glowing, rippling, flashing different shades as the light played on it. She represented the feminine force in my life — motherly and constant, infusing the magic ingredients of nurturance and home-making, ingredients we take with hardly a thank you when present, and yearn so deeply for when absent.

This scene and the conversations were all happening in my mind. Obviously I was making it up. "If you don't believe we're real, we'll give you a message in writing," my two visitors offered.

"A message in writing?" I didn't believe them. "Yep, I'll take a message in writing!"

"Well, what do you want the message to be about?"

I searched my mind. "Give me a message about Dorothy, the person who is coming this afternoon for a healing session. Tell me what is wrong with her and what she needs." That would stump them. Such a specific message. How could they possibly get a message to me, within two hours, if I didn't write it myself? My time was already fully committed to teaching. I wasn't planning to go anywhere. I wasn't *able* to go anywhere. It would be impossible.

The two imaginary figures were unfazed. They nodded their heads. They accepted. They would get a message to me in writing. The interview was over. They stood up, in unison, inclined their heads toward me in farewell and glided off the way they had come.

I opened my eyes, shook my head, like a dog, waking from a nap, rubbed my face a little and looked at my watch. It was nearly time for the next appointment.

My next client didn't arrive. I was squandering my whole afternoon waiting for no-shows. I paced the big teaching room. Frustrated with the waste of time and the discourtesy of my clientele, I wondered how I could make it up to myself? Aha! I had an original thought — I would treat myself to lunch at my favorite restaurant, round the corner.

At the end of the meal, I saw the server walking toward me, carrying the little black tray with the bill, and the fortune cookie. My bones tingled, my skin on my arms prickled — the image of a slip of printed paper, a message in writing, slid inside my head. I'd forgotten the meditation, dismissed it as stupid ramblings of an over-active imagination. Alert now, I cracked open the cookie. The fortune said: Love is the only medicine for a broken heart.

Oh, perhaps Dorothy has a broken heart. I shrugged my shoulders. It seemed far-fetched. It was just a fortune in a fortune cookie. I wasn't going to believe it. I started to crumple the paper, throw it away, but I paused, thought better of it, and placed it safely in my purse. I returned to the office to wait for Dorothy .

"I don't want an Alexander lesson," she'd said on the phone, "I want a healing session. I can tell you're psychic and I can tell you're a healer, and that's what I want."

When she arrived, we sat on the couch. "What can I do for you?" I asked.

Dorothy spoke for a long time, ten or fifteen minutes, then in her last sentence she came to the point. "Basically I'm suffering from a cardiac fracture," she said, looking at me pointedly.

"Ooh," I said, with a note of panic, doubting I had the skills to deal with a complex medical condition, "that sounds serious, what is it?"

"A broken heart," she replied, with a teasing grin, pleased with her obscure wording. She didn't know that her last three words had just shattered my view of reality.

I was speechless, but I had to pull myself together. I paused, looking at Dorothy, wondering what to do next. Then I heard myself say, "I have a message for you from my spirit guides." I took the slip of paper from my purse and handed it to her. Dorothy read the paper from the fortune cookie — Love is the only medicine for a broken heart — and looked back at me, her face registering confusion.

"I asked my spirit guides what you need in this healing session. They said they would give me a message in writing and I just got that now in a fortune cookie, so I kept it for you," I explained.

"Oh!" Dorothy said. No doubt she was wondering whether my condition was diagnosable.

"Well, let's go over to the table," I said, wanting to get on with the session.

What a strange day it had been. I had new respect for the possibility of spirit guides, crystals and Melody. I also had a question. My last missing client didn't come for her lesson because she chose the wrong exit off Cross County Highway and landed up turning back the way she had come. Considering how events unfolded, I wondered who authored that so-called wrong turn.

A few months later, I was working with Christine, a plastic surgeon. Holding her feet, I started to feel an intense vibration. It was as though I'd had too much coffee to drink, except I hadn't had any. "What's that feeling," I asked myself. "What is going on?"

"You need to open her aura, so that we can get inside," came a response, inside my head.

What now? Another sort of trance, another state I didn't recognize, another made up conversation in my head. "I'm not just going to open an aura and let you in. Who are you and what do you want?"

"We are a spirit medical team who needs to help Christine with an important surgery."

"Why? What surgery?"

"A dog bite. Someone will be bitten around the right eye by a dog and Christine will need our help in performing the surgery." A slight pause, giving me time to catch up to what was happening. "We will give you names so that you can recognize the quality of the energy, but that isn't to say that that is who we are. We want Florence Nightingale to come in through the left hand, Albert Schweitzer to come in through the right hand and an ancient Chinese Herbalist to be at the head, to lead the team." Another pause, to aid digestion. "This assistance is necessary because Western medicine is unsophisticated in treating the toxicity of dog bites." After this last sentence, I saw an image of a four- or five-year-old girl with a dog bite around the right eye.

I started to open Christine's aura, using my hands to expand her energy field by bringing them close to her body, almost touching, then pulling them away, in ever-widening sweeps. The vibration was intensifying. First it had felt like the table was shaking, then the two of us with the table, then the room, now the whole building. I couldn't stand being alone with what was happening, any more. I asked Christine, whose eyes were closed, if she could feel something weird was going on. "Oh yes," she said, not even asking what it was. I left it at that, because I wasn't ready to divulge the latest wanderings of my crazed mind to this woman of science, a doctor.

When I was done opening her aura the spirit team commanded me: "Now tell Christine about us and about the dog bite. We need to communicate with her."

"No," I defied, moving to Christine's arm, stolidly returning to a routine lesson.

"Tell Christine about us," the team insisted, vibrating the room a little more vigorously, the equivalent of a finger-wag.

"I won't," I muttered to myself. I was reluctant to expose myself, be a fool. It was one thing to be visited by spirit guides, in response to an invitation, in the comfort and privacy of a personal meditation, and quite another to have them intrude into a session and start giving doctors instructions about the inadequacies of western medicine and how to overcome them.

"Tell Christine," they admonished a third time. They obviously knew my three-time rule, knew how to make me speak.

Sighing to myself, I spoke out loud. "What surgery are you doing this afternoon?" I was hedging. I was looking for an opening, instead of diving in the deep end.

"Oh, nothing much, a revision of a scar."

"No dog bites?" I inquired hopefully.

"No," she said, "No dog bites. This is a convicted prisoner who was scarred in a bar brawl."

I hesitated, then pushed onward. "Well, there is a spirit team here who says they have come to assist you in repairing a dog bite to the right eye. . ." I edited the age and gender of the victim I had seen, not wanting to be so specific, not wanting to narrow the odds. After all, my credibility was at stake here. I embarked on what turned out to be a long explanation. All kinds of information came forth from the spirit team. The emphasis lay on treating the psychological trauma. I never should have bought that channeling crystal! I didn't like the role of giving a doctor guidelines about how to perform surgery.

Christine seemed accepting enough, even interested. She asked me some questions, which I answered. I felt like I was fabricating. Words just kept coming out my mouth and at the end, to my horror, I heard myself claim "And this is not going to happen at some time in your career, this is going to happen soon, in the next two days . . ." Where did that come from? How could I be so rash? I should have left it open-ended. Then I could never be wrong. It could just lie forever in the future. I quickly added, "to three weeks." Measly three weeks. I'd meant to buy more time than that.

Christine was quite intrigued by our visitors, but I was miserable. I would be found out. I was an irresponsible charlatan. I'd brought shame on my profession. I was an Alexander teacher, not a medium. I should stick to what I know, not go rooting around on the other side of the fence, in the forest-of-no-return. It wasn't as if I had a well-founded belief and experience in spirit energies — who did I think I was, playing around like this?

The next day, a few minutes after five o' clock, the phone rang — Christine. Now she was breathless, she was in disbelief. "Vivien," she said, then "Vivien," she repeated, unable to move on with the sentence, "I just want you to know that I have been called to Lawrenceburg, Indiana, to do surgery on a five-year old girl who was bitten around the right eye, by a Great Dane dog. I'm on my way there now." Then silence.

"No!" I said.

"Yes," she said, "I can hardly believe it. How did you know?"

"I don't know," I said, "I didn't know, it felt like I was making it up. I'm going to have to think about this, think about the implications."

"Yes," she agreed, "we're going to have to think about this. I'll let you know how it goes."

I put the phone down. Back in trance, I paced the house 'til midnight. I could feel Christine. I could feel her busy-ness, her concentration, I could feel her thirst while she was operating. I made a note to remind her to drink more water. The implications boggled my mind. If the message — the dog-bite around the eye was true, and it was — I had to accept the source. The message and the messengers were inextricably linked. That wasn't all. I had seen a future event, and it had come to pass. Did that mean that the future, like the past, is already laid out, just waiting for us to stumble into it? Why couldn't this have happened to someone else? That would have given me room to maneuver, align my thoughts into something which could sit comfortably in my mind, coexist with my doubt and skepticism.

Try as I might, I couldn't avoid the matter. No side-stepping, no back-tracking, no fumbling dance of denial. I hadn't made it up, and I could not bury my own experience.

"Everything was exactly as you described," Christine said, at her next appointment. "I handled myself and the case completely differently.

Because of the preparation, I knew how to proceed. I remembered about the significance of dealing with the trauma, so I stopped on the way and bought a fluffy toy — a bunny. Before the surgery, while we we giving the patient fluids, I sat on the bed with her and held her hand, encouraging her to stroke the bunnny. And you know what? The family raises rabbits! I was guided to exactly the right choice. Half an hour later, when it was time for the anesthetic, she was in a deep trance, very relaxed. The nurses remarked that they've never seen a surgeon spend time with the patient before going into theater."

"Did you feel the spirit energies working through you?" I asked.

"Oh, yes!" Christine smiled, "just as you said. The Chinese guide calmed the girl and put her in a trance. Then I felt this really strong force, the Albert Schweitzer energy, technical and spiritual, coming through the right and the healing, loving energy, the Florence Nightingale influence, coming through the left. I felt so calm and confident, guided, supported, not overly tense, not overly responsible."

The little girl healed without any visible scarring, no scars on her face — nothing — and no fear of dogs either.

SUPPORT FROM THE UNIVERSE

I loved the crystals, I wanted more. I wondered where and when the next opportunity like the Cincinnati Gem and Mineral Show would be. I couldn't wait a whole year for this annual event, so I phoned the organizer of the gem show and asked her, "Are there any shows like the Cincinnati show in one of the neighboring cities?"

"I don't know," she said, "let me look on the schedule. No, I don't see any. You know the Cincinnati show is one of the bigger ones. You could look in the back of Lapidary Journal. They list all the shows across the nation. They have a calendar."

I raced down to Barnes and Noble and purchased a copy. The list of shows was disappointing. Nothing in the area, not soon enough, not big enough. But I did find treasure in the classifieds — a collector, who was selling his lifetime collection. His name was Mr. Beckman, and I wasn't going to let anyone else carry off the stash.

"Yes, certainly you can come and see the minerals," Mr. Beckman said. "What time shall I expect you?"

I drove the length of Vine Street, looking for his four storey brownstone, a house with elegant proportions, once distinctive, but now swallowed by a less reputable neighborhood. Mr. Beckman was a refined gentleman. Although his demeanor showed that he was aging, his skin was soft and smooth. His stiff black shoes, polished to a shine, matched his stiff black glasses.

Mr. Beckman had removed his stones from the glass-fronted, well-lit cabinets upstairs, and rearranged them on metal library shelving downstairs. He'd brought them closer to leaving the house. These were the first steps to letting go of a lifetime of love. All I could manage was to let my eyes dart and rove over the collection, pecking like a chicken, hopping from specimen to specimen, fluttering from unfamiliar name to unfamiliar name. Time passed. At last I had adjusted, begun to attune to what I was seeing. I could begin to make choices. I looked at my watch, I'd already been there two hours. Mr. Beckman sat patiently watching me, smoking his cigarettes. He was enjoying watching a novice being bitten by the bug he'd carried for the last fifty years.

Mr. Beckman knew nothing of the metaphysical properties of the stones. He just loved them. Now that he was getting along and had no heir to share his interest, he was selling the rocks to supplement his income. Three hours after I arrived, I settled on a variety of stones, paid Mr. Beckman and extricated myself from his Aladdin's cave.

As soon as Barbara came back from her business travels I told her about my find. "Ooh," she said, "let's go."

"O.K.," I said, "I'll call Mr. Beckman."

"Of course," Mr. Beckman said, "What time? Yes, of course you can bring your friend."

Mr. Beckman installed himself on his stool again, cigarettes at hand, enjoying his new spectator sport. This time I could share the joke a little because I could see Barbara go into the same daze I had. I watched her remove her glasses so she could bring the crystals up to her nose, to look at them more closely. Minutes turned into hours before we could marshal our attention and make our pick — 'the silver pick,' Mr. Beckman told us — selecting from someone else's careful choices.

Barbara and I learned as much from spending time with Mr. Beckman's collection as we did with any other method of studying the crystals. We systematically ferried Mr. Beckman's stones from his home to ours. His minerals emitted a grand old energy, a sense of times gone by.

Dad had warned me when I was ten that mineral collecting is an expensive hobby. He was right. I was noticing its effect on my pocket. I was also noticing that my clients were joining me in my interest, relying on me to assist them in finding their own friends from the mineral kingdom. I should ask the crystals to help me financially, ask them to pay their own way. With Barbara's help, I acquired a vendor's license. I was in business.

Life was so full, there weren't enough hours in the day, or days in the week. It was hard to choose, to prioritize. I was having experiences far beyond my little South African dreams. But it wasn't just the opportunities and experiences. The quality of my life had changed. In Cape Town I didn't think about connecting with spirit, with God. I went for a walk on the mountain, surveyed life from the peak, looked across the city to the distant mountains, across the ocean to the horizon, at the place where earth meets sky. I could feel the creation all around me, know I was part of it. I didn't need a more personal relationship. Here, in Cincinnati, I had traversed a different terrain. I had gone inward, to contact spirit, and in return, spirit had come to contact me.

These reflections led me to an observation. I thought about all the people I knew in Cincinnati, who, like us, had settled here, from another country, or from another part of the U.S. A disproportionate number were healers. Every time we were asked how we came to choose Cincinnati, in the conservative mid-west — a pretty city, but a far cry from the scenic splendor of Cape Town — I remembered my Johannesburg vision of the city of Cincinnati, the red carpet unrolling toward us. I wasn't sure that we chose. I formed an intention to uncover the forces at work.

For no good reason, that I knew of, the subject came up when I was teaching a lesson. "You know, Karen," I said, "I've been thinking about Cincinnati and how many gifted healers have been drawn to live here."

"Oh" she responded, not even needing to think about it, facts and figures at her fingertips, "that's because Cincinnati is on one of the developing chakras of the Earth."

"What!" I exclaimed, "What are you talking about?"

"Well, I have this book, by Jim Hurtak, which shows the earth chakras in North America. I'll bring it next time."

"Please," I said. This sounded interesting. I knew of Jim Hurtak. Back in South Africa, I'd had an acquaintance who had studied with him. His work had been too way-out for me. But there it was. The first time I spoke the question, an answer came back. That was worth a modicum of respect.

Karen remembered to bring the book to her next lesson. Sure enough it showed a diagram of a dove drawn over a map of North America, indicating the already established chakras, as well as the two which were currently developing. The epicenter of the first, was in Kentucky, just south of the Ohio River, encompassing Cincinnati and Louisville; the second was in Canada, surrounding Toronto. That was very nice, but hardly convincing. After all, this was a book I'd avoided for years. It was food for thought, though. I would chew it over and see if more evidence came up.

I didn't have long to wait. We were at home on the Saturday night. Neil was downstairs at the computer and I was upstairs in the kitchen. We weren't great TV watchers, but for some reason we'd left the TV on in the family room. As I walked by, on my way to the bedroom, I heard the newsreader saying that *Places Rated Almanac* had voted Cincinnati the number one most livable city in the United States. "Neil," I called, running down the stairs to get him, "Neil, guess what? Cincinnati has been rated number one."

Neil emerged from his computer space. "Really? That's unbelievable. Let me see." We'd used *Places Rated Almanac* back in South Africa. Then Cincinnati had been two hundredth, or something — not very encouraging, but we'd chosen it anyway. This result made us look clever. We ran back up the stairs to catch the tail-end of the story. Cincinnati was voted the number one most livable city in North America, Toronto, number two, and Louisville number three.

My antennae were primed. Within two weeks another client told me that Edgar Cayce, the renowned mystic, had regarded Cincinnati as an important spiritual center; and the *Cincinnati Enquirer* printed a full page article on interesting facts about Cincinnati, including the information that in the early 1900's Russian psychics, who'd been asked to ascertain the most spiritual location on earth, determined it to be Cincinnati, Ohio, USA.

When Soozi had first introduced me to crystals, back in 1983, she had mentioned that for her, the best quartz comes from Arkansas. I had always hoped to become the earth-keeper of Arkansas crystal. For the winter vacation Neil agreed to take me to the crystal mines in Arkansas.

We packed our white Chevy conversion van, and on Christmas day,1994, went south on the I75 meandering through the hills of Kentucky, crossing Tennessee, passing through Nashville, and on into the mountains of Arkansas. We stayed at the formerly elegant *Hot Springs Hotel*, built in the Victorian era. The lobby was decorated for Christmas with a giant Christmas tree and a fully edible, gingerbread house, large enough to accommodate several children standing at full height. The children ran in and out, peeked through the windows, called to their parents, "Look! Look at me, look at this gingerbread house!" Aidan and Jason joined the pack. We trooped upstairs to our room to change into our swimsuits. We couldn't wait to submerge ourselves in the naturally hot, healing spring waters, wash away our travels, listen to fellow soakers tell their crystal mine stories. We were already absorbed in our newest adventure.

I itched with impatience. In the mall, in the basement of the hotel, I had seen huge quartz plates built into a fountain and decorative wall. I didn't want a leisurely breakfast. I didn't want a morning stroll. I didn't want a morning bathe in the healing waters. I wanted to get to the mines. Neil relented. He forced himself along, asking the crystal-store manager for a list of names and recommendations.

We had to drive a fair distance from Hot Springs to Mount Ida. Every few miles we'd see trestle tables laden with quartz. I couldn't contain myself. A bouncy thing was bouncing up and down inside me.

First stop, *Crystal City*. I'd been enticed by their advertisement in *Lapidary Journal*. Neil sauntered in to introduce himself to the owners, talk some male talk, shake some hands. I saw him being led into an enormous building. He came back nodding his head, wagging his chin. "Wait till you see what's in there," he said, smirking playfully.

I couldn't wait. The bouncy thing inside, bounced me up the stairs, only to come to a sudden halt. Shining clusters of crystals lined the aisles and flats of quartz were stacked, four layers deep, on long pine shelves, extending the length of the massive warehouse. I glanced back at Neil. He was standing on the stairs, laughing.

I reined in the bounce. This wasn't child's play, this was serious business. I inhaled the winter air, slowly and deliberately, galvanizing myself for action. Then I walked the aisles, gradually orienting myself. Bless Mr. Beckman and his metal library shelves. I'd been trained, I could handle this. When I felt ready, I got to work. I realized I would have to scan the flats quickly, catch the tell-tale glint of the crystal who wanted to come home with us, pull it out, move on, skilled as fly-fishing.

Up until this point, Neil had been cautiously observing my growing interest — or should I say obsession — in crystals. Perceiving the immensity of the task ahead, he pushed up his shirt-sleeves, let me explain the desirable configurations and demonstrate how the crystals, which were meant for us, would light up in response to our energy.

Despite his claims to skepticism, he caught on immediately and we methodically worked our way through the shed, while the boys delighted in watching an unsupervised glut of cartoons on the TV in the back of the van.

We were ready for the next shed, but something was going on in there. They were boxing up their entire showroom, transporting everything to Tucson, to the premier gem and mineral event in North America. We slid into the shed in time to select a few polished Brazilian points with phantoms and chlorite inclusions, as well as some exquisite laser wands. As I handled the crystals, I discovered that while holding a crystal, my mind would flash on someone specific and know the crystal was meant for that person.

Shopping for crystals proved to be tiring, even to me. The bounce turned to a dribble. We could not manage more than one or two mines in a day. Aidan and Jason grew restless. What kind of vacation was this anyway? They wanted to swim, and eat in restaurants, and tumble around on the bed with Mom and Dad. They weren't interested in hanging around muddy piles of rocks and encrusted miners in gumboots. I conceded. We struck a balance. I forced myself to sit still, eat, chew, relax, so that I could be rewarded with my own special treasure hunt in the other half of the day.

Not that Neil wasn't enjoying himself too. He was learning about crystals, rapidly, the way you learn a language when you're in the country with no other means of communication. Each mine came with its own set of lessons. We started to recognize the personalities of the crystals, know the mine that yielded them. We had depleted our budget, but local lore insisted that a visit to Mount Ida would be incomplete without a visit to *Leatherhead's*, Tony Thacker's store.

We roused Tony from his bed at ten in the morning, and he came out bleary eyed. His long hair, bearded face and lean physique declared him to be the mountain-man personified. He lectured, advised and told stories, as he showed us around his lot, balancing on long planks placed strategically over muddy puddles, enthusiastically followed by a barking pack of firm-bellied, tail-wagging mongrels. His store was a run-down shed and in it were the finest metaphysical specimens.

Tony observed us intently, as we reveled in the superior quality of his crystals. Then he excused himself, went back into his house and came out bearing a locked suitcase. He set it on the counter, swiveled the key and like a magician, held up a perfectly proportioned crystal cross. "Look at that," he said emphatically, nodding knowingly at our appreciative applause. "And this," he said, rolling a rare curved crystal between thumb and forefinger. Then he switched off the overhead light, switched on a light box and placed a polished quartz point upon it. Suspended inside, perfectly centered, was a long, slender, double terminated crystal.

"A manifestation crystal!" I gasped, never having expected to actually see such a rarity. Tony looked fit to burst. "From my own mine," he said, lowering his head, in gratitude to the earth which provides.

The back of our van was fully loaded with flats and it was time to go back to Cincinnati. At home we laid all the crystals out in the basement, and looked at each one. A disproportionate number were supposedly rare, record keepers — crystals with little triangles engraved on them, indicating they can be be used to access information from the Akashic records, the records of everything that ever was and ever will be known to Man. Supposedly such crystals only came into the hands of those ready for the responsibility. What was I going to do with hundreds of record keepers? I'd be awake at night for years accessing all this information and then what would I do with it?

I hid the little points in the garage, out of sight, out of mind, and decided to offload the big points on other people. It would be my honor to find the rightful earth-keepers for these demanding record keepers.

The next week, Dorothy arrived for her session with a smug expression on her face. She was holding something in, waiting her moment. Once the session was under way, the question popped out, "How would you like to meet Melody?" Meet Melody? What did she mean?

She was trying to keep a straight face, faking innocence. She knew my heart was hip-hopping, that I wanted her to hurry. She was savoring every moment. "I was in Kristy's rock shop, in Columbus, and she told me that Melody is coming to teach her Level One and Two workshops in April." She handed over the flyer, a green page with a photo of Melody and a description of the course.

"Of course I want to meet Melody," I yelped. "Give me that." I grabbed the paper, the bouncy thing inside had started again. I couldn't be expected to behave like a grown-up. I was going to meet Melody, I was going to train in Level One and Two, I was going to have a new teacher. I couldn't wait. And if I had to wait, no-one in their right mind could expect me to sit still.

"Are you going?" I asked Dorothy, wondering if there would be enough space for all of us.

"I thinks so," Dorothy said, "I want to."

"Well, I'm going," I said, "definitely."

I showed the flyer to the trainees on the Alexander course. Unexpectedly Jen livened up, wanting to come too. "I'll phone," she said, "I'll go reserve our places." She came back smiling, "We're all in," she said, "we're all registered for Level One and Barbara, Tina and you are enrolled for Level Two, as well." I looked at my watch, as if that could hurry the time. It was going to be a long wait to April.

Master Teachers

TRAINING

A pril. I surveyed my crystal collection in my teaching room. Who wanted to meet Melody? Who would help train me? "I will. Take me. I want to meet Melody," the crystals seemed to shout, all at once. Children asking for ice-cream, asking to go to the fun-fair. No-one wanted to be left behind. I took a box from the garage and started to wrap, cushioning my beauties in newspaper, making little travel cocoons for them, for the important journey ahead. I installed the box in the back of the chevy.

I'd forgotten my notebook. I went back into the teaching room. The air was heavy, the tone had sombered. I turned round and round in the middle of the room, disoriented, like a time traveler arriving in a familiar city, in a different era — same but different. Then I got it. The crystals were gone. My warm and friendly teaching room, my little den, stood empty and bereft. How could the presence of crystals, or their absence, be so palpable? The learning had already begun.

Barbara, Tina, Mary and I piled into the van. We would meet Jen there. With festive expectations, we pulled into Columbus, into the parking lot of the strip mall, home to Kristy's rock shop. Kristy, the owner, with her blond, coiffed hair, pink cheeks and blue eyes, looked more like a country and western singer than a crystal doyenne. She displayed the stones, and other metaphysical attractions in one store and used the adjoining space, connected by an interleading door, for presenting weekly workshops. We milled around the store, wanting to begin, but it wasn't nine-thirty yet. People, who'd driven from all over Ohio, and from Kentucky, Indiana, Illinois, Tennessee and West Virginia, were arriving. These were people on a pilgrimage, coming to learn from the master.

When I saw Melody, my eyebrows went up. She was beautiful, like her picture on the back of her book, striking. But that wasn't "it." "It" was her laugh — powerful, open-throated — something shone from her that I hadn't encountered before. Alexander teachers look different, like they've found the elixir of youth. Melody also had a look about her. She was in on one of the mysteries of life. She had joy. I took in her tallness, her lean physique, her longer-than-waist-length blond hair, her lacy, feminine clothes, and her intricate crystal jewelry. I took in her penetrating gaze, softened by the wrinkling of her nose, the crinkling of her eyes, and the way she spoke so respectfully of love, in the biggest sense of the word. I was looking at my favorite riddle, the play of opposites, the integration of opposing forces, yin and yang. I was looking at a lacy frill of a bejeweled woman with long blond hair, who was also a hard-nosed nuclear scientist, with both feet firmly on the ground. I was looking at Melody, in the flesh.

At nine twenty-nine she strode to the front of the room, took her place at the podium, cast her eye over us, and began to teach. "We are what we are by virtue of what we think and believe," she began. "And we are a mass of self-limiting beliefs. The only reason we can't do things is because we believe we can't."

"So we can fly?" I chirped from the second row.

"So we can fly!" Melody was expounding in the same moment as I was asking. She threw me a smile. "Right," she continued. "We have our personal self-limiting beliefs and we have our mass consciousness self-limiting beliefs." I thought about it. She might be right. I'd heard from reliable sources that people do learn to levitate, and I'd had countless flying dreams. It was easy to fly in dreams, you just flapped your arms, tread the air. I always promised myself I'd remember how easy it was when I woke up, but when I woke up I'd be heavy again, couldn't find the air currents, didn't believe anymore.

I brought my attention back to the room, to Melody's voice. Melody was telling a story about George Bernard Shaw and how he visited graveyards outside London, discovering that the people in the villages lived longer than the people in the city. I liked George Bernard Shaw because he used to take lessons with Alexander. Joyce had told us that he'd recommended Alexander's work to a man at his club, who'd said he couldn't afford the exorbitant fee Alexander charged. Shaw had sent him a postcard from France, and signed his name — which he didn't usually do, because his autograph was worth a tidy sum — and that had paid for the lessons. Come to think of it, I didn't know if the story was true, but Joyce used to tell it. Now Melody was using Shaw to make a point about beliefs about the normal lifespan, and how Shaw had lived to a ripe old age by moving to the country, where people were expected to live longer, and did.

The room wasn't fully persuaded. Not that we disbelieved her, we just didn't believe her — yet — we preferred the comfort of our self-limiting beliefs. After all we defined our lives by them. If we gave them up, what would happen? We'd be flying all over the place, breathing under water, walking on the moon, smoking ten packs of cigarettes a day, generally running amok. It was too big for almost nine-forty on a Saturday morning, too big for a seventy-five dollar workshop, too big a first step, even though we said we wanted it. We believed in her, but we couldn't, or wouldn't, believe her.

The next lesson was on how to clear our chakras of unwanted etheric cords. "What's a chakra?" came a voice from the back. The whole group gasped, as one. An innocent, with no background knowledge, had wandered inadvertently into this workshop with a master teacher. We held an impolite silence, while Melody patiently went over some of the basics. I don't remember anyone asking "What are etheric cords?" an equally appropriate question, but luckily Melody systematically explained that too. We send out cords from our etheric bodies, connecting us, web-like, to the people in our lives, through which we consciously and unconsciously, send thoughts, emotions and influence.

We started with some exercises which we could do individually, sitting in our chairs. We used our etheric hands to remove the etheric cords, filling the holes, with white light. We learned how to use faden crystals — flat quartz crystals with white lines, which can be used to facilitate etheric travel and mental telepathy. We did an exercise, meeting and greeting our inner selves — the equivalent of the unconscious in Hawaiian shamanism — to gain insight into the origins of our self-limiting beliefs. The two-day course had enough material in it to keep us busy for ten years. This wasn't a workshop designed to cozy us along with metaphysical treats. Melody was teaching us techniques, which we would have to go home and explore on our own time.

After the individual exercises, we unpacked our stones and practiced doing stone lay-outs on each other. First we matched the stones to the chakras by color. Next we placed stones on the chakras by following our intuition. All manner of beautiful stones were appearing out of people's boxes and bags. I saw a golden healer quartz with a black tourmaline embedded in it and a quartz point with one of its faces layered with hundreds of record keepers. It would have been fun, except for the challenge of sitting still and energizing each chakra for five minutes at a time, thirty-five minutes in all.

Melody made it look easy. She demonstrated squatting down and holding her hands over the stone covering the chakra. None of us had a five-minute attention span, so that was the first pitfall. None of us were limber enough to squat for five minutes, so that was the second pitfall. Then none of us could hold a position on the floor for five minutes, without fidgeting and scratching, so that was the third pitfall. But Melody didn't care. She just grinned at our whining. If we wanted to do it, we had to withstand the rigors. At last it was lunch-time. We limped out, tired, hungry and contorted.

Melody refused to 'give' information that she believed could be accessed, with reasonable effort, from another source. She was infinitely patient, or was it stubborn? People didn't seem to get it. "What are the properties of ruby?" someone asked. Melody swung her crossed leg, like a cat, flicking its tail. "Look in the book," she replied. They thought if they phrased it differently, in a more scholarly way, they'd get a different response. "I've heard that smithsonite can be used in place of other stones. Is that true?" Melody tossed her head. "Look in the book," she replied. "And aquamarine can be used for aligning the chakras, not so?" Smiling sweetly, "Look in the book," leg-swinging, hair tossed, wiggled eyebrows, then yielding a little, "use the index, of course." Finally, when anybody forgot and asked Melody a question which simply required straightforward research, we'd all chorus, "Look in the book!" We didn't want our time wasted either.

Melody's way of using crystals was very different from mine. I would hold the crystal in my hand and use it as an extension and amplifier of myself, and let it use me as an extension and amplifier of itself, synergizing our intentions and healing powers. Melody laid the crystals on and around the person. This could be combined with laying on of hands — putting your hands on the stones that were on the person, creating an electromagnetic grid, reaching deep into the earth to pull on the energies of unmined stones, reaching far into space to call on the energies of other entities. In Melody's method, the healer was more a technician. His or her own personality and properties were virtually insignificant, in the same way as an electrical circuit, once laid down, doesn't care who flips the switch.

I had used Melody's book *A Kaleidoscope of Crystals* on a daily basis, but her book Laying on of Stones I had left untouched on my shelf. The picture diagrams in the book had seemed inaccessible. Like any electrician, I needed apprenticeship. The effects were deep, inducing a strong state of altered consciousness. More was happening than either the healer or the recipient could consciously absorb. By the time we drove back to Cincinnati, our understanding of the universe had been stretched, the laws of nature had been expanded.

That night I went to Lois for dinner. "How's the workshop?" she asked, "Tell me about it."

I sat on the couch next to her, shifting uncomfortably. I wanted to tell her, but I couldn't engage my mouth. "I can't," I said.

"Why not? Is it a secret?"

"No, it's not a secret. I just don't know how to tell you. I don't know how to describe it."

"O.K.," she said, "we'll talk about something else." I didn't want to do that either. I felt far away, somewhere in outer space. I was an alien. I'd lost the power of human speech.

Barbara, Tina and I returned on Monday afternoon for Level Two. Until this time, my strange experiences had seemed to fall upon me from the big blue sky. In Level Two, for the first time, I went looking. The crystal layouts were designed to conjure the extraordinary, and they did. Melody had carefully researched, documented and published, a number of lay-out patterns. By intentionally selecting one of these patterns and laying the stones, I could induce a trance state and draw specific phenomena from the etheric realm.

"We're going to do *Journey to Beyond*," Melody said, "you'll work in pairs, one will be a journeyer, the other a guide." This layout involved a very large number of stones and took up a lot of space. Half of us lay down on the floor, instructed to feel the currents as the stones were laid out around us. I could sense a mounting force, which soothed me, transported me above the hubbub.

Silence. The room was ready, the journeyers were ready, the guides were ready. "Now," Melody said, "imagine you're climbing a tree, a rainbow or a mountain. Listen to the drum, it will beat to the heart rhythm. Guides, keep your journeyer talking, don't ask any leading questions. Journeyers, narrate to your guides, keep them informed of what is happening." The drummer began, lub-dup, lub-dup, lub-dup, lub-dup. I visualized myself climbing a mountain, felt myself plodding along. Lub-dup, lub-dup, lub-dup, lub-dup. Suddenly, I was flipped to the inside of the mountain. I was climbing a stone, carved staircase. The stairway was a feat of engineering and design. Skylights had been cut into the mountain at angles, creating windows, invisible from the outside, lighting the stairway.

I was no longer alone. Climbing the stairway were people from many different cultures and times. I could tell by their outfits, we all had one thing in common — we were the shamen, priests and healers of our communities. Our collective intent motivated a smooth ascent to the summit of the mountain. From there we floated upward beyond the clouds into a place of vibrant colors, where thought and action fused. I wondered if I could fly. I found myself flying. I thought of playing in the sand dunes. I was a child, laughing, skipping, rolling and tumbling in the sand. I was bathed in peace and joy. I was one with the universe.

Duh-duh-duh-duh-duh. The drumbeat changed, calling me back. I didn't want to come back. And I didn't want to climb back down the mountain. Instantly I was sliding, from the peak, toward the foot, with increasing speed. I slid off the slope into the image of a huge light being, arms outspread — my Tibetan spirit guide. I passed through him and I was back — back in ordinary reality.

Back from eternity, to the fickle world, we think is real. I broke into a grin, I'd been to heaven. I floated around the room.

"How often do you do that?" I asked Melody.

"At least once a week," she said. Now I knew why she looked like the cat who got the cream — she was the cat who got the cream.

I didn't need any more, but intense experiences continued to come, thick and fast. "It's the Psychic Olympics!" Barbara exclaimed. I was vibrating at a different frequency, like the time the spirit team came to ask me to open Christine's aura, so they could get inside. I could actually see the energy flow passing from crystal to crystal, in the layouts.

At the end of the workshop I felt pushed to speak to Melody. "I just want to say goodbye and thank you," I said. She nodded at me. I was already turning away, I turned back. "I also need to tell you that your book was the first metaphysical text my guides have ever given me permission to read and consult. They said it wouldn't interfere with my intuition."

She looked up from her crystal packing, really connecting with me. "It shouldn't. Nothing must interfere with your own intuition. I wrote it in a way that it wouldn't."

She was letting me know that my words meaningfully acknowledged her work. I was turning away again, when Melody caught my eye. "I'll be in touch," she said.

"In touch?" I repeated to myself. I wondered what she had in mind, knowing she was not one to say something lightly.

A couple of months later, in June, when the training course took a summer break, Barbara, Tina and I, dedicated a week to exploring the stone lay-outs. One of the lay-outs we selected was *Venus*, a lay-out which 'attracts people, experiences, or objects necessary to one's growth.' First Alexander came to me and clarified some aspects of the Alexander Technique, which I had not yet grasped, followed by a lesson. I was lying on the floor surrounded by stones, but I could feel hands, and the movement inside my body, as clearly as if there were a live person working on me. Directly after that Melody arrived. She smiled. That's all. She didn't say or do anything. I watched her, not comprehending at first, and then said, "Oh, I see, you're here to show me that we can be in two places at once."

"Now you're getting it," she nodded, and disappeared. I wondered if that was what Melody had meant by saying she would be in touch.

PAST LIVES

Just shy of a year after I'd done the Melody training, in March 1996, as I was walking into my Taekwondo lesson, Paul announced, "I've found it. I've found the next book." We had an agreement to tip each other off on exciting reads.

"So, what is it?"

"Here," he said, "look at this, you'll love it." He handed me a copy of *Many Lives, Many Masters* by Brian Weiss. I recognized the title. Christine had told me about it after she'd been inspired by our spirit rendezvous. She had been especially pleased, because like herself, Brian Weiss was a doctor.

I settled down on my bed, ready for a good read. From the opening paragraphs, I could feel a spiral, which had begun thirteen years earlier, with Soozi Holbeche, coming back around. Brian Weiss was describing his startling experiences as a psychiatrist, when a patient, under regular hypnosis, spontaneously went into past life regression and stranger yet, conversed with master guides in the spirit world. He'd had a difficult time reconciling his conventional medical training with these supernatural mind wanderings. He could have ignored it, refuted it, or dismissed it as imagination, except the master guides took care to prove themselves to him. They talked to him through his patient, about his own life, reminding him of personal events which no-one else could know. He didn't want to ruin his good name, but he'd been chosen by the spirit community to bring a message to the world. He'd stepped off the edge and written this book, publishing his firsthand witnessing of verifiable past lives and master guides. In quick succession I read all three of Brian's books, recommending them to virtually every one of my clients.

For the first time I was willing to believe my past life recall was actually about past lives, not limited to important symbolic constructs of my unconscious. I thought about the session I had with Soozi in 1983, the evidence which had come forward over time and the way the past life memories now meshed with my current life. I'd never told Mom about my memory of being sacrificed, or the pearl gift, because I didn't expect her to understand, or like the role I'd cast her in. Yet, for ten years since, whenever she gave me a present, it contained pearls — pearl stud earrings, pearls set in gold, a single string of pearls, a pendant with amethyst and pearls. Even without the words of the story, Mom knew about the pearls.

But there was an even more chilling parallel — a parallel no-one would plan, just to prove a point. Seven years after the memory, someone stood above my mother's son, dagger in hand, and plunged it into his head, sacrificing him to the raising of social conscience.

Equally, I resonated with my Celtic memory as a wizard who rejected his daughter. The story of Dad's remark, "Oh, but I wanted another boy," when I was born, was a family joke. Of course Dad was thrilled with his little girl. Yet, I seemed primed to have that story stick in my heart, remind me from the start of consciousness, that I wasn't a boy. I always felt that I had to prove to him, and to everyone else, that I was "as good as" a boy. I was dressed in boy's clothes, my hair was cut like a boy's because that was what was practical and when I was mistaken for a boy, Dad would say, "Well, what do you think, boy or girl? A boy of course!" and he'd glow with pride, and I'd glow with pride — on the outside — that such a perfect mistake could be made.

When Aidan was born, and I'd said, "That's Aidan!" I'd wanted to add, "That's my little girl, and she's now a boy, and I'm now a girl, and I will take care of him, and I won't take up magic. My child will come first." I was unreasonably fearful that Aidan would die, until he passed the age of three, and then my irrational fear evaporated. Aidan was unreasonably fearful of separating from me, and wouldn't, or couldn't, draw the roof on a house, even though he could draw Superman in every detail when he was three. His teacher said, "Vivien, I know I can tell you this because of who you are, but when a child can't draw a roof on the house it means he has a problem with his mother." She knew that there was no apparent problem, but I suspected what the problem really was. "Yes," I said, "it could be from a previous lifetime. I think Aidan was my daughter and I neglected her, and let her die, when she was three, because I was too obsessed with my work."

Those words sounded like nonsense, but I found out some facts over the years: the Celtic wizards, of the order of Merlin, came from the village of Iona and Bishop Aidan, who became St. Aidan, came from the village of Iona. Then, Mom called me one day, from Cape Town and said, "We just got the blueprints of our house, and our house has a name and guess what it is."

"What?" I asked, unable even to begin to guess.

"Iona!" she said, "what do you think of that?" and she didn't know about any of this, except for Aidan's name.

I read *The Cunning Man* by Robertson Davies and right at the end of the book I found out that Merlin's lover's name was Vivien. Robertson Davies had spelt it with the same spelling as mine, a coincidence, to highlight the significance of the discovery.

I asked myself: "If we only have one lifetime, how strong must the unconscious be, how much must the unconscious know to create such random events? And how can it be possible to weave such a complex web, that engages every person in our personal drama, as if we, alone, are all that mattered?" No, that didn't seem possible. It was more likely that we live many lives, and that we do design our destinies before being incarnated here on earth. I began to believe in reincarnation.

In April, Tina, Lois, Barbara and I went to Columbus again, to do another workshop, hoping to reconstruct the camaraderie and learning of the year before. Lois was also on our Alexander training course now, fulfilling her dream. We had fun, but the workshop was frustrating. It wasn't a training. It was experiential.

Monday morning, after the weekend, I was standing at the stove, frying an egg, musing that the next time I committed my time, it would have to be to learn a new skill. "Yes, yes," I encouraged myself, pushing myself along this track, becoming more specific, "hypnotherapy." I wanted to learn hypnotherapy so that I could do past-life regressions.

I took my egg on toast to the dining room table and sat down, looking around for reading material, from Neil's stack of newspapers, magazines and books. My eye fell on a bright red magazine. It was the cover of the *Omega* Summer 96 catalog. We hadn't been to Omega, the New Age campus offering week-end and week long residential courses in upstate New York, but David Stern had given us glowing reports of his time there. The year before I'd salivated over the offerings, not having either the time, or money, to participate. I picked up the catalog. The page fell open at a picture of Brian Weiss. For the first time, he was offering a professional training in hypnotherapy and past-life regression. Omega was hosting it.

It was 8:15 am. The Omega office was only open from 9:00 am. I shuffled in my chair. The bouncy thing was pushing around inside me again. I knew this workshop was going to fill up fast. I wasn't going to miss a place, I was going to be first in line.

The phone rang — Lois. "My dishwasher flooded my house," she wailed, "and I pulled my back, and I can hardly bend, and there's a big mess here, and I have to take Amanda to school. What should I do? Can you help me?"

I must help Lois. My rational mind knew that the workshop couldn't possibly be full yet. Most people wouldn't even have received their catalogs, let alone looked at them, made a decision, got round to calling. But I wanted to call straight away. I forced myself to go and help Lois, because she would have helped me. I lost my opportunity to phone, because after that I was busy for the rest of the morning. Three hours later, noon, I spoke to the representative, explained what I wanted. The bouncy thing wouldn't lie still and it had been joined by something sticky and hot in my throat that made it hard to speak and swallow. "Fine, yes, you're enrolled," she said. This time I had to wait until July.

Now that I could think straight again I went back to studying the Omega catalog. I noticed Family Week in August. I was on the look out for vacations we could enjoy as a family. Last summer we'd gone to visit Neil's brother, Tony, in Bishop and the boys wouldn't hike in the mountains with us. They wanted to watch TV and play video games. They needed friends their own age. Neil and I had paced up and down at the window, eying the mountains jealously, stuck in the valley, so close, but so far. Of course we'd forced the boys to go walking with us, insisted that they appreciate nature, forsake their electronic world for just a couple of hours. That wasn't relaxing, it was sheep herding. Now here was an option. We could go to Omega, together, yet share our interests with others our own age. Aidan could do art, Jason could do Little Rangers, Neil could do Outdoor Trails and I could do Heartsong. I hadn't been to Omega before. This year I was going to go twice.

When did the Omega experience begin for me? Was it at breakfast, three months before, when I picked up the red-orange catalog and the page fell open to the photo of Brian Weiss and the write-up of the past-life regression training? Or even, the moment before that, when I was making breakfast, dreaming and scheming, while frying an egg, deciding to train in hypnotherapy so that I would be able to do past-life regressions? Was it at the pick-up point, waiting at Grand Central, in New York, able to distinguish, with such ease, by colorful dress, dangling earrings and purposeful gait, who was arriving for the Omega shuttle? It was impossible to tell, what was the seed, what was the shoot, what was the tree, but I was looking forward to the fruit.

The shuttle pulled into the Omega parking lot — summer staff helping summer residents, backpacks, bags and suitcases, standing in line, signing up, receiving a key and a map — this was like arriving on kibbutz. I walked up the slope to find my cabin. I had to share with at least one other person. What if I didn't like my room-mate? What if my room-mate didn't like me? I just had to trust. Sharing was going to be a part of this experience — it would work out exactly right.

I opened the door. Sunlight, filtered by the woods, streamed in through the window. There was a green carpet, wooden floors, simple furnishings. Someone else's belongings were set down thoughtfully. There was a note of "Hi" and "welcome" from my room-mate. I put down my luggage, put my overnight bag in the bathroom, unpacked my traveling crystals, unfolded my celestial fabric with the gold stars and moons and suns, and laid out my stones — my signature — on the chest of drawers, under the mirror. Then I wrote a note back to my room-mate, "looking forward to meeting you," and went down to the cafe, to find friends and food.

All the food at Omega, was vegetarian or macrobiotic. For nine years of my life I had yearned for this facility. I wasn't vegetarian nor macrobiotic anymore. I was learning to live life without special rules and regulations, able to order something easy from the menu, break bread with friends without having to remove the wheat first. Still, it did something for my soul, gave a home to the piece of me that had wistfully read East West Journal, back in South Africa, wishing I could go to the American resorts which catered for people like me. I sat on the deck, with my vegetarian food, looking at the garden — a central mandala — under the almost invisible presence of a presiding Buddha.

I wanted to soak up this place, but I was waterlogged. First I needed to wring myself free of responsibilities, desires and goals. Omega commanded a state of being, like Alexander school — so much to learn — and everyone sitting around doing nothing. The bouncy thing was pushing and pulling inside me, making me look at my watch twice every minute, making me want to spill out a tirade of letting someone, anyone, everyone know who I am and why I'm here. I couldn't chew my salad — too slow. I wanted to gulp soup.

Almost everyone at the café had come to do Brian's training. Over one hundred and twenty people had registered, mostly psychotherapists, psychiatrists, psychologists and social workers; but there were also other health professionals, from traditional and alternative backgrounds, yoga teachers, body workers, healers, even an Alexander teacher — me.

"And what is the Alexander Technique?" my deck companions asked politely. I sighed against the bouncy thing. It was a reasonable question, but that didn't mean I liked it, and I knew I would probably have to answer it one hundred and twenty times that week. Some would be interested in my answer, but most would be categorizing it, incorrectly, with something else they'd already heard of, and thought they knew, but didn't.

"Would it help my knee? I'm having trouble going up and down stairs," a woman asked. She looked hopeful, one of the interested ones. I softened.

"Yes," I said, and explained why and how.

I ambled back to my cabin. This time my room-mate, Gail, a clinical psychologist from Long Island, was in the room. "Ha! There you are. I've been waiting to meet you. I thought I brought a lot of stuff, but look what you brought," she said, pointing at the crystals. Gail was very lean, with short hair, compassionate eyes, and a perceptive, no-nonsense voice. The curve of her back, announced to me, her generous heart. Gail took me next door, to the adjoining cabin, and introduced me to Pat and Ina, and Clyde. These four colleagues, from New York, were my new friends.

As taken as I was with the campus, the atmosphere and the people, I couldn't stop the bouncy thing. By the time Brian stepped forward, I was looking at my watch every fifteen seconds. Brian looked like a nice Jewish man — gray hair, glasses, broad hands with slender, strong fingers. I was impressed. There was no pomp and ceremony, no pedestal. He just stood there, in front of the stage, on the hardwood floor, holding a microphone, speaking to us, like a favorite uncle at a Bar-Mitzvah.

Brian proceeded to hypnotize all of us en masse. His soothing fatherly voice enveloped us. Then he taught us two main methods of hypnosis: the slow, twenty-minute, systematic technique of progressive relaxation, taking someone deeper and deeper into trance, and the quick, three-minute, rapid induction, which drops someone into trance through intense focus and sudden command. We had to pair up, work with different people, get to know each other. I looked around the room. Who would I approach? We broke apart, formed diads, practiced techniques. We followed the instructions, and voilà, the subjects were hypnotized.

That wasn't entirely true. Some people were having a little trouble — couldn't smooth their voices enough, couldn't flow. Others were having trouble going into trance. They were sitting hunched in their chairs, jaws clenched, fighting to relax. I stood frozen in the middle of the hall. An unarticulated thought was pulling at my sleeve. I took a moment to listen to myself — cocking my head to hear the noise in the house, the close of the door, the footfalls. Is someone there? Then I heard the footsteps of my heart — faint, timid — a little voice. "Look who you're with," the little voice breathed, "you're with psychologists, and psychiatrists, and social workers, and psychotherapists. Look who you're with. Remember?"

It had been twenty years since I'd kept company with this profession. Twenty years since I'd been barred, pushed out. "Look at them," the little voice continued, "what do you think now? Still wish you were one of them?" No, I didn't. I was grateful I'd found the Alexander Technique. I could see, with my tendency to somatize experience, how pulled down I would have been, had I lingered in the profession.

"You look like you've got it," a psychologist approached me. "I'm having trouble going under. Will you help me?"

"Of course," I said. "Come over here, come sit in this chair. Now, first you need to sit properly." I eased her back against the back-rest, placed her feet squarely on the floor, widened her shoulders, lengthened her neck, "and let yourself breathe deeply, evenly, feel the breath move your rib-cage, close your eyes a moment, let yourself be with yourself. Now we can begin." We'd already begun. As soon as you grasp your subject's attention, you've begun. We were ready to apply the rapid induction technique.

"O.K., now lean forward. . . Look into my eyes. . . Place your hand on mine. . . ," I intoned, putting my left hand out at chest height, my right hand on her head. "Yes, very good, now keep looking at me, keep looking at me, yes, look, look, press down with your hand, press down, harder, firmer, keep pressing down, keep looking at me." Then pulling my hand away, suddenly, commanding, "sleep!" catching her upper body with my right hand as her head fell forward, easing her back on the seat, eyes closed, rhythmic breathing. She was under. It only took that first afternoon to learn how to hypnotize someone. The part we needed to cultivate, was the skill of interviewing someone under hypnosis.

Dinner in the dining room. "What's this?" people were asking, pressing the tofu, peering at the tabouli, poking the buckwheat, helping themselves to bread and jam. We sat round big tables, chirping like budgies, eagerly reviewing the day's events. After dinner, we went back to our cabins — time to practice.

Every day, Brian hypnotized the whole group, taking us through either a past-life regression or a guided healing meditation. There was leeway for individual differences, other opinions. "And that's O.K. too," he would say, again and again. Guidelines were minimized, self-discovery was maximized.

Spending long tracts of the day, consciously functioning from the unconscious, impressed upon me how the unconscious operates by different rules, speaks a different language from the conscious.

I already knew that the unconscious is a slippery beast. It's that creature behind the curtain in the A. A. Milne poem. The one you know is there, but it slithers away, disappears, just in time, when you take a peek. You're never fast enough to catch its tail. It's always quicker than you, always will be. The question is, if you can't take a peek, how are you going to recognize it? How are you going to study it, how are you going to master it, control it? That's the point. The unconscious is in control, wants to stay that way.

Under hypnosis, you can coax the unconscious to come out, break the surface, a little at a time. Big and burly in the dark, it shrivels and shrinks in the daylight. Big brother Conscious stands guard, keeping up a running commentary. "Nonsense, all nonsense, you're making this up. You don't really believe this, do you? Say nothing, say you don't remember, say you aren't getting anything. Go back in the dark, all black, nothing, you'll be safe there." So the unconscious, a timid four-year old, goes back underground.

What a disguise! The unconscious is a subterranean force. It is the heaving, seething, molten center of the planet, ready to spew up into volcanoes and earthquakes. It is the center of our being, shaping us, our motive and meaning, as the mountains and the oceans shape the earth.

The unconscious is ambivalent, and it is literal, childlike, slow to comprehend and slow to yield its secrets; and then, just as truly, the unconscious is a sly old fox, stealing chickens from the hen-house, breaking eggs, quick to grasp metaphor, free associate, weave a complex plot out of a chance occurrence.

We formed into groups of four, taking turns to be hypnotist, subject and two observers. I was the subject. I had been regressed into a past life, when I was a Viking.

"Why don't you tell me about it?" my interviewer asked.

"Why don't I tell him about it?" I mulled — then puzzled, "was I supposed to?" I played with the inside of my mouth, my thoughts were trance-slow. I was in alpha-wave time. The image of the ocean and the Viking ship receded. My mind emptied. "Why don't I tell him about it?" I got lost in the confusing question, rolled around the words, looking for meaning. My tongue was too heavy to speak. I wanted to say, "Ask me differently." I wanted to communicate from the facile place of words, but my brain couldn't go there.

Then the question was repeated, differently, a simple command, without idiom. "Tell me more about your life as a Viking. What is happening?" The images returned, we were back on track.

As always, I'd learned more from a mistake than from doing it right. The idiomatic wording made patent the difference between interacting with a subject in ordinary consciousness and interviewing a subject in trance. It taught me the helpless, slow, childish sensation. I'd met the unconscious, theoretically, when I'd studied psychology and I'd observed its effects, working with clients for sixteen years, but this taught me how it feels to be swimming in the sea of my past, the sense of being dependent on the interviewer, the struggle for words, the loss of time. And that it is important to visit there, only occasionally, with wise intent.

There we were — one hundred and twenty individuals, spending most of our day in an altered state, unlocking the unconscious, giving it voice, en masse — anything could have happened. And what happened was that we were all learning, feeling successful. We were raising our arms, holding our hands out for the microphone, standing up and telling our significant stories out loud, to the whole group. I sat between my friends, Gail and Pat and Ina and Clyde, and felt so good.

The river of good feeling was fed by several tributaries. I was receiving support and acknowledgement, in quantity, from my peers. "***You*** should be giving a workshop here," Clyde said. "I want to learn more from you." I lowered my eyes. It was chivalrous of Clyde to say those words. In the lunch and evening breaks a line formed outside our cabin, people looking for relief from pain, looking for healing. "Vivien, are you in there?" they called through the window.

"I have terrible headaches," one woman, Caren, ventured. "My friend said you might be able to help me."

"Come lie on the floor," I soothed, setting her up with her head supported on books. I passed my hands over her. Her aura was very flat, her eyes were dull, her skin was too yellow. "I think you have liver damage," I said.

She started in surprise. "How did you know," she said, "that's true. I was given prolonged medication and the doctor's just told me my liver is damaged. Can you help me?"

"Well, I can certainly energize your aura, help relieve your headaches, but we'll have to work every day while we're here. You need to take care with what you eat and drink, let your liver recover."

"Yes," she said, "I'll do that. Thank you, thank you. I can't believe you knew that. That's amazing." We did some healing work. Her cheeks took on a rosy glow. The next day she brought her husband. "Can you check my husband?" she asked, "tell us what he needs."

Ordinarily I should have felt imposed upon, drained, but this felt different. There was something life-giving in the whole scenario and I knew what was making the difference. It was Brian — Brian's leadership, Brian's manner. Put in front of an adoring audience, he fared well, but in his heart, Brian was interested in the one-on-one relationship. He responded deeply to the individual, wanting to connect. Throughout the week he remained available, opening his heart bigger and bigger, to include the whole group in his awareness and attention, giving of himself without reservation.

Leaving the dining-room one lunch-time, he was walking a little ahead of me on the path. I hung back, not wanting to rupture his space, not wanting to 'suck up to the teacher.' He hung back too, turning slightly toward me, a subtle beckoning, letting me know that he wanted me to catch up to him, talk to him. We chatted a little about South Africa, the once hallowed medical training there, the caliber of South African trained doctors, casual, collegial conversation, respectful. On the surface it was nothing, a brief politeness, yet it was very healing for me. It made me feel like a whole person — Brian made me feel like a whole person.

While I was at Omega, I wanted to do a soul retrieval, a session where the shaman asks spirit help in retrieving parts of the recipient's soul, which have departed because of traumatic or stressful life-conditions. Christina, the resident shaman at the therapy center, was fully booked. At first I was disappointed. Then I remembered we were coming back in August. I called Neil — yes, he wanted an appointment too. As consolation, I had a *Phoenix Rising Yoga* session in the mean time. I didn't know what to expect. It had something to do with stretching and having my body taken through yoga movements.

The practitioner was a young woman. She was comfortably talkative, relaxed and professional at the same time. *Phoenix Rising* seemed to be a way yoga teachers were breaking into the bodywork movement, getting a hands-on approach, using the insights of yoga to fuel a new discipline. In the supportive manipulation of my body and the overall pleasure of the session an awareness overtook me. I realized that I had no pain! Like a tongue probing a tooth, I pushed at all the edges, but no, there wasn't any fire in my shoulders, no throb in my head, no spasm in my colon.

I'd spent the last twenty years, systematically clearing myself. Starting with the Alexander Technique, going through process, after process, twenty years, exactly half my life, exactly equal, twenty years building pain, twenty years clearing pain. What a milestone! I felt lucky, yes — and no — I deserved it.

Thursday afternoon Brian said, "We're going to do a guided healing meditation now — the one at the bottom of the ocean, by request."

Brian took us to the bottom of the ocean, where we found a treasure chest, opened it and found many secrets, many keys to our lives. I enjoyed the meditation. It was filled with blues and greens and coral colors, with the ebb and flow of the tides, with the rise and fall of the waves. I found a silver chest at the bottom of the ocean, overflowing with jewels.

That night Caren brought me a gift of appreciation for the work I'd done with her. "Here," she said, "I bought this in India a few months ago. I bought it as a gift, but I didn't know for whom. I want to give it to you." It was a silver jewelry box, the chest of jewels I'd found at the bottom of the ocean, earlier that day. It was my turn to be surprised, and grateful. I took the box with me to the Friday morning session.

Brian caught the glint, before I even showed it to him. "Look at that!" he said, stopping mid-sentence. He walked over to me, put out his hand for the box, held it up for everyone to see, "where did you get it?"

"It was given to me last night, directly after the meditation. Its exactly what I found at the bottom of the ocean."

Brian raised his eyebrows at me, acknowledging the magic, handing me the microphone. "I've always said, if you want something in your life, you have to make a space for it. This is the space for the jewels of my life, thanks."

We were going through one of the last pieces of our training. Lata, Brian's assistant, was demonstrating an age regression on a volunteer. Brian had pointed out to us previously how we get hypnotized along with the subject, how even the hypnotizer gets hypnotized, by his or her own voice.

Lata was interviewing the subject under hypnosis. "Go back to the time which brought you here today," she directed. I was hypnotized too. My mind skipped to ten years old. I was in the doctor's office. I was with Dr. Mervish, being hypnotized to sleep at night. "No, this is wrong," I argued, "I have other reasons for being here, more sophisticated reasons, sensible, professional reasons." My unconscious tuned out my protests, continued to play this memory, turning up the volume. This was when my interest in the unconscious began, when the seed had been planted. The hypnotherapy, which I'd considered a mistake, because I'd really needed psychotherapy, had brought me here, today.

The course was over. We picked up our belongings, looking around regretfully, hugging our comrades goodbye. I went back to the cabin, not ours anymore. Time to hand back the key, let someone else have the space, the new ones would be arriving in the afternoon. I didn't want to say goodbye to Gail, I wanted her to come with me, stay with me. We'd grown very close, we had so much in common, including the untimely deaths of our only siblings. Sharing a room was definitely a part of the Omega experience. I was glad that I knew I would be coming back in a few weeks. It eased the wrench.

I returned to New York on the shuttle and flew home. A month later we packed the van and drove back to Omega. I couldn't wait to introduce my family to the calm of the campus, the hills, the woods and the lake.

Family week. The grounds teemed with children and parents and games. I did the Heartsong course with Michelle, a big strong woman with a big strong voice. We sang for a whole week, sang to open our hearts, then sang from our hearts. A different teacher, a different group, a different course, but it was the same thing. "I want to sing a song," Richard said, one of the few men in the group. "I want to sing this song that feels like it has come to me from a past life."

"Yep," I thought to myself, "same thing. Omega is a place for tapping into the essence. Doesn't' matter what we do here, all roads lead to Rome."

Neil and I each did our soul retrieval sessions with Christina. We went for a walk along the back roads, to talk, compare notes. "Let's train in shamanism," I said. "I think that should be our next step."

"Yes," Neil said, "Let's train in shamanism."

ANOTHER LEVEL

As soon as I got back from Omega, Dorothy, my personal bearer of crystal tidings, reported to me that Melody would only be giving a few more Level One and Level Two workshops, and then she was going to stop teaching in North America. Soon Melody would be visiting Columbus again for the Universal Light Expo. Should I go to Columbus? Should I speak to Melody, ask her to train me to present her workshops?"

I played the conversation in my head, over several weeks. "Who do you think you are? *You* aren't Melody."

"No I'm not Melody, but someone has to continue teaching her work. I can make a contribution."

I decided not to go to Columbus. The timing wasn't good. I was preparing for my black belt test. Two and a half years had passed since I'd recommitted to Taekwondo. I would be testing for black belt in December. But I did not dismiss the thought. I released it into the universe. I watched the thought of training as Melody's representative float out of the window, into the ether.

In November, I opened the mailbox and took out a letter. The address label had quavers and crotchets on it. The letter was from Melody. It started, as most other letters ended, with the word 'Love.'

"Dear Vivien," it said, "Love. You have been selected from the Level Two participants as someone who would be eligible to train as a Melody Crystal Healing Instructor." Melody was inviting me to attend a Level Three training, in Denver, in April '97.

The letter felt hot as a baked potato. I couldn't hold it, I had to put it down in the kitchen, on the counter with the other mail, the catalogs and bills, like it wasn't significant. I roamed around the house, looking for a space that would accommodate the bouncy thing, which had, started up again. The letter pulled me back, a fish on a line. I reread it. It said what I thought it said. I hadn't made it up, not wishful thinking. Now I knew what those musical notes were for. My heart was singing. I sat down and wrote an immediate response. "Yes, I would be coming. I want to train as a crystal healing instructor."

I had to focus my mind, pull myself back into the present. Never mind what was going to happen in April next year. I had to get fit and strong, practice my forms, self-defense, sparring and breaking techniques. I had all kinds of fantasies about what it meant to be a black belt. None of them were accurate. The physical training wasn't the hard part, after all. It didn't require superhuman strength, or agility. The hard part was winning the battle against myself, overcoming the part of me that wanted to give up, make excuses, didn't believe that I could do it. When I was a lower belt, I had found reasons not to go to class week after week. I had to make a rule: not allowed to miss, ever, for any reason. I realized that the way to get my black belt was to make sure that I went to class every week. If I simply took care of that, the day would come.

With my test coming up so soon I diverted my attention, teaching a minimal number of Alexander lessons, conserving my energy for Taekwondo. "Is it so important?" I asked myself. It wasn't like I was ever going to be a star athlete — I didn't even have hopes of being better than mediocre. I had to settle for accepting that it just *was that significant*, give myself permission to let everything else slide.

I tested for black belt on a Friday night. I walked into the dojang, anxious and eager. Everything went smoothly, as practiced. At the end of the test, Paul tied the black belt on me, and everyone clapped. I examined my belt. It was new and black — otherwise, nothing. The belt was empty, it was the process that earned it and the process that lay ahead, that held the power.

Afterwards Paul said, "Now that you're a black belt, I want you to do the instructor training."

"Me? An instructor?"

"Of course," he said, "you're a teacher. That's what we need."

"What kind of irony is this?" I asked. "I already teach people how to relax. Now I'll be teaching them flexibility and sequences of movement. All the things I struggle with most." Paul shrugged his shoulders.

"I guess we teach best what we have the most difficulty learning," I continued.

"Yin yang," Paul agreed, "our weakness becomes our strength."

Me as a martial arts instructor! It was a tight squeeze. But then so was the thought of me teaching Melody's work.

I was cutting myself up into pieces, taking on too much, doing too many different things. The Alexander Technique was still my great love, and my livelihood. "How is this all going to come together?" I wondered to myself. I stored the question in the back of my mind. I was going to have to wait and see.

Level Three was held in a Holiday Inn in Denver. We dribbled in the night before. My room looked onto an indoor courtyard of miniature golf and arcade games. I had decided not to share. I believed I would need space and time, would want to be on my own. Omega had worked out, but I didn't want to push my luck. The down-side was that I felt isolated, stuck in my on-my-own bubble. I eyed the other arrivals hungrily. There was no need to wonder who was there for the same reason as me. I could see by the crystal jewelry. I walked round and round the courtyard, wishing someone would talk to me.

Next morning, an army of crystal healers trooped into the hotel, stones in hand (and boxes.) I emerged from my room, with my special, pink-handled, craft tote of travel crystals. We were all heading for the conference room. Melody stood in the lobby, beaming and nodding. The others were hugging her, hanging on her like old friends, punching shoulders, laughing and joking. I pressed up against the sides of my on-my-own bubble. How come they all knew her so well and how did I land in this group? I was a lucky outsider.

Melody started the nine-thirty class at nine twenty-five. "Good morning," she greeted us. "Good morning," we chorused back enthusiastically. A few introductory remarks, then she marched to the center of the room and began unfolding a mobile partition, dividing the room and the group into two. Something about the crease of her eyebrows showed she meant business. My heart began to thump. She nominated someone from each group to come stand up front, at the podiums. If like me, the others were expecting a review of the Level One and Two material, with tips on how to present the workshop, we were rapidly realizing we were out of luck, moving into dismay. It was dawning on us that the nominee was supposed to know the syllabus, sent to us in the mail. We were already being tested on presenting the material.

The unwitting man, standing before us, was turning pages, rubbing his face, wiping his neck, looking for a place to begin. We were squirming in our seats. We hadn't learned the script either. The invitation had made it clear that the standard would be challenging, but I wasn't expecting this. This was too demanding. I thought back to the letter. Melody had said "beleaguered and besieged." She'd meant it. I should have known. After all, this was Melody.

The man mumbled and fumbled, then accepting there was no way out, found the place in his notes and lurched into a reasonable presentation. We all settled. Melody watched from the side, a vulture on a high stool. But she wasn't saying anything. She wasn't giving any guidance. She wasn't correcting. She wasn't giving any information. What if what he was saying wasn't correct? I looked over at Melody. She wasn't just watching him, she was watching us too. She was going to make us teach ourselves, teach each other. She was going to make us listen, make us sweat. The man in front, was saying something about grounding stones. I had a question. I put up my hand.

"Yes?"

"The book recommends not to use grounding stones in a layout. Does that mean that you don't use any black or red stones, or does that mean you can use black and red stones, for their other properties, but you don't intentionalize for them to have a grounding influence?"

"Yes, that one." Everybody laughed. He wanted to move on, get away from my question, but I wanted an answer.

"Which one?" I persisted.

The man looked over at Melody. Melody stared at him, not giving anything away. He tried his joke again, "Yes, that one, the one you said." Everybody laughed again. He continued with his presentation.

I put my hand up in the air. He glared at me, "Yes?"

"Sorry," I said, "I really want the answer."

He turned to Melody again. "Did you plant her?" he asked. Melody roared. Everybody roared. I felt a little guilty. I didn't know the answer and I didn't expect him to know, but we all needed to know. It was a set-up. We weren't going to learn the material, and we weren't going to learn how to present, unless we challenged each other with our questions. If we could deal with each other, we would be able to deal with the students in our workshops.

When he got to the end of the first section, Melody let him return to his seat. She glanced down at her list, called another name. The next unfortunate had to go stand at the podium and present the following phase of the workshop. Melody drilled us each, in turn, section by section, piecing our way through the Level One course, until every single one of us could walk to the front, without hesitation, speak the content clearly, field the questions confidently. After two long, intense days of constant repetition, she was satisfied. We would be allowed to move on to Level Two, but not without a caution. "Don't forget, you have to get ninety percent to pass the written exam," she warned us again — must have been the twentieth time in forty-eight hours.

I wasn't so worried about the written exam. I'd done enough of those to know I could cope. Besides, give me a written exam any day, rather than a Taekwondo test.

There were other challenges. Imprisoned in a Holiday Inn, without a car, I didn't know how to stick to my *Weight Watcher's* diet. There was a *Healthy Habits* buffet restaurant right next door, which offered extensive salads, soups and entrées, as well as chocolate chip cookies and sugar-free ice cream and no-fat hot fudge sauce. This test was too difficult for me. I was falling back into buffet habits, piling my plate high, making multiple trips, eating too much. I was longing for the squareness of my *Ezekiel* toast and *Jarlsberg* lite cheese, the roundness of my bowl of portabello mushrooms and brown rice, the packaged pleasure of my *Wendy's* chili and baked potato. I didn't know how to stick to my diet and I didn't know how to break out of my on-my-own bubble. I'd had lunch and dinner with some of the people on the course, but I didn't feel connected yet, hadn't found the one that hits the sweet spot. It wasn't possible that I could be in a room with thirty-four crystal healers, hand-picked by Melody, and not one of them was my soul-mate. I wanted to find her.

Wednesday morning I came into the room and saw a display of crystal wands on a card table. "Hmm," I thought to myself, "Wonder what those are for, they look interesting?" I liked the leather binding round the copper tubes, the delicacy of the Tibetan crystal points, the balancing stones placed at the other termination.

At the end of the morning session, Melody said, "Ro and Georgia have a gift for you. O.K. Ro, come on up."

A woman with short, bright red hair and purple-blue eyes stepped forward. I didn't know her, because she was in the group on the other side of the partition. "Georgia and I wanted to make you something to commemorate our training experience. We have inscribed these wands with the symbol of the Hale-Bopp comet to mark the year. We'd like you each to choose one." I sat in my seat, pondering. I thought of the time it must have taken to hand-make a selection of wands for thirty-four people. Their generosity made me envious. I wished I had time to make crystal wands. I wished I knew how to make crystal wands. Their generosity made me greedy. I wanted more than one.

After everyone had chosen their wands, I hung around, wanting to ask Ro a question. "How much are the wands if you want to buy some as gifts for other people?" I asked.

"I don't know," she said, "we hadn't thought about that. I'll need to speak to Georgia."

"O.K.," I said, "let me know. I'd like to buy a few."

"What are you doing for lunch?" Ro asked.

"I'll just have to have something around here," I said.

"Do you want to come with me?" she asked, "I live in Denver. I have my car here. We can go to Wendy's."

"Wendy's!" I said, my eyes lighting up. It was a sign. I'd been craving the food sold under the icon of the girl with the bright red pigtails, and now here was this woman, with bright red hair, inviting me to go with her to Wendy's. I grabbed my purse. "Let's go," I said. I'd found my soul-mate.

Once I was out of the square mile containing the Holiday Inn, zipping along in a Saab, dashboard lined with plush gray dolphin toys, I breathed a sigh of relief. There was still a world beyond the crystal healing training. We got to Wendy's. Ro wanted the kid's meal. I looked at her quizzically. Well, it was obvious. They were giving out dolphin toys in the kid's meal.

Ro broke the surface tension of my on-my-own bubble. I emerged, and started to connect properly with other members of the course. It was fun having dinner out in a big group, shouting and laughing, getting to know each other.

Thursday morning. I sat on the edge of the bed, letting a gestalt take over my mind. Puzzle pieces were coming together. I was reflecting on the history of the Alexander Technique — what had happened after Alexander had died — how in all systems started by a founding master, there are claims and counter-claims about who now wears the master's mantle, who truly represents his work, who really knows. I shook my head, wanting to free it of this massive thought, with all its implications. I wanted to get away from the insight that now, at the beginning of our identity, we should form ourselves into a professional association. Inner conflict jostled me. I had just declined becoming the chair of NASTAT. I'd been on the Board. I was chair of the training course director's committee. I had an inkling of what was entailed. I'd seen enough to know I didn't want more of it in my life — tidal waves of e-mail, calls across the country, stacks of paperwork on Sunday mornings — misunderstandings with friends, surprise opposition and simple tasks gone awry in the abyss between good intentions and group consensus. Yet I recognized the sense in establishing ourselves under Melody's guidance. Once the idea had occurred to me, I could not shake myself free. I was too far along — I even had a name for our association.

Next morning I approached Melody. "I've had an idea," I said. "I was thinking about this group, and I was thinking about the inevitability of group dynamics, and I was thinking that, depending what you think, we should form ourselves into a professional association, right now, with you to guide us, before the in-fighting even begins." Melody looked me up and down, assessing me and my idea.

"Yes," she said, "you're right."

Encouraged, I continued, "I even have a tentative name," I said, "or rather a choice. The one is Association of Melody Crystal Healing Instructors, which would form the acronym AOMCHI, the other is The Association of Melody Crystal Healing Instructors, which would form the acronym TAOMCHI, a combination of Tao, Om and Chi."

"Yes," Melody said, "I like it."

"Which one?" I asked.

"The second one," she replied, "TAOMCHI."

"Good," I said, relieved. I'd got it off my chest.

"I want you to speak," she said. "I want you to present this idea. I'll give you time to put this forward." Not quite what I'd had in mind. She caught my hesitation, the sideways glance of my eyes. "*You* must do it." Too late to back out. The wheels were in motion.

Later that morning, Melody summoned me to the front to address the class. "Vivien has had an idea," she announced. "I want her to tell you about it." Everyone's attention was on the forthcoming exam. I could feel the spikes of tension, the flicker of nervous eyes, wishing me and my idea away, so that they could rush to their notes, to study. I explained myself. The room began to buzz. Yes, a professional association was a good idea; yes, we should form one; yes, let's play politics. Our first general meeting would be held Friday morning, just before our final exam.

Melody went to sit in the back of the room, expecting an orderly progression — an affable exposition on how to run a general meeting, consensus on using Robert's Rules of Order, an election of office-bearers in accordance with a presumed conclusion that I would be the founding chair. I would make a statement of what would happen next and then we would return our attention to crystal healing. But I'd burst open a hornets' nest. Nominations for chair popped out, smelling like burnt corn. People wanted to speak, address the assembly, argue their point of view. There were factions in the room. There was competition. There was human nature.

Melody's face was getting blacker and blacker. I couldn't decide whether the proceedings proved me stupid or wise. The contest gradually simmered down to a vote between me and, of all people, Ro. Not that I wanted to be chair, but I'd promised Melody one year to get the association up and running. I was elected, and I asked Ro to accept the position of vice-chair. Melody was not pleased with our unbecoming conduct. We were all stressed. We'd needed a good fight. We sat the exam in the afternoon.

Saturday, Melody stood at the podium, waiting for us to take our positions. The atmosphere was somber, electric. Who would fail, who would be disappointed, who would be left behind? Too late to pray. Melody turned her head from left to right, surveying the crop. "You all passed," she announced. A whoop of relief resounded through the room. "All results are final and cannot be discussed," she added with finality.

Graduation. A ceremony at an Ethiopian restaurant, dressed up, posing for photographs, receiving certificates, the glow of relief and the glow of accomplishment. I returned home with another dream come true, and a lot of work ahead of me.

Spirit Voices

⟨⟩

MESSENGER

Two months later I needed to be in New York. I was going to the NASTAT annual meeting and then on to Omega, for a weekend of shamanic training. Neil and I were following up our inspiration of the year before, following the soul retrieval sessions. We'd selected core shamanism, the training offered by Michael Harner and *The Foundation For Shamanic Studies*.

The advantage of going to Omega was that we could take the boys. The disadvantage was the cost of the weekend — flights, tuition, board, lodging and child care came to a staggering two thousand dollars for the two days. We swished it around in our minds, swished it around in our mouths. We didn't have a choice. It was cough up or don't do it. We really wanted to do it. We were going to have to pay.

Neil dropped me off at the airport Wednesday morning. He would be flying up with the boys on Friday. We'd meet at Omega. Walking into the *Delta* terminal the eye, in my mind, caught a flash — an image of a man sitting down next to me, engaging me in a significant conversation. I dismissed the scene. "Nonsense, my time alone is precious. I'm not open to idle conversation with strangers. No-one will be sitting next to me. No-one has something to tell me."

Of course it was nonsense. There wouldn't even be an opportunity for me to sit down — had to go to the bank, go to Starbucks, rush around the airport doing errands. Standing at the glass sliding doors of the Comair shuttle pick-up point, I felt something soft and pleasing, comforting as a cotton blanket on cold feet. Someone was sending me energy. "That's unusual," I thought to myself, "here in the airport, of all places." The thought stopped there. The shuttle bus was bobbing and bucking outside. The doors slid open. A man in pilot's uniform motioned me to step ahead of him, and I boarded.

I sat down next to the baggage rack, one of my privacy-guarding maneuvers, making sure there was no space next to me. The pilot strode on last. His gaze was fixed. He waved me on a seat, indicating that he wanted to sit next to me. The martial artist in me asked no questions. This was a man in uniform. I should trust him. As soon as he was seated, he dipped his hand into his left jacket pocket, pulled out a quartz pebble, white, with a brown-orange cast, stained by the earth. "I'm supposed to give this to you," he said, "it's a healing stone from the Cherokee Reserve. You are a healer who will transform many peoples lives. You are supposed to have it." He paused momentarily, then introduced himself. "My tribal name is Black Wolf."

I stared at his ginger hair, blue eyes and fair skin. He didn't look black and he didn't look like a wolf. He didn't look Cherokee. He looked like a big, amiable Irishman. I wanted to doubt, to disbelieve. How could boarding a shuttle bus at the airport turn into a spiritual adventure? And how could it not? The purpose of my journey, after all, was to seek training as a shaman. I tuned in to the vibration of the man sitting next to me. He felt powerful, kind, gentle. He felt credible. I wanted to question him. "Do you say this to all the girls?" But this was no ordinary line, and, I had to admit, it wasn't like he was wrong.

"Well, that's interesting," I said, for want of a better response. "I've just come back from being trained as a crystal healing instructor, and I'm presently on my way to do a training in shamanism." I opened my bag, showed him some crystals, stones, feathers and books I was carrying. He nodded. He wasn't surprised. There was nothing incongruous about two strangers, a pilot and a passenger, talking about crystal healing, shamanism and personal transformation, on their way to the *Comair* terminal.

"Do you have some time?" he asked. "I just have to check-in, let them know I've arrived."

"Yes, I have an hour before my flight leaves."

"I'll meet you here," he said, gesturing to a bank of chairs.

I went to the phone to call Neil. "You won't believe what just happened!"

"What?" he asked, "Is everything O.K."

"Yes, yes, everything's O.K., but listen to this." I told him the story.

"No!" he said, "You're joking, I don't believe it." Neil knew I wouldn't have made it up, couldn't have made it up, not even if I tried. I could feel him shaking his head.

"I guess we made the right decision about the shamanic training. It's already been worth the money."

"Yes," said Neil. "Got to admit, it looks like we made the right decision."

"Black Wolf" and I, sat in the concourse together. I noticed how the Comair personnel would stop and greet him, the way they lit up, on the inside, and the outside. I was feeling lucky again. Lucky to be sitting next to this gentle man, lucky to be chosen, lucky to be alive. As a parting gift, Black Wolf lifted his hands, slipped the fetish he was wearing around his neck, over his head, and gave it to me — a bear, in champagne jasper. I understood that I was meant to pass it on to Neil.

I sat on the plane, a little shocked. I needed to process the incident. What a good story. I couldn't wait to tell my friends. This would shake them up, make them see me for who I am! But it went deeper than that. There was something eerie about the way the pieces hung together, especially the precognition, letting me know these were not random events. There was a plan, and I was on track — in the right place at the right time, making the right choices. The universe was speaking to me, not with the usual signs and riddles — directly, clearly, through the voice of a stranger.

THE SPIRIT WORLD

Neil and the boys arrived later on the Friday night. Although this was a beginner workshop — the 'gateway' basics — the weekend was being led by the master himself, Michael Harner.

Michael reminded me of Uncle Harry. Not that Uncle Harry would have been remotely drawn to shamanism, but the shine of Michael's bald head, the folds at the back of his neck and the learnedness of his glasses, jogged my childlike faith. My uncle had been a worthy authority, a man of the world. Michael's see-for-yourself attitude reassured me. He had traveled the world studying the shamanic traditions of numerous cultures, harvesting — and giving back — reviving skills which hung by a thread, restoring spiritual customs where they'd become extinct. Michael brought to life the other side of my social anthropolgy course, the part we'd been allowed to scoff at when I was eighteen years old.*

A few sentences from Michael let us know that we were in the company of a remarkable messenger. He knelt on the floor, lit the herbs and incense. "The spirits like certain fragrances," he explained. He mumbled a prayer and the weekend of drumming, dancing and journeying began.

The boys were disgruntled. They wanted it to be like family week. "We came for us, we wanted to do this course," we tried to explain. "You

 * See p. ? Chapter 2

didn't want to be left behind, so we brought you. But this isn't family week, you have to make do." They looked unconvinced. Our boys weren't the only ones who were frustrated. Richard, the man who had sung the song, from a past life, in the Heartsong course, had also returned to Omega, with his wife, looking for another shot in the arm. He didn't like his course. He looked sad. "What are you doing?" he asked.

The shamanism course," I said.

"Do you like it?" he asked.

"I love it," I replied, "you should try it.

He stood at the back of the room, on the Saturday morning, already too late to catch the wave. He asked me to help him. I gave him a healing session on the floor of his room. "Perhaps he was supposed to come this weekend to see you," his wife suggested.

"I don't know," I said, to both of them. "I hope you find what you're looking for. Don't give up, it's worth the search."

The forty-eight hours sped by. We learned to do divination using a rock, we journeyed to the lower world to meet our totem animals. We journeyed to the upper world to meet our teachers. We danced our spirit energy and we journeyed on behalf of a partner, to retrieve a lost power animal. Every time Michael started to drum I'd hear voices singing, a heavenly choir. I opened my eyes, looking for the singers, convinced they must be real, live, in the room.

Finally I went to Michael. "Who is singing?" I asked.

"No-one. It's not in this reality," he said, "it's on the other side."

I couldn't believe it. The sound was too sweet and pure, too uplifting, more real than reality. On the way to the airport I asked Neil, "Did you hear the singing voices?"

"No," he said, "I didn't. Sometimes I heard one voice, sort of."

"This was a choir," I said, "not words, but voices harmonizing. It was very clear. I opened my eyes to see who was singing, but there wasn't anyone."

"No," Neil said, "I didn't hear a choir, but I did hear other things."

Our two thousand dollar weekend had yielded a sixty-four thousand dollar question. Despite my experiences, I still wasn't a believer. I justified myself — I didn't want to be a flake. On the other hand, every time I'd consulted a psychic in the last five years, I'd been asked the same question. "You are very psychic, but you're blocked. What is blocking you?" I'd shrugged in response. I knew I was blocked, but I was hoping they'd tell me what the block was. After all they were the psychics.

I was ready to admit to myself that I did have psychic ability, so much, that I could develop my potential in almost any way I wanted. That was the block. I was standing, stuck, at the crossroads. I needed to decide which path I wanted to follow.

I didn't want to be a fortune teller, or a medium, or a card reader, or a palmist — I wanted to be a teacher and a healer. I made a choice — I would develop my psychic ability to support my teaching and healing work. I had learned how to cross from one reality to another, how to access the spirit world in an orderly manner. Now that I had technique and system, I needn't fear being overwhelmed.

Still, I wanted to test the etheric world again, before I surrendered.

A client, Colleen, was getting desperate. She'd had a sore shoulder for years. Nothing she'd done seemed to help, "What should I do," she asked, "should I get acupuncture?"

"Let's tune in," I said, "let's ask the guides." I felt brave in Colleen's company. Colleen was more faithful than I.

A Chinese spirit doctor came in to give us counsel. "Yes, he said, acupuncture will help. I will do acupressure through you to relieve the pain for now, open the meridians." He took over my hands, poking, prodding, pressing, holding. It seemed to help. The muscles were relaxing, the energy was flowing. "Give me proof that you're real," I challenged the guide. "Give me proof that I'm not just making you up."

He smiled at me. His eyes jigged, plotting a little joke. "Tell her I know her granddaughter, Rosie."

"I'm not going to say that. I know that's not her granddaughter's name."

"Just tell her," he said. "Tell her I know her granddaughter, Rosie." He was teasing me.

I sighed. Colleen's infant granddaughter was not called Rosie, but I couldn't remember her actual name. I'd asked for proof, I'd wanted to test the good faith of the guide, and he'd turned it into a test of my good faith. I yielded. I said out loud, "He says to tell you he knows your granddaughter, Rosie."

"Oh, that's nice," said Colleen, smiling with pleasure.

I was more puzzled than ever, "But Colleen," I whined, "why is he calling her 'Rosie,' I know that's not her name?"

"No," she responded, "her name is Julia, but she's my rose. I call her my little Rosie."

How much proof was I going to need before I would trust the spirit world, before I would trust myself? It was time for me to release my doubt, move into a committed relationship. It was time for me to remember that I could discriminate between the real thing and a fake. After all, I always could tell the difference between cocoa and milo.

THE MESSAGE

Chairing committees and founding associations was highlighting for me why I prefer to be self-employed. I was getting impatient with group dynamics. I wanted my time back. I wanted to write, to exercise, to be with my family. I wanted time to lie on my bed and do nothing.

I had found an ear to listen to my grumbles. I was in the car, on my way to pick the kids up from school, my favorite opportunity for communicating with my master guide. I'd imagine him sitting in the passenger seat next to me, in his robe and hat, and ask him questions. "What's going on?" I asked. "Why do I have to do all this board work, chair these organizations, write these bylaws. It's too much work. Why do I have to do it?"

"Its training," was the curt response. That should have warned me, let me know to keep my mouth shut. It was too late, my thoughts were being heard.

"Training? Training for what?" I pouted.

"You need to know," responded the master. "You need to know how to chair a board and how to establish a non-profit organization. You need to know how to hold a vision, inspire others, direct group energy."

"Why?" I demanded. This wasn't making any sense in terms of my life as I knew it.

"Because you're going to establish a college."

"A college?"

"Yes, a college to train healers."

"Train healers?" It sounded like a good idea, except I didn't like the role I'd been allocated. "Why me?" I asked.

"Because of the way you've trained to become a healer. You need to pass this on."

"Me? I haven't trained as a healer."

"Yes, you have. What do you think you've been doing all these years? You've systematically trained as a healer — Psychology, Alexander

Technique, Crystal Healing, Martial Arts, Past-Life Regression, Homeopathy, Aromatherapy, Flower Essences — you never stop. You've put in the time, you've put in the discipline. Not only have you worked consistently in private practice, but you've also been training teachers and healers. You know what it takes."

I remembered the box of record-keeper crystals and Melody saying, in a matter of fact voice, "That many record keepers? You obviously have a lot of knowledge to pass on."

"We are a spirit team who will stand by you," my guide continued. "We will assist you and guide you. The college already exists in the etheric. We need you to help us bring it into physical reality."

I took a deep breath. I didn't want to hear anymore. I needed to let my mind rove the avenues of possibility. This could explain my drive to learn, not one, but three disciplines which each demanded a lifetime commitment. I thought about two other effective healers I knew. They also had multi-disciplinary training. They also had masters degrees, several certifications in complementary techniques and a foundation of demanding physical training. I perceived that the whole is greater than the sum of its parts — the way we worked went beyond the information we had learned. Our effectiveness depended on a synergy, a transcendence of our knowledge and skills. I thought about a frustration I never give voice to — how I only have opportunity to teach people bits and pieces of what I know, but not everything I believe in — and that really, there are no short cuts. My spirit guide was right, a truncated version of my own process could not yield the same effect.

As soon as I thought this, he interrupted me. "We want the college to teach a pyramid of learning — general foundation courses, rising to a more and more focused specialty. When you reach the apex of the pyramid, you will be transformed by the learning, so that you are able to energetically ascend from the pyramid of 'concrete' knowlege, into the etheric, yet live on the earth plane, as the embodiment of a healer. This was the skill of the lost civilization, Lemuria. It is time for this knowledge to be restored to mankind, and combined with all the new knowledge."

Lemuria? I had a block against Lemuria, even though I'd visited there in crystal journeys. I went back to my own train of thought. I visualized a college where the faculty were well-steeped in the Alexander Technique. Where healers, were required to train in a Martial Art. Where students were supported through the study of Anatomy, Physiology, Biochemistry, Physics and Psychology. And where students learned the principles of

Naturopathy, Homeopathy, Herbalism, Flower Essences, Aromatherapy and Crystals. I visualized the transformation of the role and standing of healers in our society. I was tempted ... until I visualized the work this project would entail. Mercy. I was at the school. Time to pick up the kids.

"I won't say anything," I said to myself. "I'll see if this persists. It's too much, it's too big. It will take the rest of my life. If it's supposed to happen, someone else will do it."

For months the idea hung in the air, on the other side of my teaching-room window. Hovered behind the door in my bed-room, filling the gaps in conversation, waiting for me to take up the cause, willing me to speak it out loud, give it a voice. I went to a psychic, to ask about the book I was writing. "Yes, yes, I see your book. In fact I see a series of books. But I see something else. I see a much bigger project, what's that?"

"Must be the college," I muttered.

She leaned forward. "What college?" I explained, reluctantly.

"Yes, that's it, very good . . . very important . . . a lot of spirit support." The rest of the reading revolved around the college. I rolled my eyes. I wanted to know more about my book.

I had to go to another reader. "Let me see what guide came in with you," the psychic said. She lit a candle and held it to a piece of white paper, letting the soot form an image. "Oh," she said, "a master guide. Look here's his hat, and here is the collar of his robe. A very old guide, he's been around a long time." She was looking at me gravely, with eyes magnified by glasses, to see if I was understanding the significance of what she was saying. I looked back at her. It was more significant than I wanted it to be. I didn't want to know about my guide. I knew about him. I wanted to know about my book.

"Yes," she said, "a very important book, a teaching book. It's repre-sented by this small wheel here, which leads into this big wheel here." She pointed at interlinked circles formed by the pictures on the cards. "What's the big wheel? That's really important. The book sort of leads into it, but is also separate. The big wheel is what the spirits want to talk about."

"The college," I murmured. This consultation was going the same way as the previous one.

"What college?"

I explained.

"Oh," she said, "I want to work there. Will there be a place for me? It's just what we need." Wrong answer. She was supposed to say it wasn't my destiny. She was supposed to say I should redirect my thinking.

At the TAOMCHI annual meeting, Ro presented me with a gift from the association, to thank me for my work as founding chair. It was a brass star, engraved with the words: "A dream come true, thanks, Vivien." I felt guilty. The words seemed loaded with meaning. Yes, there was TAOMCHI, but there was another dream, too. The spirits were resorting to dirty tactics, symbols and metaphors and similes.

I surrendered. I tentatively began to speak about the college. I expected people to say, "How do you think you're going to do something like that?" but they didn't comply. They said the opposite. They said, "What a good idea." They said, "It's by time," and, "You can do it, Vivien!" If anyone was thinking it couldn't be done and if anyone was thinking it was absurd, the spirits were doing a good job of keeping them out of my way. Everyone wanted to join in, help establish a college. Didn't they understand how hard it was going to be? Didn't they understand how long this would take? They didn't seem to care. They only wanted to know one thing: "When can we begin?"

We couldn't begin until we had a name. While I was standing in the kitchen washing dishes, I asked the master guide, "What will the college be called? Tell me the name."

"The name is under your nose," the master replied.

More riddles? "Just tell me the name," I thought, "I don't want to play any more games, just tell me the name."

"The name is under your nose," the spirits bantered.

Week after week, I waited for the name to come to me. I worked at it, putting together different combinations. I meditated, waiting for the name to pop into my mind. I asked others, hoping someone would tell me.

Standing in the kitchen again, looking out the window, holding a letter addressed to me, I heard the words, "The name is under your nose." I saw the street name below the window — under my nose. I saw the address on the envelope that I was holding — under my nose. I saw the name — "FourWinds."

That was it. I could hear the voices singing — that was it — *FourWinds Academy for the Healing Arts and Sciences*. Four. The four seasons, the four directions. Winds, the winds of change, the wind of spirit. FourWinds, the college, was born.

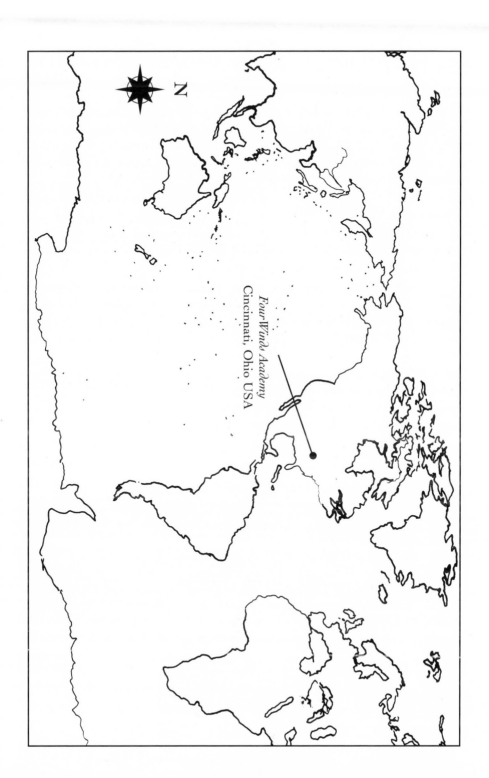

FourWinds Academy
Cincinnati, Ohio USA

ACKNOWLEDGMENTS

I would like to thank the following for their contribution to creating this book:

All my test readers, for your invaluable feedback.

All my students and colleagues at *Alexander Technique of Cincinnati, Cincinnati Taekwondo* and *Four Winds Academy.*

All the members of my small and large groups at *Women Writing for (a) Change.*

Nancy Dawley, Jennifer Hetzler, Lou Hemmer, Jeremy Gibson, Lois Cone, Alicia Lampe, Paul Korchak, Yvonne Barkie,Claire Kupferle, David Stern, Naomi Stoehr, Susan Tew, Janet Kalven, Josh and Cathy Sands, Yvonne and David Cooper, Jeannie and Charlie Kabenji, Tom and Kaska Firor, Tom and Sally Harding, Marcie Strasser, Jen Knarr, Pat Kolata and all my friends who have supported and encouraged me.

Yvonne Becker, personal mentor, for your precious time and knowledge.

Doug Schar, publishing mentor, for your generous guidance.

Dana Kadison, photographer and friend, for your special eye.

Kathleen Noble, graphic artist, for your style.

Kevin Cole, editor, for your expertise.

Kathy Wade, teacher, for nurturing me as a writer.

Alec and Renee Singer, my parents, for inspiring me.

Neil, Aidan and Jason, my family, for letting me be me.

Dedication
* **Women Writing for (a) Change**
  4850 Madison Road, Cincinnati, OH 45227

Chapter 1 - Childhood
* Peter O'Donnell, *Modesty Blaise* (1984)
* Lyall Watson, *Supernature A Natural History of the Supernatural* (1973)
* Ambrose A Worrall and Olga N Worrall, *Explore Your Psychic World* (1989)
* Ambrose A Worrall and Olga N Worrall, *The Gift of Healing: A Personal Story of Spiritual Healing* (1989)
* Leonard Cohen, *The Favorite Game* (1997)

Chapter 2 - University
* Adelle Davis, *Let's Eat Right To Keep Fit* (1988)
* Michael Gelb, *Body Learning* (1981)
* Glynn MacDonald, *The Alexander Technique* (1995)

Chapter 3 - Journey
* Arthur Frommer, *Frommer's Europe* (1997)
* Carlos Castenada, *Teachings of Don Juan: A Yaqui Way of Knowledge* (1985)
* Carlos Castenada, *A Separate Reality: Further Conversations with Don Juan* (1991)
* Carlos Castenada, *Journey to Ixtlan: The Lessons of Don Juan* (1992)
* Carlos Castenada, *Tales of Power* (1992)

Chapter 4 - Choices
* Thalassa Caruso, Making Things Grow (1976)

Chapter 5 - The Alexander Technique And More
About the Alexander Technique
* **The Society of Teachers of the Alexander Technique (STAT)**
  20 London House, 266 Fulham Road, London SW 10 9EL
  +44(0)171 351 0828 E-mail: info@stat.org.uk
* **American Society for Teachers of the Alexander Technique**
  (AmSAT, formerly NASTAT 0, alexandertech@earthlink.net
  (800) 473-0620

There are also national societies for the Alexander Technique in Australia, Denmark, Germany, Israel, The Netherlands, Spain, South Africa, Switzerland, France, Brazil, Belgium and Canada.

* W.H.M. Carrington, **The Constructive Teaching Centre**
  18 Lansdowne Road - Holland Park W11
* Ken Dychtwald, *Bodymind* (1986)
* Soozi Holbeche, *The Power of Gems and Crystals* (1989)
* Soozi Holbeche, *Journeys Through Time: A Guide to Reincarnation and Your Immortal Soul* (1996)

Chapter 6 - Milestones
* Dolores Krieger, *The Therapeutic Touch* (1992)
* Michio and Aveline Kushi, *Macrobiotic Diet* (1985)
* Janet Balaskas, *Active Birth* (1992)

Chapter 9 Powers
* **Cincinnati Taekwondo Center** - www.cincytaekwondo.com
* James Redfield, *The Celestine Prophecy* (1993)
* Melody, *Love is In the Earth* series (1991)
* J.J. Hurtak, *The Book of Knowledge: The Keys of Enoch* (1977)

Chapter 10 Master Teachers
* Brian L. Weiss M.D., *Many Lives, Many Masters* (1988)
* Robertson Davies, *The Cunning Man* (1996)
* **Omega Institute -** 800.944-1001 - www.eomega.org

Chapter 11 Spirit Voices
* Michael Harner, *The Way Of The Shaman* (1990)
* **The Association of Melody Crystal Healing Instructors (TAOMCHI) -** www.TAOMCHI.com
* **FourWinds Academy for the Healing Arts and Sciences**
  www.4WindsAcademy.org

* *In some cases the dates refer to the most recent release.*